MAKERS OF ARAB HISTORY

MAKERS
OF
ARAB
HISTORY

BY
PHILIP K. HITTI
Professor Emeritus of Semitic Literature on the
William and Annie S. Paton Foundation
Princeton University

ST. MARTIN'S PRESS
New York

Library of Congress Catalog Card Number 68–20139
Manufactured in the United States of America
First Printing

Maps by Joseph P. Ascherl

ST. MARTIN'S PRESS INC.
175 Fifth Avenue New York NY 10010

MACMILLAN AND COMPANY LIMITED
Little Essex Street London WC2
also Bombay Calcutta Madras Melbourne

THE MACMILLAN COMPANY OF CANADA LIMITED
70 Bond Street Toronto 2

To the memory of
MY FATHER
who labored hard and long
to support a large family
and give his children the benefits of higher education
which he was denied

PREFACE

THIS is an attempt to give the student and interested layman an introduction to the religious, political and other cultural movements in Arab history through the lives of representative leaders. Other authors would have chosen other personages, and given at times different interpretations. It would be surprising if that were not the case. Makers of Arab history—of any history—are at the same time made by history. They themselves are the products of surging movements whose waves they ride to guide or modify the courses thereof. They could be styled creators of their people's tradition, architects of their nation's way of life.

The material for this study was drawn from original sources checked with the results of modern scholarship in the East and West. The design does not require new researches. The author utilized data already worked out in his *History of the Arabs* and histories of Syria, Lebanon and the Near East. He hopes that this modest introduction might lead the reader to a more intimate acquaintance, if not friendship, with the complicated but absorbing subject of the study.

P. K. H.

Princeton, N. J.
March 15, 1968

The medallion on the title page, bearing the Moslem profession of faith, reads in Arabic La ilaha illa Allah; Muhammadun rasulu Allah (no God whatever but God; Muhammad is the messenger of God).

PAGE

PART I: RELIGIOUS AND POLITICAL

PART II: INTELLECTUAL

MAPS

Part 1
Religious and Political

Muhammad:
Triple Initiator of Religion, Nation and State

> *Thus have We sent to you a messenger from amongst yourselves to recite to you Our revelations, to purify you and to instruct you in the "book" and the wisdom and to teach you what ye do not know.*
> —Koran 2:146

HISTORY records the names of several men who founded religions, others who fathered nations, still others who instituted states; but if ever there was a man, other than Muhammad, who initiated all three institutions, history must have forgotten his name. The three founded by Muhammad were originally inextricably interwoven and to an extent interdependent. Throughout their careers the first—religion—provided the integrating force and proved to be the most enduring.

I

The religion founded by the Prophet of Arabia—Islam—claims today the adherence of some 450 million people of all races, speaking a multitude of languages, dominating almost the entire area from Morocco and Nigeria to Indonesia and Malaysia. Every seventh or eighth person in the world today calls himself Moslem. The nation Muhammad called forth—the Arabian—is presently represented by 100 million from Morocco to Iraq who call themselves Arabs. The state he started in the peninsula developed into the caliphate, the mightiest empire of medieval times, and has now successors in North Africa and western Asia dreaming of coalition into one unified state.

Nothing in the early life or environment of this man presaged what destiny held in store for him. His birthplace Mecca, whose name is now used as a common noun for a center of pilgrimage, had never figured on a national or international level. Nor did his country Hijaz. The limelight was then shining on the Eastern Roman Empire in the northwest and the Persian Empire in the northeast, leaving the entire Arabian peninsula in darkness. The name he bore, Muhammad (highly praised), is now borne by more children in the world than probably any other name. It never occurs before his time and sounds like an honorific title, not the real name given him by his mother at his birth in 570. In the Koran (*surah*[1] 61:6) he is referred to as Ahmad, and to his tribesmen he was known as al-Amin (the trustworthy).

All the established facts about the early life of the future prophet can be squeezed into a paragraph. His father 'Abdullah died while on a caravan trip to Syria before the child was born. His mother Aminah died when he was barely six. His grandfather 'Abd-al-Muttalib, in whose house the orphan was reared, passed away two years later, leaving the boy in the custody of his uncle abu-Talib. The blackout which here begins was not lifted until his marriage to Khadijah seventeen years later.

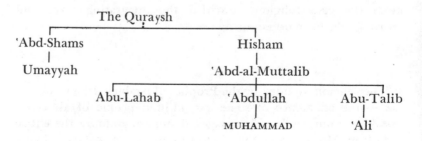

To the two dominant features of Muhammad's childhood—domestic tragedy and clan impoverishment—the Koran (93:6–10) bears clear testimony.

1 Chapter, of which the Koran has 114.

Did He not find thee an orphan and give thee a home?
Did He not find thee astray and guide thee?
Did He not find thee destitute and enrich thee?
Therefore the orphan oppress not,
And the beggar drive not away.

The enrichment referred to in line three accrued from his first marriage.

If fact and history denied young Muhammad wealth and happiness, faith and tradition enriched his life and embellished it with miraculous phenomena comparable to those cherished by believers in Christ and Buddha. His mother never felt his presence in her womb until the time of delivery, when an angel announced the good tidings to her. His Bedouin wet-nurse felt "milk swelling mysteriously her long-dry breasts" the moment her eyes fell upon the infant. Her sons, while playing with him in front of their desert tent, saw two white-robed persons lay him on his back, open his chest and extract a black clot. The skeptic is referred to Allah's words (sur. 94:1–4) addressed to His prophet:

Have We not opened thy chest,
And eased thee of thy burden,
Which galled thy back,
And exalted thy fame?

When on a caravan going north with his uncle abu-Talib, the twelve-year-old lad met a Christian monk, Bahira, who recognized between his shoulders the seal of prophethood. The cycle of Moslem and Christian legends around Bahira telescopes the early relations between the two religions and the influence of Christianity. An alleged visit of Muhammad to Damascus prompted his remark, as he hesitated at the city's gate, that he wanted to enter Paradise but once. It is hard to believe, however, that a visit to a city so radically different from his birthplace, at such an impressionable age, would not have left an echo in the Koran.

The Koran, as it refers to episodes in Muhammad's life, becomes unwittingly the most authentic source, mirroring the strong as well as the weak points in his character. The first biography of Muhammad (*Sirah*[1]) was compiled by ibn-Hisham, who died in Egypt as late as 833. By then a halo had developed

1 Tr. Alfred Guillaume, *The Life of Muhammad* (London, 1955).

around the Prophet's head, and deeds and qualities were ascribed to him which neither he nor the Koran ever claimed. The second biography was included by al-Tabari, who died in Baghdad in 923, in his multi-volume *Annals*. Muhammad's campaigns (*Maghazi*) were written up by al-Waqidi (d. 822), also of Baghdad. Meantime the Byzantines had developed their own image of the founder of Islam, first delineated by Theophanes (in 813). To him Muhammad was "the ruler of the Saracens and the pseudo-prophet." This image persisted until modern times.

II

Fortune began to smile on Muhammad when, at the age of twenty-five, he married Khadijah, a wealthy widow of his tribe. Fifteen years his senior, she was his employer in her caravan trade. He therewith took the first step on the threshold of clear history. As long as this high-minded strong-of-personality lady lived, Muhammad would have none other for wife. After her death (619) he married nine, besides having concubines.

The competence that now entered into his economic life enabled him to engage in his two favorite indulgences: contemplation and seclusion. A cave in a mount outside Mecca provided the locale. Two fires must have been burning within him: conciousness of the ills of the society in which he lived—a society in transition from nomadism to urbanism—and the realization that the Christians and Jews he met had a "book" and were more progressive, more highly developed than his people. Arabia was then ringed by Christian countries. The Christians he met must have been Syrians, Copts, Abyssinians and Christianized Arabians on the borders of Syria and Iraq. They came as merchants, slaves or visitors. The Jews must have been native Medinese and Yamanis or foreign traders and slaves.

Mecca had by this time become a meeting place and crossroads of trade from the frankincense and spice lands of Yaman and Abyssinia on one hand and Syria, with its Mediterranean ports, and Iraq on the other. The city evidently owed its existence to the Zamzam well, whose water—tradition assures us—gushed forth miraculously to save Ishmael from death by thirst when he and his mother Hagar were lost in the desert. Ishmael became the ancestor of the Arab people. His father Abraham renovated a cube-like structure nearby, now the Kaabah, and instituted the pilgrimage (surs. 3:90–91; 22:27). The area thus became a sanctuary to which any man could go without fear of molestation. Muhammad's grandfather redug the well and earned his living by apportioning its water to pilgrims.

Mecca's trade was changing its Bedouin society into a settled, mercantile, capitalistic society. The socio-economic gap between the "haves" and "have nots" was widening. Old loyalties were giving way to new ones. Tribal solidarity, essential for survival in a desert, becomes downgraded in a settled community, where individualism counts for more. Courage and military power determine mobility and prestige in a nomadic state, whereas in a mercantile one wealth is the determining factor.

On one of the last nights of Ramadan (sur. 2:185) in 610, as Muhammad was pondering problems that had been haunting him, he all of a sudden heard a voice commanding: "Read, in the name of thy Lord. . . ." Startled, the unschooled Muhammad must have asked, "How can I?" and the voice repeated:

> Read, for thy Lord is the most bounteous,
> Who teacheth by the pen,
> Teacheth man what he did not know.
>
> Sur. 96:3–5

Muhammad must have used reading and writing in his business, but evidently he did not think he could manage sacred writing. After a brief interval the voice came again like the "reverberating of bells." Under the stress of great emotion he rushed home and asked his wife to put heavy cover on him. As if in a trance he then heard:

> O thou, enwrapped in thy mantle,
> Arise and warn.
>
> Sur. 74:1–3

There was no doubt about it. The voice must have been that of an angel, later identified as Gabriel. The Prophet had received his first call. Unlike the visual-auditory visions of Moses, Isaiah and Saul-Paul, it was entirely auditory. Khadijah was his first convert. It was her faith and confidence that sustained and encouraged him as he made his faltering debut on the stage of prophethood.

The essence of his early message can be summed up in a few simple words. There is only one God, Allah. He is the creator, all-powerful, ever-living. Muhammad is His messenger. There is a judgment day. Splendid rewards in Paradise await those who obey His commands. Terrible punishment in Hell is the lot of those who disregard them.

Allah (contraction of *al-ilah,* the God) was not an unknown deity to the Meccans. In fact he was the principal deity of their Kaabah, which was known as "House (*bayt*) of Allah." " 'Abdullah," the name of Muhammad's father (which may not have been his original one), meant servant of Allah.

Polytheism by its nature is more tolerant, more accommodating to new deities than monotheism. But in this case, the exclusive nature of Allah was its objectionable feature to Meccans. The new dogmas would alienate the conservative Arabians from the deities of their fathers and to that extent from their fathers themselves, whom Muhammad would consign to Hell. True, the new preacher posed as a prophet only, but his gospel had economic, social and political implications which the Quraysh were not slow to grasp. It might undermine pilgrimage, next to trade the main source of income. The generosity he preached stood high in their scale of values, but the novel concept of wealth as a stewardship on which the poor had a rightful claim (sur. 70:24–5) was too bitter a pill to swallow. In Arabic the same word, *karam,* means both "generosity" and "nobility." Moreover the new teaching would substitute faith for blood as the social bond: "Verily the believers are naught but brothers" (sur. 49:10). This would undermine family, clan and tribal unity in favor of religious unity. Finally the Quraysh sensed that religious success was bound to entail political success, jeopardizing their own authority. Thus did opposition mount.

Consecrated and fired by the new message he felt commissioned to deliver, the Messenger (*rasul*) of Allah went among his people teaching, preaching, warning. They laughed him to scorn. Verbal attacks multiplied. He is possessed by the jinn (sur. 81:22), said some; a falsifying magician (38:3), claimed others; a soothsayer (69:42), asserted still others. In all such allegations the opposition unwittingly acknowledged some unusual power in the adversary while trying to explain it on a mean basis. The early response to the voice in the wilderness came from outcasts, destitute and slaves—the "meanest," to use the koranic word (26:111). Five years of labor yielded a disappointing, albeit not discouraging, harvest.

When ridicule and sarcasm were deemed ineffective the Quraysh resorted to more violent tactics. This necessitated the migration of Muhammad's followers to Christian Abyssinia, where the Prophet had reason to believe they would not be molested. Eighty-three families or more responded (615). These were the first batch of Emigrants (*muhajirun*) who with the Companions (*sahabah*) constituted the nobility of the new community. Muhammad's patron abu-Talib chivalrously refused to deliver his nephew, not because he believed in his prophethood—which he did not—but because he felt bound by the clan code of honor. A change in faith did not justify outlawing a member of the family. Economic boycott was the only weapon left. All the other clans of the Quraysh cooperated. The Prophet and his clan were isolated in their part of the town, denied business transactions or marriage dealings with the rest of the tribe. The quarantine lasted three years, ending in 619, about the time both Khadijah and abu-Talib died.

Muhammad's position deteriorated. A fresh field for missionary activity was considered desirable. Taif, seventy-five miles southeast of Mecca, was the place favored. Unlike Mecca, described in the Koran as lying in a barren valley, Taif was an agrarian settlement on a high plateau. It served as a summer resort for wealthy Meccans and housed a shrine for Allat ("the goddess"), one of the three mighty "daughters of Allah" whom Muhammad in a weak moment accepted as intercessors. But later, revelation came to him (22:51) abrogating the verse in which the intercession was authorized as one "prompted by Satan."

In Taif Muhammad received a rude welcome. A mob flung stones at him. He sought refuge in a garden which turned out to

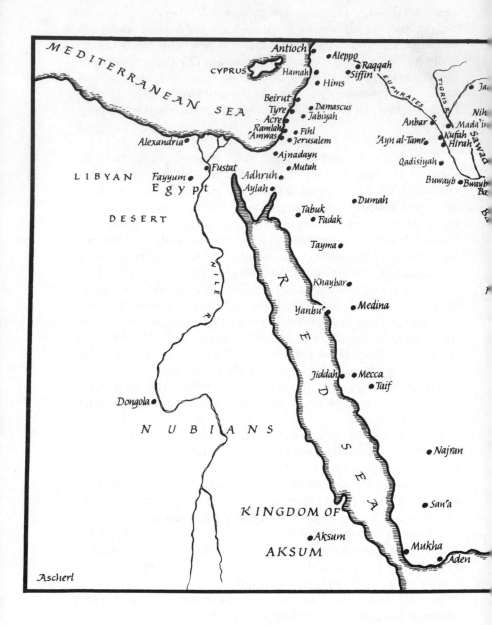

MEDITERRANEAN SEA

CYPRUS

LIBYAN

DESERT

Antioch
Aleppo
Hamah
Raqqah
Hims
Siffin
EUPHRATES
TIGRIS R.
Ja

Beirut
Tyre
Acre
Ramlah
'Amwas
Damascus
Jabiyah
Fihl
Jerusalem
Anbar
Mada'in
Kufah
Hirah
'Ayn al-Tamr
Nih
Sawad

Alexandria
Ajnadayn
Mutah
Qadisiyah
Buwayb
Bwayb
Ba

Fayyum
Fustat
Adhruh
Aylah
Dumah
Ba

Egypt

Tabuk
Fadak

Tayma

NILE R.

Khaybar

Yanbu'
Medina

RED SEA

Dongola

Jiddah
Mecca
Taif

NUBIANS

Najran

San'a

KINGDOM OF

Aksum
Mukha
Aden

AKSUM

Ascherl

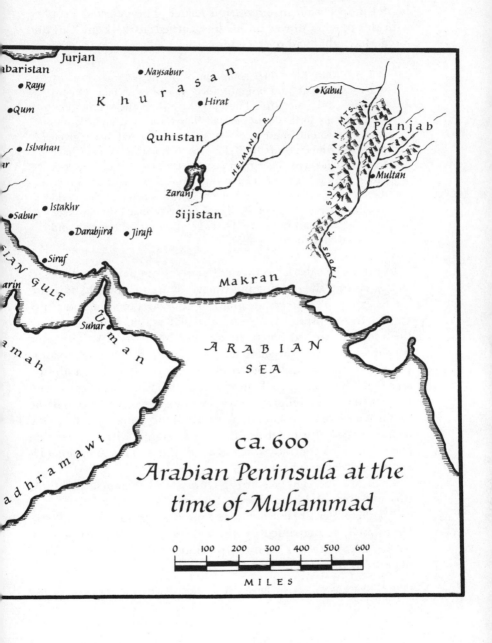

ca. 600
Arabian Peninsula at the
time of Muhammad

0   100   200   300   400   500   600

MILES

be the property of an opposition leader. The dejected Prophet, with this moving prayer on his lips, turned his back on Taif and faced Mecca that had rejected him:

> O Lord, unto Thee do I complain of my helplessness, paucity of resourcefulness and insignificance vis-à-vis other men. O most merciful of the merciful, Thou art the lord of the helpless and Thou art my lord. To whom wilt Thou abandon me? To one afar who would abuse me? Or to one who has been given power over me? Assuredly if Thy wrath is not upon me, I have no worry. For Thy favor then encompasses me. I therefore seek refuge in the light of Thy countenance, the light by which darkness is illumined and all affairs of this world and the world to come are rightly ordered. May it never be that I should incur Thy anger or fail to satisfy Thee. For there is no resource and power save in Thee.[1]

In Mecca he calculated that tribesmen from neighboring desert camps visiting the city for pilgrimage or frequenting its fairs for the exchange of their goods might be the ones to stretch the proverbial Arab hospitality to the spiritual realm. Interviews with their shaykhs turned out to be an exercise in futility. The same occasions, however, provided a new opportunity. He met visitors from Yathrib (250 miles north of Mecca) who seemed mildly interested. They had vaguely heard from their Jewish fellow townsmen that a great religious leader was expected and thought he might be the one. Muhammad's mother had some uncertain connection with Yathrib. On a lucky day he signed with a delegation from that city a contract which assured him and his followers protection in their new home.

To escape the vigilance of the Quraysh, Muhammad had some two hundred of his followers slip quietly into Yathrib, to be called thereafter al-Madinah (Medina, the city [of the Prophet]). He himself, accompanied by abu-Bakr and 'Ali, arrived September 24, 622. With this hegira (*hijrah*), not exactly a "flight" but a migration, the Meccan period ends and the Medinese begins.

[1] Ibn-Hisham, *Sirah,* ed. Ferdinand Wüstenfeld (Göttingen, 1858–59), p. 280; cf. Guillaume, p. 193.

III

The hijrah marked the turning point in Muhammad's career, the starting date of the annals of Islam and the first step of the crucial stage in the development of Allah's religion and His community (*ummah*). It turned the Prophet's life from frustration to self-realization. Seventeen years later Caliph 'Umar chose the beginning of the lunar year in which the hijrah took place—in preference to the year of Muhammad's birth or call—as the starting date of Moslem chronology. The Islam of Medina became the Islam of the world and the community of Medina served as the nucleus of the Arab nation and its government became the prototype of the Moslem empire.

In Medina the seer in Muhammad receded to the background, the practical man of affairs pushed to the fore. First among the new problems was feeding and housing the destitute Muhajirun. This was solved by boarding them among the new converts (*ansar*, supporters). Thus was the theory of the new religion as a fraternity put early into practice. It worked. The Ansar must have increased rapidly. The socio-economic malaise of Medina was the same as that of Mecca, transition from nomadism to a stationary culture—except that Medinese settlements were chiefly agrarian, whereas in Mecca the way of life was essentially urban and mercantile. Both involved conflict between the old and the new. On the political side, however, the situation differed. Mecca presented a unified authority under the Quraysh, whereas Medina had no such leadership. Here the situation was characterized by feuds and petty wars between the two leading tribes, the Aws and the Khazraj, and complicated by the existence in the city of three tribes which followed a strange religion, Judaism. Lack of political unity and the presence of a community with Messianic expectations must have predisposed Medina to accept a prophet with authority anchored in religion.

But in two years the strained economy of a host city with limited resources was approaching the breaking point. Meccan caravans returning from Syria laden with dinars and merchandise offered an irresistible temptation. A blow at the caravan was indeed at the lifeline of Mecca. The hour struck on a day of Rama-

dan (mid-March 624), during the "holy truce." If Christ could
justify his disciples' behavior on a Sabbath on the ground that
the Sabbath was made for man, why could not Muhammad justify his truce-breaking raid on the same ground? The locale was
Badr, a watering place southwest of Medina, where Muhammad
waited. The expected caravan consisted of 1,000 camels under the
leadership of abu-Sufyan, head of the aristocratic Umayyah clan
of the Quraysh. Abu-Sufyan got wind of the possible interception
at the wells of Badr and sent to Mecca for reinforcements. They
came, about 900 strong, accompanied by female singers to spark
the courage of the fighters. Muhammad commanded 314 Moslems
according to the standard report in ibn-Hisham.

The battle began, as usual, with single combats between champions, followed by a general melée. The instructions to the Moslems were to fight in closed ranks, using their arrows and keeping
swords for later. So confident were the Quraysh of victory that
they fought with no plan and under no discipline. While they
battled for their possessions, the foe battled for its very survival
and for Allah. The defeat was catastrophic. The Meccans fled,
leaving about seventy dead and seventy prisoners. Only eighty
"martyrs" fell. The distribution of the booty, assigning to Allah
and His Messenger one fifth (sur. 8:42), established a precedent.

The Prophet offered magnanimously to accept ransom. One of
the prisoners, the husband of his daughter Zaynab, presented her
necklace, a wedding gift from her mother. Muhammad remem-
bered it on the neck of his beloved Khadijah. After a sleepless
night he ordered his son-in-law freed, with no ransom, but on
condition of restoring Zaynab to her father.

While as a military engagement this first encounter of Islam
with polytheism cannot be considered of major significance, psy-
chologically it was. The Quraysh fell in prestige and self-con-
fidence as Muhammad and his followers rose. The victory was
interpreted as a divine sanction of the new faith and as a long-
foretold punishment of unbelievers. Even the angels, a thousand
of them, took part in it (sur. 8:9–12, 17). True, the second year at
Uhud abu-Sufyan and his Meccans avenged their defeat, even
wounded the Prophet (March 625), but the glamor of Badr was
not tarnished. Islam soon recovered and its propagation seemed
assured. Hitherto a religion within a state, now it became more

than a state religion, it itself became identified with the state. Then and there Islam came to be what the world has ever since recognized it to be—a militant polity.

Taking courage from Uhud, the Quraysh with Jewish allies and Bedouin mercenaries (the *ahzab* "confederates" of sur. 33) dared a final attempt on Medina. They reached the city (627) with 10,000 men—Muhammad could muster 3,000—to find it surrounded by a series of trenches, a novelty in Arabian warfare. A Persian follower of Muhammad is credited with the innovation, which disgusted particularly the Bedouins. The besiegers withdrew after a month, leaving twenty dead and determined never again to measure swords with the Moslems.

The turn of the Jews came. Throughout his early career Muhammad had endeavored to work out a coexistence within the framework of the two older monotheisms (2:127–31). A number of their essential features were adopted. His prophethood was in the same series as that of Abraham and of Jesus. Prayer was ordered toward Jerusalem, eating the food of the People of the Book and marrying their women were lawful (sur. 5:7). It was not long after migrating to Medina that Muhammad began to be disillusioned, however. Any Messianic hope he might have cherished was dashed. Jews considered themselves God's chosen people, the only seed of Abraham, unwilling to integrate or be integrated.

A cold war ensued. Early in his second year at Medina he ordered the direction of ritual prayer (*qiblah*) changed from Jerusalem to Mecca (2:139, 144, 145). The muezzin's voice replaced the trumpet and the gong. The People of the Book were charged with having corrupted the pure religion, concealed and falsified the revelation (3:57–62; 5:17). The two sides found themselves at irreconcilable odds. Polemic attacks developed into military ones. The *casus belli* was provided shortly after Badr by a Jew playing a prank on a Moslem woman customer in his shop by so fastening her skirt at the back that when she stood up a considerable portion of her body was displayed. A Moslem witness killed the prankster and was in turn killed in revenge. The entire Jewish tribe was thereupon attacked, fled from its quarters and landed in Syria, leaving behind its weapons and property. The following year (625) another Jewish tribe was expelled, leaving their houses and palm gardens to be parcelled out among needy Emigrants and Supporters. Certain exiles found refuge in Khaybar, a fertile Jewish oasis a hundred miles north of Medina. Khaybar was protected by strongholds impregnable against Bedouin raids. The colony became a center of intrigue against Islam and sent a contingent to the Meccan siege of Medina. After a two-week attack, ending June 628, Khaybar surrendered, agreed to yield annually to Muhammad half the income of its gardens and fields—a needed relief—and was rendered innocuous. Thus was the Jewish problem in Arabia solved.

The Prophet's checkered career in Medina as a politician, warrior, leader and administrator is reflected in the difference in the revelation of this period from the revelation of the preceding one. Surahs revealed in Mecca are concise, incisive, musical with rhythm and rhyme and rich in ideology. They emphasize God's oneness together with His attributes, and man's subservience to and dependence on Him. In an early surah (112) God addresses Muhammad:

> Say: He is God alone,
> God, the eternal,
> He begetteth not, nor is He begotten,
> And none is comparable unto Him.

Another early surah is called "the Opener," the first. This simple and meaningful surah, often compared to the Lord's Prayer, is reiterated by the faithful about twenty times a day, making it one of the most often repeated formulas ever devised.

> Praise be to God, Lord of the worlds,
> The merciful, the compassionate,
> King of the Judgment Day.
> Thee only do we worship and on thee do we call for aid.
> Guide us on to the straight path,
> The path of those to whom Thou hast been gracious,
> Not those with whom Thou art angry, or those who go astray.

In contrast Medinese surahs are lengthy, verbose and prosaic in style and more secular in content. Additional to laws governing prayer, fasting, pilgrimage and other religious practices, there are social and economic, military and political ordinances relating to marriage, inheritance and divorce, usury and slavery, food and drink, prisoners of war and booty. The richest in such material is number two. This is the earliest of Medinese surahs and the longest of all (286 verses). Legislation here extends to fighting "in the path of Allah," debts and trade, orphans and widows, menstruation and marital intercourse, suckling of children.[1] Alongside, we find one of the most impressive passages (256) on the sublimity of God:

> God! There is no God but He, the ever-living, the eternal. Slumber seizeth Him not, nor sleep. His is whatsoever is in heaven and whatsoever is in the earth. Who is there that can intercede with Him but by His own permission? He knoweth what is before them and what is behind them, yet naught of His knowledge do they comprehend save what He willeth. His throne extendeth over the heavens and the earth, and the upholding of both burdeneth Him not. And He is the exalted, the great.

IV

Shortly before he scored his military victory over Khaybar (628), Muhammad had scored a peaceful one over Mecca. He signed with its Quraysh oligarchy what is known as the pact of al-Hudaybiyah (a settlement nine miles north from Mecca), in which Moslems were so recognized as to leave no room for fear from that quarter. He thereupon became conscious that all serious local opposition had been overcome. Tradition ascribes to him letters addressed to neighboring heads of state inviting them to Islam. Delegations, we are told, flocked to him from all over the peninsula offering homage and with it their alms. In January 630, at the head of a thousand followers, Muhammad made his triumphal entry into his city of birth. No opposition was offered. His archenemy abu-Sufyan embraced the faith he had so vigorously and so long fought. By proscribing only ten of the opposition leaders—against the advice of 'Umar ibn-al-Khattab and other aides—the Prophet showed self-restraint worthy of his

[1] Sur. 2:186, 245, 247; 275, 282; 218, 234; 222, 223; 233.

statesmanship. Hardly a triumphal entry in ancient annals is comparable to his.

He, we are told, made his way into the Kaabah and smashed the three hundred and sixty idols while exclaiming: "Truth hath come, and falsehood hath vanished!" Thereby the great heathen sanctuary was purified and Islamized. By adopting the Kaabah with its Black Stone and the neighboring Zamzam, Islam entered upon its greatest legacy from heathenism and to that extent alienated itself from its two monotheistic sisters.

Two years later Muhammad led the annual pilgrimage to his religious capital and performed the rites. This proved to be his last visit and is therefore styled the farewell pilgrimage. In it he delivered a noble sermon considered the culminating point in his oratorical career. In part he said:

> Hearken, O ye men, unto my words and take ye them to heart. Know ye that every Moslem is a brother unto every other Moslem, and that ye are now one brotherhood.[1] It is, therefore, not legitimate for any one of you to appropriate unto himself anything that belongs to his brother unless it is willingly given by that brother.[2]

Three months after his return to Medina, Muhammad unexpectedly took ill and died complaining of severe headache on June 8, 632.

V

Muhammad and his Koran lived through medieval Christendom in infamy. This may seem strange in view of the fact that of all religions, Islam is the nearest of kin to Christianity. A Christian would find only a few dogmas in Islam objectionable. The alienation was due not to theological differences but to historical developments. Zoroastrianism, Hinduism, Buddhism posed no threat to Christianity. Islam did. Islam's early empire was built at the expense of the Byzantine. Its Saljuq champions threatened

---

[1] Cf. sur. 49:10.
[2] Philip K. Hitti, *History of the Arabs,* 9th ed. (London and New York, 1967), p. 120.

eastern Europe, provoking the Crusades. Its Arab armies occupied Spain and Sicily for centuries and raided France and Italy. Its last champions, the Ottomans, stood twice at the gates of Vienna.

Throughout that long period of conflict the portrait of Muhammad was that of a false prophet, an impostor, an oversexed dissolute. His coffin hung between heaven and earth, for neither would accept his corpse. Dante, however, split his body from the head down to the waist and consigned him to one of the low hells to become the chief of the damned souls who brought schism into religion. In his tragedy *Nahomet,* Voltaire portrays the hero as a camel dealer who receives from Gabriel that "incomprehensible book" whose "every page does violence to sober reason." Even Thomas Carlyle, whose choice of Muhammad for the role of the hero as a prophet was an indication of a new trend, considered the Koran "a wearisome confused jumble, crude, incondite, endless iterations, long-wordiness, entanglements; most crude, incondite; insupportable stupidity, in short! Nothing but a sense of duty could carry any European through the Koran." [1] The English essayist forgot that the Koran, like any other world classic, cannot be understood if studied by itself with no regard to the context of the economy, politics and religion of the period, and without projection against that vast background of culture of which it is a religious and literary monument. Happily, the researches of modern Western scholars[2] have rehabilitated the founder of Islam and rendered the Koran more comprehensible.

Muhammad suffered injustice not only from enemies but from friends. While he and the Koran were emphatic in their assertion that he was nothing but a man, with no superhuman quality, his followers endowed him with miracle-working power and lifted him from the stage of idealization to that of idolization and at least in folk religion to adoration.

[1] Thomas Carlyle, *On Heroes, Hero-Worship and the Heroic in History* (London, 1897), pp. 64–65.
[2] Such as W. Montgomery Watt, *Muhammad at Mecca* (Oxford, 1953), *Muhammad at Medina* (Oxford, 1956); Tor Andrae, *Mohammad: The Man and his Faith,* tr. Theophil Menzel (New York, 1957); Richard Bell, *The Qur'ān, Translated,* 2 vols. (Edinburgh 1937–39).

Stripped of all legendary accretions the historical Muhammad, Muhammad the man, the leader of men, the consummate statesman, the triumphant warrior, the impressive orator, the effective author, remains the ablest Arab in history.

'Umar ibn-al-Khattab: Founder of the Moslem Empire

The Arabians are truly an unruly camel and, by God, I am he who can keep them on the right path.

—'Umar ibn-al-Khattab

I

ON that sultry day in June 632, as Muhammad lay dead in 'A'ishah's hut at Medina, his infant community was thrown into a state of wild confusion. Some, accepting the fact of his mortality, wailed. Others, rejecting it, objected. Still others, stunned and bewildered, could not make up their minds. Amidst the tumult a voice, thunderous and threatening, rose: "By God, he of you who claims that the Prophet is dead, his limbs shall be severed from his body." The voice came from a towering, athletically built, thin-bearded middle-aged man, 'Umar ibn-al-Khattab. Soon another voice was heard, more serene and persuasive: "Remember ye men, if ye worship Muhammad, Muhammad is dead and gone. But if ye worship God, He is the ever-living, never-dying." It was the voice of an aged, wiry man, abu-Bakr, with tears still dripping from his eyes. He had just uncovered and kissed the Prophet's face. The storm subsided. The dead body was interred where it lay. A more serious, more practical problem was faced: Who was to be the successor?

As long as Muhammad lived he performed the functions of prophet, ruler, legislator, judge and commander in chief of the army—all in one. Specifically the question now arose as to who should succeed him, in all but his prophetic function. As the last of the prophets, Muhammad could have no successor.

Throw a debatable question before a house and invariably parties form. In this case the first party was the Emigrants, mostly Qurayshites, early believers and fellow sojourners of the Prophet in Medina. Their claim was obvious. Then came the Ansar. They argued that had it not been for the hospitable reception they had tendered the Prophet and his migrants and the subsequent military aid they gave, the cause would have been nipped in the bud. Last but not least the legitimists presented their claim. 'Ali, first cousin and son-in-law of the Prophet, father of his two grandsons and one of the first believers, was by Divine right and Muhammad's wishes the sole and only legitimate successor. In 'Ali's progeny the privilege should ever abide. Such an office, they continued, could not be left to the discretion of the people.

The first party won. It had two contenders for the highest honor: abu-Bakr and 'Umar ibn-al-Khattab, both fathers-in-law of the Prophet, both his intimate friends, close associates and confidants, both highly respected by all believers. The two men differed sharply in personality, physique and style of action, but agreed in their measure of dedication to Islam and loyalty to the memory of its founder. Of the two, 'Umar was undoubtedly the abler. In fact he was the best mind in Muhammad's entire entourage. But the sixty-year-old abu-Bakr was 'Umar's senior by eleven years, an earlier believer and the one designated by the fatally ill Muhammad to officiate in public prayer. He was generally favored. 'Umar was the first to shake his rival's hand and declare his allegiance. Abu-Bakr was proclaimed caliph (*khalifah*), the first in a series that was to last, at least in name, until 1924.

'Umar stood by his former associate, now his chief, as a loyal counselor, showing no signs of any jealousy or resentment he might have harbored. Chroniclers say he was the supreme judge (*qadi*, cadi) under abu-Bakr but his influence went beyond that. It was manifest in the two main events of the two-year-reign of abu-Bakr (632–34): the attempted compilation of the Koran and the "wars of apostasy." 'Umar is credited with having been the first to suggest that the Word of Allah be assembled and committed to writing, because its memorizers (*huffaz*) were being rapidly decimated by the current wars. The caliph demurred. "How can I," said he, "undertake what the Prophet did not?" Zayd ibn-Thabit, Muhammad's amanuensis and the logical man to head the undertaking, offered the same objection.

These wars, so the classical report goes, were prompted by the refusal—on Muhammad's death—of tribes throughout the peninsula to pay the legal alms (*zakah*) enjoined in the Koran. The caliph was adamant in his determination to fight them to the bitter end. In reality the wars must have been waged not so much to bring back defectors to the fold of Islam as to press new believers into it. For how could tribes as far as Bahrain have been converted in Muhammad's lifetime? Even Mecca did not yield until a couple of years before his death. Arabia had to be Islamized before it could Islamize other lands. It had to conquer itself before it could conquer the world.

The hero of these early campaigns was a brilliant young soldier of the Quraysh, Khalid ibn-al-Walid, destined to rise to giddy heights of success and fame. The carnage of his arms won him the title "sword of Islam." His severe treatment of Moslem prisoners of war sparked a feud between him and 'Umar that was to end on the plains of northern Syria with the humiliation of the general.

Equally influential was 'Umar in the Prophet's councils. He is credited with, among other things, having prompted the prohibition of wine (sur. 5:92), to which he was addicted before Islam, and with having pressed upon Muhammad the desirability of isolating and veiling his wives (sur. 33:53). He is also said to have recommended the choice of the site near the Kaabah, where tradition claims Abraham had prayed, for a mosque, and the use of the human voice for calling to public prayer as against the use of instruments, practiced by Christians and Jews. In other cases his opinions were rejected. Ever ready to unsheathe his sword, he suggested after the battle of Badr that all prisoners be beheaded. Later, on Muhammad's triumphal entry into Mecca, 'Umar recommended the death sentence for its leading citizen, abu-Sufyan, father of the future caliph Mu'awiyah. Indicative of the esteem in which the Prophet held his companion was the honorific title he gave him, Faruq (distinguisher between truth and falsehood). This must have been the source of two sayings ascribed to the Prophet: "God laid the truth on 'Umar's tongue and heart"; "Had God willed another Prophet after me, that would have been he." "Faruq" has since been proudly borne by many, including Egypt's last monarch.

Unlike his predecessor abu-Bakr, and second successor 'Ali, 'Umar could not claim the honor of priority in Islam; he was about number forty-five when converted. For years he was its bitterest opponent. But once espoused, Islam became to him the focus of the same intensity of emotion as it was previously of hatred. Among the victims of 'Umar's persecution, before his conversion, was his newly converted girl slave, whom he would whip, wait to recoup his breath and start again whipping her. Another victim was his sister. On a fateful day in 616, when Muhammad with a small band of followers was shut up in tight quarters and boycotted by his townsmen, 'Umar, with fire in his eyes and a sword in his hand, rushed to attack the band. The doorman confronted him with a shocking remark: "Why not begin with your sister and brother-in-law?" 'Umar hurried back and entering his sister's house he noticed her trying to hide something under her. He guessed it was something written relating to the new religion. Both she and her husband were thereupon attacked. As the blood streamed from her body, she screamed, "Do what you will; Islam will never depart from our hearts." Saying this, she handed him the sheet of paper in which he read:

> A revelation from Him, who created
> the earth and the high heavens,
> The merciful one, established on
> the throne.
> Unto Him belongeth whatsoever is
> in the heavens and whatsoever is in the
> earth and whatsoever is between, and
> whosoever is beneath the sod. . . .
> Verily, I am God; there is no other
> God whatsoever but Me. Serve me then. . . .
> Sur. 20:3–14

That was enough. A changed 'Umar retraced his steps to the Prophet's door and heard a voice from inside: "Let him in. If he is intent on peace, peace he shall have; but if intent on slaughter, he shall be slaughtered with his own sword." The peace the new convert sought and found turned out to be the gateway of a turbulent career the like of which perhaps no other Arabian ever experienced.

Stripped of its dramatic overtones, this story of the conversion of the greatest figure of Islam after Muhammad (told by ibn-Hisham, ibn-Sa'd in his *al-Tabaqat* and by other early biographers) brings out the impulsive character and fiery temper of the man. He was then about thirty-four years old. The circumstances of his conversion prompted the appellation "St. Paul of Islam," but the analogy stops there. In the roles the two played in the spread of their respective faiths, they differed radically. In fact in his impatient temperament this early Moslem reminds us more of St. Peter.

It is interesting to note that in his condemnation of Muhammad, 'Umar put first the splitting of the Quraysh by that fake of a religion the new prophet was preaching. Tribal solidarity, dear to the heart of every Arabian and an ancestor of our modern nationalism, was especially dear to 'Umar. He was then serving as an ambassador of his tribe to other tribes, allied or alienated. His qualifications were two: oratory and physique, both developed at the annual fair of 'Ukaz.

To 'Ukaz in the neighborhood of Taif flocked in the months of the annual tribal truce men and women from the area with the products of their herds, oases and handicrafts as well as the products of their brains. The last were orations and poetry. Athletes also had here their field day. This made of the fair a combination of supermarket, *salon littérataire* and gladiatorial arena. As poets recited their original compositions vying for the coveted prize, champion wrestlers fought their duels and merchants exhibited their wares. All the while visitors moved along sipping date wine and listening to singing girls. The prize for poetry, legend asserts, consisted in having the winning composition inscribed in golden letters and suspended on the door of the Kaabah. No Nobel Prize winner of today could be prouder than were such prize winners. Seven such odes (*mu'allaqat*) have come down to us. They constitute the literary masterpieces of pre-Islam. Poetry was then Arabia's only cultural asset.

As a youth, 'Umar must have been a habitual visitor to these fairs. His main interest was in poetical and oratorical compositions. He must have memorized much of what he heard. 'Ukaz' stylistic influence, together with that of the Koran, is evident in 'Umar's later speeches and correspondence, concise, incisive, rhythmic and rhymed. On the physical side his whip was as effective as his pen or tongue, giving rise to the saying " 'Umar's whip is as painful as his sword." 'Ukaz held another attraction to 'Umar, wrestling, in bouts of which he sometimes participated. On at least one occasion he floored a Bedouin champion. He could also, so we are told, jump onto an unbridled racing horse and land erect on its back. Meccan damsels acclaimed their townsman's feats and sang his praises. When he dropped from sight, they were told he had become a merchant (*tajir*), concerned with the support of a family.

Mecca, we learned before, was a merchant republic. 'Umar presumably dealt in barley and other cereals and had an interest in the caravan trade centered in his native city. But that he visited Syria and Persia (claimed by a late historian al-Mas'udi in his *Muruj al-Dhahab*) does not inspire credence. Commerce required some knowledge of reading and writing. 'Umar was cited first of seventeen Qurayshites who could do that.

Domestic affairs are not reckoned by Moslem biographers a theme worthy of their treatment. From sporadic references, however, we gather that in pre-Islam 'Umar had four or five wives, one of whom, 'Asiyah (rebellious) had her name changed to a more befitting one, Jamilah (beauteous). Islam deprived him of one of his two favorites, wine, but not of the other, women. He continued to specialize in youthful, beautiful women. In all he married nine—of whom three had been slaves and then concubines—and divorced three, one of them because she refused to follow him into the new faith. When later in life he sought the hand of a young daughter of 'Ali for the "honor and blessing" of being associated with the Prophet's family, he had to pay 40,000 dirhams as a dowry. In one proposal he was rebuffed. A daughter of abu-Bakr consulted with her sister 'A'ishah and judged him "rude of manner, austere in living and severe on women." Clearly some of these marriages, as in Muhammad's case, were political. One of his wives, 'Atikah, remained closely attached to him to the last day of his life and mourned him in an elegy that has come down to us.

'Umar fathered nine boys and four girls. The most distinguished of his daughters was Hafsah, whom Muhammad married in the third year of the hijrah. In all conjugal disputes, not excluding a crucial one, 'Umar sided with the husband. When Mariya the Copt gave birth to a son and began to be favored by Muhammad, Hafsah and 'A'ishah put up a fight that almost led to divorce. The episode was considered of sufficient importance to warrant a revelation (sur. 33. 28–32). No affairs of 'Umar the husband or 'Umar the father were ever allowed to interfere with the discharge of the heavy duties and responsibilities of 'Umar the supreme head of the Moslem state.

II

The removal of abu-Bakr (August 634) and before him Muhammad from the scene left 'Umar and Khalid ibn-al-Walid as the two leading actors on the stage of Islam.

In what might be termed his inaugural address, 'Umar declared:

> Remember all ye people: I have been given the rule over you on the assumption of being the best qualified and strongest among you and the ablest of you to conduct your general affairs.[1]

Later, and as if on second thought, we hear him pray: "O God, I am harsh, soften me; I am weak, strengthen me; I am stingy, render me generous." From such early utterances (review the one at the heading of this chapter) we gain a glimpse of the dynamics of this caliph's life, faith—faith in a trinity of God, Muhammad and

[1] In this and other cases where the quoted material varied in its Arabic versions, the translation is composite and at times rather free.

self. His faith in self stemmed from physical prowess and intellectual talents; in God, from his wholehearted espousal of Islam; in Muhammad, from 'Umar's acceptance of him as the Prophet of God. But his confidence in self ended where his faith in God began. Listen to this soliloquy when, in a fit of anger, he whipped a Bedouin seeking his aid against an oppressor and the Bedouin refused to retaliate with a blow as ordered:

> Lowly thou wert, O Son of al-Khattab, and Allah exalted thee; stray and Allah guided thee; weak and Allah strengthened thee. He also made thee rule over the necks of thy people; and when one came seeking thy aid thou didst strike him. What wilt thou say to thy Lord when thou standest before Him? [1]

At 'Umar's accession war was the preoccupation of the people of Arabia. Their wars were conducted on foreign soil, their land having been at least nominally pacified and consolidated in abu-Bakr's reign by the sword of Khalid under the banner of Islam. A few non-Moslem pockets in the peninsula had remained and, in pursuance of his predecessor's nationalist policy, 'Umar expelled the Christians from Najran. They were compensated and allowed to migrate to Syria.

The war machine developed in the conquest of Arabia acquired a momentum that had to be directed into new arenas. The new religion, we learned, made of the Arabians presumed brethren. Even tribal raids, a national institution from time immemorial, were now discouraged. But the urge remained and had to seek a new outlet. Significantly, the early campaigns beyond the peninsula were called "raids" (Arabic, sing. *ghazwah*, razzia). The early chronicler al-Waqidi entitled his book *Kitab al-Maghazi*. As in raids, booty was an objective.

Raids into Iraq and Syria, initiated by abu-Bakr, were reinforced and escalated by his successor, who fittingly assumed a newly coined title, commander of the believers (*amir al-mu'minin*), in preference to caliph. The two titles were thereafter used synonymously. The leading figure in the Iraq campaign was Khalid ibn-al-Walid, in the Syria campaign abu-'Ubaydah ibn-al-Jarrah. Abu-'Ubaydah was an early convert and Companion of

---

[1] Ibn-al-Athir, *Al-Kamil,* in Hitti, *History of the Arabs,* p. 176.

the Prophet. He was the third member of the triumvirate that
exercised decisive influence over the Prophet's policies and the
developments following his death, the other two being abu-Bakr
and 'Umar. Khalid's advance as far as the Euphrates was facilitated by the presence of tribes from Arabia domiciled for centuries in the area. Their kingdom, a satellite of Persia, was centered
in Hirah on the lower Euphrates. Though Christianized, they
spoke Arabic. Their city offered no opposition to the Moslems
(633), pledged itself to pay tribute and served as a base for forays
into neighboring Persian territory.

On orders from Medina Khalid had to interrupt his successful
march and rush to relieve the Moslem army attacking Syria and
harassed by the Byzantine defenders. The first major victory he
scored was over Damascus. The capital of the Byzantine province
of Syria, which extended from the Taurus into Sinai, opened its
gates in September 635 after six months' siege. The besiegers
found collaborators inside the city walls, headed by the native
bishop and by the state treasurer. The state treasurer was the father of St. John Damascene, the celebrated hymnologist-theolo-
gian of the East Syrian Church. The populace received the newcomers with unreserved joy. To them Arabians were closer ethni-
cally and linguistically than their Byzantine overlords. Both were
Semites; Aramaic and Arabic were cognate languages and had
little in common with Greek.

As in the case of the western frontier of Iraq, the eastern frontier of Syria had been infiltrated by Arabians, headed by the
Ghassan tribe, who in the centuries immediately before Islam had
established an amirate based in al-Jabiyah, fifty miles south of
Damascus. Though by this time Christianized, Syrianized, and
acting as satellites in the Byzantine orbit, they had retained their
Arabic tongue and maintained some consciousness of their Arabian origin.

To the Christians of Syria and Iraq the new religion from Arabia had the appearance of a Christian sect. Though it had been
under Greco-Roman rule for about a thousand years, inland
Syria was not as Hellenized as the coastal region and as the north
with its Antioch, Seleucia, Laodicea (al-Ladhiqiyah, Latakia)
and other Greek-founded cities. Damascus was not unique in its
treatment of the invaders. In Shayzar, a suburb of Hamah, the

welcoming committee included singers and tambourine players.

The Syrian Church was considered by the Byzantine as unorthodox, and subject to conversion if not persecution. The main issue was the nature of Christ. The rituals of the two Churches differed in origin, development and language. The adherence of the Syrians to their church was one form of expressing their nationalist feeling as a suppressed minority. In addition to the religious there was the political alienation, aggravated by heavy state taxation. Syrians hoped for better treatment from the new conquerors.

The terms of the Moslem treaty with Damascus served as a model for later ones.

> In the name of God, the compassionate, the merciful. This is what Khalid ibn-al-Walid would grant the people of Damascus if he enters it: He shall give them security for their lives, property and churches. Their city walls shall not be demolished and no Moslems shall be quartered in their dwellings. Thereunto we give them the pact of God together with the protection of His Prophet (God's blessing and peace be upon him!), of the caliphs and of all believers, so long as they pay poll-tax, nothing but good shall befall them.[1]

The second victory scored by Khalid was more difficult to win. The locale was the juncture of the Yarmuk, an eastern tributary of the Jordan, with a tributary of its own. The Moslem army numbered some 25,000, the Byzantine twice as many. But more than half of the Byzantines were Armenians, Syrianized Arabs and other mercenaries with no deep loyalty to Constantinople. The will to conquer was on the other side. Paradise with special privileges was promised by Islam to him who died on the battlefield. After some skirmishing the two enemies joined in battle. It was a hot August day in 636 clouded by a fierce sand storm, to which sons of the desert were not strange. Arabian generalship succeeded in maneuvering the enemy to a tight triangle between two streams facing the gust-driven, needle-like particles of sand. The chants of the accompanying priests proved less effective than the battle cry *Allahu akbar!* (God is greatest!). Those who were not mercilessly slaughtered were relentlessly driven into the

[1] Philip K. Hitti, *Origins of the Islamic State* (tr. of al-Baladhuri, *Futuh al-Buldan*) (New York, 1966, reprint Beirut, 1966), p. 187.

stream beds; only a few escaped. The fate of Syria, one of the fairest of Byzantine provinces, was then and there decided. In his headquarters at Antioch, Emperor Heraclius, who had mustered the largest force possible and pinned his hope on it, realized the sad fact. "Farewell, O Syria," were his parting words, "and what an excellent country this is for the enemy."

Heraclius' unceremonious exit from the Syrian scene left northern Syria demoralized. In the south Jerusalem, third holiest city in Islam after Mecca and Medina, yielded after a prolonged siege.

From the pinnacle of his glory and fame Khalid, "sword of Islam" and double hero of Iraq and Syria, was toppled down by 'Umar. The caliph, it will be recalled, had harbored ill feeling against the general since abu-Bakr's days. Rumors of Khalid's extravagance in living and of lavish bounties conferred on his friends and admirers jarred in the ears of the austere caliph. A poet who sang the military feats of the general received 10,000 dirhams. We are even told that when asked to render an account of his local expenditures and the share for the national treasury, Khalid referred 'Umar to an earlier reply he had made to his predecessor, in effect: Mind your own business. The treasury's share (fay'; sur. 59:6–10) amounted to one fifth of the spoils.

'Umar then ordered his generalissimo abu-'Ubaydah to question Khalid and, if guilt was established, to tie his hands with his own turban and deliver him bare-headed. The shock to the people must have been greater than that when President Truman bluntly recalled and dismissed General MacArthur, hero of Japan and Korea. Khalid, it seems, voluntarily relinquished his Syrian post and delivered himself to the commander of the believers in Medina. He reimbursed the treasury in the amount of 20,000 dirhams, and in a public statement was absolved by the caliph of insubordination. To explain his orders, 'Umar said that public adoration of Khalid had reached such dimensions that it could detract from adoration to God. He unwittingly revealed the probable real motive: jealousy. In 'Umar's firmament there could not be two suns.

Khalid was the first of military heroes to be driven into the limbo of Arab history. He died (ca. 642) in a suburb of Hims, where his name is commemorated in an elegant modern mosque.

The turn of the administrator came. How to govern such a newly acquired, highly developed country baffled the unsophisticated mind of a novice at international affairs. In his wisdom 'Umar summoned his army officers to a conference at al-Jabiyah, headquarters of the Syrian army. There he arrived (638) dressed "in tattered clothes" and on "camel back," accompanied by the principal Companions and aides. No band, no singers, no ceremonial procession hailed the advent of the chief. The nearest thing to a song came later, in the form of the chant of the call to public prayer by the Prophet's muezzin, Bilal, whose stentorian voice had not been heard since the master's death. The first thing 'Umar did was to chide his officers for arriving on horseback and dressed in Syrian brocade.

We have no proceedings from this first significant state conference in Islam. But from subsequent developments we can surmise certain decisions. The Byzantine framework of the administration was retained. The districts into which the province was divided were not altered. A basis for a system of taxation was laid. With that went the creation of the bureau of registry (*diwan*) for pensions the amounts of which were determined by relationship to the Prophet and seniority in Islam. Abu-'Ubaydah was confirmed as governor general of the Syrian province.

While in Syria, 'Umar visited Jerusalem. The impression he left on its Christian population was expressed by Theophanes in no less exaggerated terms than the impression made on his Moslem subjects:

> He entered the Holy City clad in a worn mantle of camel's hair and bearing a diabolical expression of piety. He asked to be shown the temple of the Jews, built by Solomon, that there he might worship his own blasphemies. On seeing him, Archbishop Sophronius exclaimed: "Truly, this is the abomination of desolation spoken of in Daniel the Prophet [11:31] as standing in the holy place." [1]

Arab chroniclers have a footnote to add to this dramatized episode. The hour for Moslem prayer having come while the archbishop was guiding his guest at the Church of the Holy Sepul-

[1] Theophanes, *Chronographia*, ed. Carolus de Boor (Leipzig, 1858), p. 339.

cher, he offered him a rug to perform his religious duty. But the
caliph refused lest his action encourage his people to claim the
site. On the spot where he prayed, in front of the church, a
mosque arose bearing his name. It still stands.

Shortly after that spread a virulent plague, originating in
'Amwas, biblical Emmaus and site of the Palestine Moslem army
camp, devastating the entire province. 'Umar authorized abu-
'Ubaydah and others to return to Medina, but the governor general protested. "How could we," wrote he, "flee from God's
decree?" 'Umar's characteristic reply read, "You flee from God's
decree unto God's decree." The governor was one of the 25,000 victims claimed by the plague. His tomb became a place of pious
pilgrimage. It was visited by the amir 'Abdullah of Transjordan
(1933) as an atonement for having rented a large estate to Zion-
ists.

Syria served as a springboard for further conquests in Egypt
and Armenia. The hero of the Egyptian campaign was 'Amr ibn-
al-'As, a general in the Syrian army. He wrote to 'Umar for authorization, offering as a qualification that he had been a cara-
vaneer on the Hijaz-Egypt route and knew the country well. The
caliph's reply, so the story goes, read: "If this reaches you before
crossing the border, return. Otherwise, proceed and God's aid be
with you." 'Amr got wind of the message and did not open it
until he had entered Egypt.

In dash and military brilliancy 'Amr had only one rival in
early Islam, Khalid ibn-al-Walid. Like Khalid he was a Qurayshite but a late convert. At the head of some 4,000 men, later augmented to 20,000, he crossed the Syro-Egyptian border. The
march through Egypt from east to west was even easier than that
through Syria from south to north. Basically the reasons were similar. Its people felt alienated from their Byzantine masters by
blood, language and denomination. Their governor Cyrus, who
held also the patriarchate of Alexandria, pursued an ecclesiastical
policy involving attempts at converting the Copts, and a civil policy entailing onerous taxation. Copts shared the Christological
view with Syrians, and like them hopefully looked to the newcomers for relief.

'Amr offered Cyrus the usual three choices: tribute, Islam or
the sword. The choice was a foregone conclusion. Seven months'

siege of the strongly fortified Babalyun (outside modern Cairo), ending in 641, opened the way to Alexandria, the capital. The impression left upon Cyrus' envoys, as reported by the Arab historian of Egypt's conquest (ibn-'Abd-al-Hakam, *Misr*) was thus expressed:

> We have witnessed a people to each and every one of whom death is preferable to life, and humility to prominence, and to none of whom this world has the least attraction. . . . Their leader is like unto one of them; the low cannot be distinguished from the high, nor the master from the slave. And when prayer time comes none of them absents himself; all wash their extremities and humbly observe their prayer.[1]

In the west Alexandria, with its 50,000-man garrison, double wall, moat and mighty fleet, was considered impregnable but offered little resistance. Political factions inside the city and demoralizing reports from fugitive generals played into the hands of the invaders. In September 642 the Byzantines evacuated the city. 'Amr's laconic report to 'Umar read:

> I have captured a city from the description of which I now refrain. Suffice it to say I have seized therein 4,000 villas, 40,000 baths, 40,000 poll-tax-paying Jews and 400 entertainment places for the royalty.[2]

The treaty terms followed those with Syria. The new rulers took over the substance of their predecessors' administrative system, kept the functionaries (mostly Copts) in their posts and imposed their usual tax. The told and retold story that the caliph ordered his general to burn the contents of the famous Alexandria library, whether they agreed with the Koran and were therefore useless or disagreed and were therefore unwanted, is one of those stories that make good fiction but bad history. It was first told six centuries after the alleged act. The books, which reportedly supplied the city baths for six months with fuel, were mostly parchment. Moreover no library of such dimensions was extant at that time.

[1] Hitti, *History of the Arabs*, p. 163.
[2] Ibn-'Abd-al-Hakam, in Hitti, *History of the Arabs*, pp. 164–65.

Politically the newly acquired possession provided a base for further expansion in Africa. Economically it served as a granary for Arabia as it had done for the Roman Empire. From his military camp and new capital Fustat (outside of Babalyun), 'Amr sought to rule his conquered domain as independently as Khalid had done. But he was a more wily politician than his Syrian counterpart, and when Medina appointed a civilian governor, limiting 'Amr's responsibility to army command, he protested: "This amounts to having one man hold the cow's horns while another milks it."

In the meantime things were not quiet on the eastern front. Khalid was succeeded in the command of the Iraq-Persian expedition by Sa'd ibn-abi-Waqqas. 'Umar may have considered limiting expansion to the territories already conquered, as Persia had no comparable geographical or historical ties with the peninsula. But how could he? His generals were already drunk with victory; their men had whetted their appetites for further booty; the people at home had "never had it so good" thanks to the flow of their share in spoils and tribute. The logic of developments was inescapable. On the other side the internecine wars in which Persia and its Byzantine rival had been long engaged left them both enfeebled and played into the hands of the new enemy.

From his headquarters at Hirah on the Euphrates Sa'd sent envoys to Emperor Yazdagird in his capital Ctesiphon (al-Mada'in). The envoys were received in the imperial palace, one of the most sumptuous in the world. Yazdagird and his courtiers, in their resplendent uniforms, wondered how such wretched-looking men, with cloaks on their backs, sandals on their feet and desert weapons in their hands, dared challenge the mighty empire of the Chosroes. Explained the spokesman:

> Wretched and erring were we, but God sent us His Messenger whom we first opposed but later followed. He replaced our lowliness with dignity, our weakness with strength, our poverty with prosperity and set us out to bring to His faith all those who differed. Hence the offer we now make you: Islam, tribute or the sword.[1]

1 Hitti, *History of the Arabs*, p. 163.

Such clichés, in varied forms, are put in the mouths of practically all envoys. Enraged, the emperor dismissed them unceremoniously with the remark: "Had you not been envoys, I would have ordered you executed." [1]

Sa'd lost no time. From Hirah he pushed on to its neighbor al-Qadisiyah, gateway to Persia. Here in the spring of 637 the first encounter with Persian forces took place. Sa'd commanded about 10,000, his opponent Rustam possibly six times as many. The strange appearance of war elephants on the battlefield was no less puzzling a phenomenon than the appearance of tanks in the first World War. Arabs saw them as "huge monsters manned with warriors, bedecked with banners and looking like moving castles." A Persian prisoner offered the right advice: Concentrate on the white elephant leading the corps and aim at its eyes. It worked. Consternation seized the herd. Soon the imperial commander in chief was seized and slain. Consternation spread into his herd. All Iraq west of the Tigris lay at the feet of the conqueror.

The news of the decisive Qadisiyah victory, followed by that of the successful fording of the Tigris, reached the capital and struck terror into the hearts of its people. The river, across the bank of which Ctesiphon lay, was considered a natural defense line, especially when, as at that time, it was swollen by spring floods. So precipitous was the flight of the emperor with his court and warriors that they had no time to carry along the accumulated imperial treasures of centuries. The remaining garrison offered but little resistance. Thus fell the proudest city of western Asia, heir of Nineveh and Babylon and rival of Constantinople. That day of May 637 when the muezzin's voice was raised from the "palace (Iwan) of the Chosroes" registered one of the most glorious moments in the long annals of militant Islam.

The royal booty dazzled the eyes of the warriors from the desert, and stretched the imagination of the reporters. Their stories were accepted by the greatest of Arab historians, such as al-Tabari. They assure us—without the benefit of a computer—that the value was exactly nine hundred million silver pieces. There were rich embroidered silks, gold vases and other kitchen utensils, gem-inlaid chairs and sofas all in quantity. Two *objects d'arts* were unique: a horse of solid gold with a saddle of silver and a

[1] Cf. Hitti, *Origins of the Islamic State*, pp. 41–42.

body studded with turquoise; and a carpet at the center of which
was a parterre of verdure surrounded by plants with fruits, flowers and birds glittering with precious stones.

One Persian city after the other tumbled. The ill-starred fugitive emperor fell victim to the greed of one of his own men. His
death marked the end of a twelve-hundred-year-old empire. The
new acquisition brought Islam into vital contact with a new ethnic group, Indo-Iranian, related more closely to Greeks and Romans than to Arabians, using a non-cognate tongue and practicing a strange religion, Zoroastrianism.

III

Had someone in 634, the year of 'Umar's accession, prophesied
that within a decade a new power from hitherto little-known
Arabia would emerge, destroy one of the two greatest world
powers—Persia—and strip the other—Byzantium—of its fairest
provinces, he would have been considered out of his mind. But
that was precisely what happened—and all in the reign of one
man. The question then arises, what specific role did this man
play in these world-shaking events?

In the minds of the chroniclers there was no question about it.
The early wars were conceived by the first caliph, continued and
executed to the minutest detail by orders from his successor in
Medina. This is hard to believe. From scattered bits of evidence
we infer that 'Umar was a semi-reluctant builder of the empire he
built. "Let not the sea intervene between you and me," he enjoined his generals. To the son of the desert, the sea was prohibi-
tive. His half-hearted authorization to 'Amr to cross the Egyptian
border may be recalled in this connection. 'Umar insisted that his
armies remain isolated, avoiding integration and thus maintaining a state of mobility. Hence their camps in Kufah, al-Jabiyah,
and Fustat. Arab historians, mostly theologians writing a couple
of centuries after the events, viewed those events in the wrong perspective both chronologically and ideologically. Hence their
Providential interpretation, not unlike the Hebrew interpretation of the conquest of Palestine. Two of the sources used in this
study were entitled *Futuh*, "opening" the way for the admission
of Islam the religion.

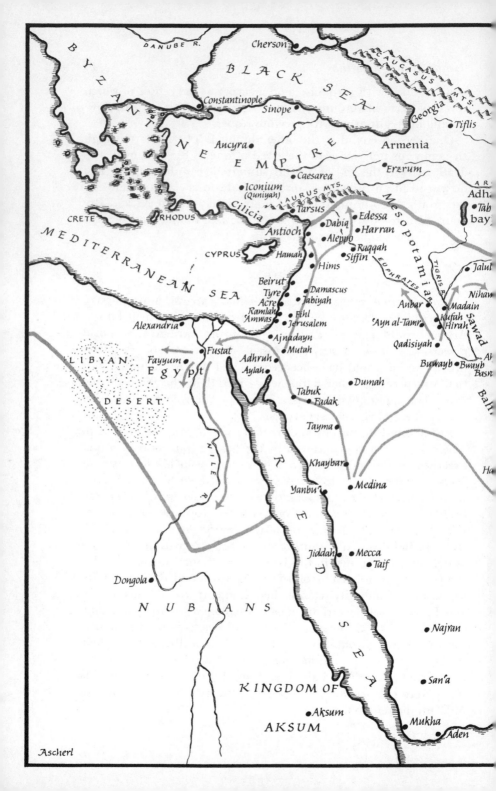

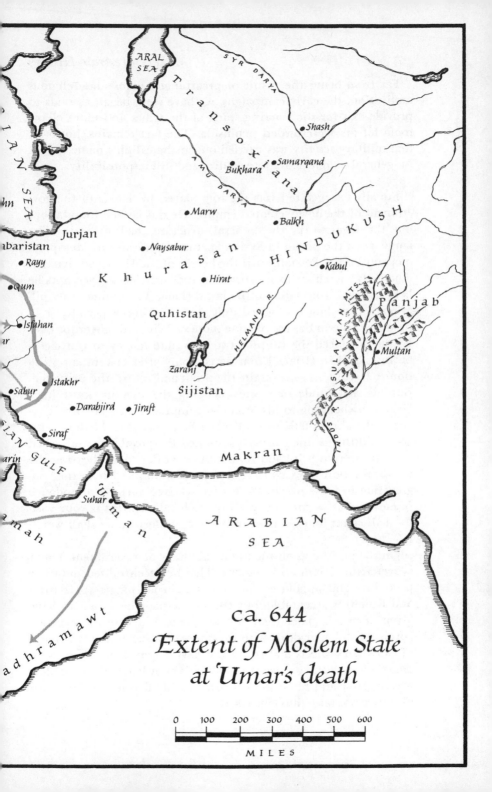

ca. 644
Extent of Moslem State
at 'Umar's death

0   100   200   300   400   500   600

MILES

Far from being the result of prearranged plans and religious motivation, the early campaigns, we have seen, began as raids to provide exit for the warring spirit of the tribes and more elbow room for an overcrowded peninsula. The fact remains, however, that military activity was carried out in the caliph's name, under his general guidance, remote control and full responsibility.

Equally exaggerated was the role played by 'Umar in the government of the newly created empire. He did lay the foundation; but the framework, the general structure, had to wait. The language of the diwan in Syria remained Greek and in Mesopotamia and Persia, Persian until the height of the Umayyad dynasty. The early merchant in him insisted that provincial governors be held strictly accountable to the last dirham. The annual holy pilgrimage gave him the opportunity for checking. Especially scrupulous was he in the use of state moneys. When his governor over Basrah advanced the caliph's two sons state money to transact a business deal in Hijaz, 'Umar agreed only after fervent supplication to having his sons retain the profit and return the principal. But the magnitude of money flooding the treasury must have been overwhelming to his financial comprehension. His first governor of Bahrain tells us that when he reported to Medina with 500,000 dirhams, the caliph questioned the possibility and asked him "to sleep over it" and report the next day. After hearing the identical report the second time, 'Umar announced it to the congregation in these words: "We have received such an abundance of money that we are not sure how to handle it. If it is your wish we shall count for each person his share; otherwise we shall weigh it."

On the judicial as on the financial aspect of government 'Umar is overcredited with achievement. That he decentralized judiciary procedure and appointed the first provincial judges (to Basrah and Kufah) is acceptable, but the instructions he is said to have given them echo later legal developments. Likewise the so-called covenant of 'Umar deals with questions relating to the treatment of Christian subjects that could not have arisen then. There is no denial of the fact, however, that 'Umar's knowledge of Islamic law was superior and his sense of justice highly developed. His ideal of justice was once thus expressed:

> By God, he that is weakest among you shall be in my sight
> the strongest until his rights have been assured for him; and
> he who is strongest shall be treated as the weakest until he
> complies with the law of Islam.

His ideal was put into practice. At the destruction of the Ghas-
sanid state in Syria, its last dynast Jabalah ibn-al-Ayham embraced Islam and undertook a pilgrimage to Mecca. While circum-
ambulating the Kaabah, a Bedouin stepped on his robe and
received a slap on the face. The caliph ordered a retaliatory slap
by the Bedouin. Shocked, the new convert turned his back on the
egalitarian society of Islam in favor of the Christian aristocracy of
Constantinople, where he lived happily thereafter.

More tragic is the case of 'Umar's son 'Abd-al-Rahman. He was
caught drunk in Egypt and Governor 'Amr administered less
than the prescribed penalty. The caliph ordered his son back
home, where the full number of lashes were administered in public, despite the young man's plea of illness. He thereupon died.
Even contemporary biographers of the caliph fail to note the in-
human element in the story, as they deny the unfair element in
'Umar's treatment of General Khalid. Idolization leaves no room
for the belief that the man could do wrong, although 'Umar himself at least once, in the case of the Bedouin cited above, had
admitted his wrong doing. Only Shi'ites, who never forgave him
for thwarting 'Ali's aspirations for the caliphate, and Sufis, to
whom he seemed too practical, do not share in the adoration.

IV

When on Friday, November 3, 644, the congregation of believers flocked to the noon service at the Medina Mosque, little notice
was taken of a man wrapped in a black cloak leaning on a col-
umn at the entrance. As the caliph, conspicuous because of his
towering height, approached, the man's arm emerged from inside
the cloak and plunged a dagger deep into his chest. 'Umar fell to
the ground, a stream of blood gushing from his wound. A "surgeon" poured milk into the victim's mouth and as "he saw white
with the blood" he declared the prognosis unfavorable. 'Umar
was buried under the floor of 'A'ishah's hut, beside his two friends

abu-Bakr and Muhammad, in the hope he would join them in sharing the delights of Paradise. In the confusion the murderer, a Persian Christian freedman, was not forgotten. As he attempted to escape he was torn to pieces. It was recalled that he had once complained to the caliph against his patron's treatment and that the caliph thought he had no case. Some believed, without sufficient evidence, that the crime was more than a personal one, the murderer being an instrument of a conspiracy by Persians resenting the loss of their country.

'Umar was the first caliph murdered in Islam. His two immediate successors met the same fate. He remained to the end simple, frugal and dedicated. His triangular belief in God, Muhammad and self never forsook him. In life, power did not erode his character, and in death, time did not tarnish his fame. To a Pakistani biographer, "he was at once Alexander and Aristotle, Messiah and Sulaiman [Solomon], Timur and Anūshirwān [Persian emperor], Imām Abū Hanīfa [Arab jurist] and Ibrāhīm Adham [Sufi saint] all in one." [1]

Dedicated believer, fiery and impassioned leader, destroyer of one of the two greatest empires of his time and builder of the caliphal institution that for thirteen centuries served as a bond of Islamic union, 'Umar ibn-al-Khattab takes his place as the second greatest in Arab history.

[1] Shibli Nu'mani, *'Umar the Great*, tr. Muhammad Saleem (Lahore, 1957), vol. II, p. 351.

Mu'awiyah: Architect of the Arab Empire

> *I apply not my lash where my tongue suf-*
> *fices, nor my sword where my whip is*
> *enough. And if there be one hair binding*
> *me to my fellow men, I let it not break.*
> *If they pull I loosen, and if they loosen I*
> *pull.*
>
> —Mu'awiyah ibn-abi-Sufyan

THE year 661 signaled the fall of the Orthodox caliphate in Medina and the rise of the Umayyad dynasty in Damascus. The
change was more than dynastic and geographic. It involved political philosophy, religious outlook and cultural orientation. This
makes the year 661 perhaps the most momentous in the first century of Islam. The two heroes of the act were 'Ali ibn-abi-Talib
and Mu'awiyah ibn-abi-Sufyan.

I

'Ali, we learned before, was first cousin of the Prophet, husband
of Muhammad's favorite daughter Fatimah and father of his only
two surviving grandsons, Hasan and Husayn. His father was
young Muhammad's protector. 'Ali was the first or second male
believer. Mu'awiyah was a scion of the aristocratic Umayyad clan
of the Quraysh, son of none other than the archenemy of the
Prophet. He was a late believer, his conversion dating from the
year of Muhammad's conquest of Mecca. 'Ali had a record of mil-

itary exploits beginning at Badr, where and after which he served
as Muhammad's standard bearer and figured prominently in the
slaughter of the enemy. Mu'awiyah had no such record. 'Ali's
sword dhu-al-Faqar (breaker of vertebrae) became proverbial.
With it, we are assured, he could bisect a horseman leaving the
lower part of the body on the mount while the upper rolled on
the ground. "No sword comparable to dhu-al-Faqar," sang the
ancient bard, "and no youth can match 'Ali." Incomparable also
was 'Ali's religiosity, expressed through strict observance of Islamic rites and spurning worldly affairs. Mu'awiyah's Islam was
suspect; it looked more like one of convenience than conviction.
The two contestants, however, had one point in common: birth
at Mecca about 600.

The struggle for power began with the murder of the third
caliph 'Uthman June 17, 656. 'Uthman, an Umayyad, was considered worldly and charged with nepotism and laxity in the enforcement of the Divine law. His was the first caliphal blood shed
by a Moslem and in connivance with other Moslems, including
probably 'Ali. The event sparked a series of civil wars (*fitnah*),
the first in the fraternity of Islam. So irreconcilable were the con-
flicts thus engendered that they not only plagued 'Ali's entire reign
(656–61) but passed on to posterity.

On his ascension to the throne the new caliph found himself
confronted with two formidable Meccan rivals, Talhah and ibn-
al-Zubayr, backed up by 'A'ishah. The "mother of believers"—
who was so young when she joined Muhammad's harem that she
took along toys with her—hated 'Ali with all the bitterness of a
wounded pride. Once, when she loitered behind her husband's
caravan, 'Ali had suspected her fidelity, necessitating Allah's intervention on her behalf (sur. 24:11–20). 'Ali who, unlike his
predecessors and most of his successors, led his troops in person to
and on the battlefield, won an easy victory (December 9, 656)
over his adversaries. The battle was fought outside Basrah and
was styled the "battle of the camel," after the camel on which
'A'ishah rode and which served as the rallying point for the rebel
warriors. The magnanimous victor bewailed his two fallen rivals,
prayed over them and ordered the "first lady of Islam" escorted to
Medina and treated with befitting consideration. He then proceeded to replace governors appointed by or sympathetic to his

predecessor. With one of them, Mu'awiyah of Syria, he did not
reckon.

Mu'awiyah had been sent as an army officer to Syria by abu-
Bakr, appointed governor by 'Umar and confirmed by 'Uthman.
Any personal ambitions he might have harbored must have been
kept in the background. He posed not as an avenger of a relative
but as a champion of legitimacy in the caliphate. He managed to
put 'Ali on the horns of a dilemma: "Produce 'Uthman's assassins
or accept the responsibility of an accomplice." The Koran did not
fail him as he searched for support for his position: "And slay not
the person whom God hast made inviolable except with justification. If anyone is slain wrongfully, We give to his next-of-kin authority, but let him not be extravagant in slaying; verily he will
be helped" (sur. 17:35). Meanwhile he exhibited in the Damascus
mosque the blood-stained shirt of the murdered aged caliph and
the two severed fingers of his wife, who tried to defend him as he
read the Koran he had compiled. 'Uthman's compilation became
the accepted text. His blood, we are told, flowed upon the sacred
leaves and—conveniently—stained the passage: "And God will
suffice you for defense against them" (sur. 2:131).

'Ali recruited an army of reputedly 50,000, mainly from Iraq,
where he had established a residence. The Iraqis had a personal
interest in combatting Syrian hegemony. The two armies stood
face to face on the plain of Siffin on the west bank of the Euphrates. Skirmishes dragged on for weeks. The climax came July 28,
657, when the tide turned in favor of 'Ali. On the advice of his
cavalry commander, the cunning 'Amr ibn-al-'As, Mu'awiyah ordered 500 copies of the Koran suddenly hoisted on soldiers'
lances, a gesture interpreted as an appeal from the decision of
arms to that of the Koran—whatever that might mean. Both sides
must have been worn out. Chroniclers swell the number killed to
70,000. Urged by his aides, the simple-hearted 'Ali ordered a halt
to the hostilities. He accepted his opponent's proposal to spare
Moslem blood and arbitrate the case. His will must have been by
this time paralyzed by the avalanche of problems besetting his
regime. He was about sixty years old and had fourteen sons and
nineteen daughters by nine wives and several concubines.

Mu'awiyah appointed 'Amr ibn-al-'As to represent him. Against
his better judgment 'Ali appointed abu-Musa al-Ash'ari, a man

of undoubted piety but of dubious loyalty to the 'Alid cause. Armed each with a written authorization and accompanied by 400 witnesses, the two arbitrators held their final public session in January 659 at Adhruh halfway between Ma'an and Petra on the pilgrimage route. What exactly transpired at this historic conference is difficult to ascertain from the conflicting sources. Probably both referees deposed both principals, which left only 'Ali the loser. His acceptance of the arbitration had raised Mu'awiyah's position from that of a rebel governor to a rival for the supreme office of the state; it lowered 'Ali's to that of a pretender. The judges' sentence therefore deprived 'Ali of a real office he held and Mu'awiyah of a fictitious office he had not yet dared publicly to claim.

This weak-kneed vacillating policy on the part of the caliph alienated a sizable body of followers who became known as Kharijites (those who went out). They rose in arms against him. He attacked their camp and almost annihilated them, for which he had to pay with his life. One Friday in January 661, as he was on his way to the mosque at Kufah, one of them stabbed him fatally with a poisoned saber. This he did to win the hand of a girl friend who had made her consent contingent upon it. 'Ali dead proved more effective than 'Ali living. Lacking in the foresight, resolution, alertness and expediency essential to political leadership, he was nevertheless rich in those traits that make an ideal Arab. Orthodox in religion, valiant in battle, eloquent in speech, true to his friends and magnanimous to his foes, he became to his followers the paragon of Moslem nobility and Arab chivalry. In anecdotal literature he has lived to the present as the Moslem Solomon. Unwittingly he became the author of a great schism in Islam. His Shi'ites constitute today the largest and most important minority in Islam. To "No God but God" and "Muhammad is the messenger of God" they added a third dogma, " 'Ali is the friend (*wali*) of God." In fact, in Shi'ite folk religion he looms higher than Muhammad. Extremists even deify him and surround his successors with a halo of sanctity.

II

Months prior to 'Ali's death Mu'awiyah's aides had proclaimed him caliph in Jerusalem. For twenty years as governor he had made his province the most prosperous and progressive in the caliphate. His starting point was "modernizing" the army following the Byzantine model. Hitherto, its unit of organization was the tribe, led by its own shaykh, a relic of an archaic patriarchal system fit for desert warfare. Mu'awiyah whipped his Syrian troops into a trained, disciplined military body, the first of its kind in the caliphate. He recruited it largely from among Christian Syrians and Yamanite Arabians long domiciled in Syria, in preference to new immigrants from Hijaz. By doubling the soldiers' pay and seeing that payment was regular and on time, he won their unbounded loyalty. The conquest of Syria won him possession of well-equipped Byzantine shipyards (*dar al-sina'ah,* whence Eng. arsenal), which he utilized to build the first navy in Islam. This made Mu'awiyah the first admiral (from *amir al-bahr,* commander of the sea) in Arab history. His navy was initially manned by Byzantine Syrians, as North Arabians had no seafaring tradition.

In Syria the Moslem governor found not only military but also administrative institutions and personnel which he could utilize. This he did for building a dependable and efficient governmental machine. Next to defense, finance stood high in importance. Here was the Syrian Christian Sarjun (Gr. Sergius) family, in which the office of controller of finance had been hereditary. A member of this family, it will be recalled, had figured in the capital's surrender to Khalid ibn-al-Walid. Greek remained the language of the books until the time of Mu'awiyah's two successors, 'Abd-al-Malik (685–705) and al-Walid (705–15). Not until then could Arabic-writing officials handle the exchequer's books. Simultaneously a parallel change was taking place in Iraq and Persia, where Persian had been retained. Under Byzantine influence Mu'awiyah also developed the bureau of registry (*diwan*) of which the nucleus, we learned, had been laid by the second caliph. In the meantime he initiated a postal service system, the first in Islam. De-

signed primarily to meet government needs, it was conducted by
relays of horses and was developed further by his great successor
'Abd-al-Malik. It served to link the varied parts of the far-flung
empire.

With the change of language went a change in coinage.
Mu'awiyah and other early caliphs contented themselves with the
foreign currency, Roman and Persian, already in circulation. In
certain cases koranic superscriptions were stamped on the coins.
The first Arab copper coin was struck by 'Abd-al-Malik at Baalbak (Ba'labakk), in imitation of a Byzantine coin. Thus it took
more than fifty years to Arabicize the Moslem state.

Mu'awiyah's maintenance of his provincial as his imperial capital was a master stroke. It recognized the fact that the early conquests had shifted Islam's center of gravity northward. Arabia
was no longer and Iraq not yet its locale. Iraq had to wait ninety
years for the expiration of Syria's hegemony. As for Hijaz, never
again did it figure on a national scale until the twentieth century.
In Syria the coastal towns were now vulnerable to naval attacks.
Inland Damascus had served as royal capital for Aramaeans, but
was abandoned by the Seleucids in favor of their creation, Antioch, which was also used by the Romans. Medina stood for status
quo, Damascus stood for change. In Syria, as against Hijaz, Islam
became less oriental to the desert and more to the west.

Early in his career as governor Mu'awiyah must have sensed
that the Byzantines posed the greatest single threat to his realm.
A hundred miles off his shore lay Cyprus, pointing like a gun at
his province. The island had a minor naval base, the major Byzantine one lying in Alexandria. No sooner had Mu'awiyah built
and equipped his naval unit at 'Akka (Acre) than he asked 'Umar
for permission to invade the island. But the caliph wanted no sea
to intervene between him and his generals. 'Uthman, however,
yielded after repeated requests—in one of which Mu'awiyah assured him that roosters could be heard across the water—on condition that he take along his wife. In or about 649 he conducted a
number of raids which did not yield permanent results. Al-Baladhuri's confused account[1] makes the number of ships in one of
them 500 and credits him with exacting tribute equivalent to that

[1] Hitti, *Origins of the Islamic State*, pp. 235–43.

paid the Byzantines. Wood for ships was provided as in Phoenician days by the cedars of Lebanon.

Rhodes lay next on the way to Constantinople. In 653 a naval expedition against it met with temporary success. The island had to be reoccupied by an Umayyad successor. Rhodes boasted a colossal statue of the sun deity rising to a height of 105 feet and counted among the "seven wonders of the world." The Arab conquerors sold its metal ruins to a junk dealer who employed 500 camels to haul them away. Crete and other islands in the Aegean and eastern Mediterranean waters were repeatedly attacked and pillaged. In 664 distant Sicily, destined to become later a flourishing adjunct of an Arab African state, was reached. Emboldened, a Syro-Egyptian flotilla ventured an expedition (655) against the Byzantine capital. Constans II, grandson of Heraclius, met it at Phoenix (Finike) on the Lycian coast but suffered a crushing defeat. By tying each Arab ship to a Byzantine vessel, the Arabs transformed the maritime engagement into a hand-to-hand encounter and scored the first major naval victory in Islam.

Egypt in the following year passed into 'Alid hands. Taking advantage of 'Ali's entanglement in a network of domestic problems, Mu'awiyah entrusted his right-hand man and first conqueror of Egypt, 'Amr ibn-al-'As, to reconquer it in his name. This 'Amr did without much difficulty, after defeating its youthful governor and killing him. From this military victory (658) he proceeded to the peaceful victory at Adhruh.

'Ali's death confronted Mu'awiyah with pressing problems. There was first 'Ali's eldest son Hasan, whose Iraqi partisans had declared him the legitimate successor by Divine right. Knowing that his new opponent's interests lay more in the harem than in imperial administration, Mu'awiyah wrote him: "I admit that your blood relationship gives you a clearer title to the high office. And if I were sure of your ability to fulfill its duties I would unhesitatingly swear allegiance to you. Now then, ask how much you want." Enclosed was the equivalent of a blank check. After some bargaining agreement was reached on a subsidy plus a stipend involving millions of dirhams largely from the income of Kufah and a district in Persia. The Prophet's grandson thereupon retired to a life of ease and indulgence at Medina. He died at the age of forty-five after making and unmaking reportedly no less than a hundred marriages. His death was probably due to poisoning by harem intrigue, but his partisans blamed it on Mu'awiyah and listed Hasan among their highly honored martyrs.

Next to Iraq as a hotbed of Shi'ism came Persia. Its governor, Ziyad ibn-Abih, one of the ablest in the caliphate, refused to lower the 'Alid flag. His second name, meaning "son of his father," was given him because of doubt shrouding the identity of his father, his mother having been a slave girl of Taif. Abu-Sufyan, among many others, had known her. Now Mu'awiyah unshamefacedly acknowledged Ziyad as a half brother, following a recognized procedure (*istilhaq*). He added to his governorship Basrah and later Kufah, with which went eastern Arabia, thus making him viceroy over the eastern wing of the empire. Mu'awiyah's personal interest was in the west. Ziyad transferred his loyalty, with its enthusiastic implementation, from the 'Alid to the Umayyad cause. With a bodyguard 4,000 strong, who functioned also as spies and police, he ruled his realm with an iron hand, tracking down mercilessly any who professed to favor 'Ali's descendants or reviled his new master. Even Bedouins, more interested in booty than ideology, were checked. Historians rank Ziyad as the third, after Mu'awiyah and 'Amr, of the four political geniuses of Islam.

Mecca and Medina as to be expected were lukewarm to Mu'awiyah; they favored 'Ali's sons because of their relation to Muhammad. They pinned their hope on Husayn, Hasan's younger brother; but neither he nor they dared rise against the lord of Damascus. On Mu'awiyah's death Husayn led a small band of Hijazis and Iraqis which was cut down (October 10, 681) by an Umayyad force of 4,000 at Karbala twenty-five miles northwest of Kufah. The decapitated head of the leader was sent to Damascus. Yazid, Mu'awiyah's son and successor, ordered the trophy returned for burial at Karbala in a way befitting the Prophet's grandson. Husayn joined his father and brother in martyrdom. In Persia and other Shi'ite centers his death is still commemorated annually with lamentations, recitations and other public demonstrations.

III

The year 661 divided Mu'awiyah's political career in Syria into two almost equal periods of near twenty years each. In neither period of governorship or caliphate did he suffer a major reverse. Throughout he looked more forward than backward, leaving a record that makes him the least Oriental among early Moslem rulers and the most "modern."

As caliph, Mu'awiyah was not content with geographic pacification. He insisted on human *rapprochement*. His initial approach to dissidents was through persuasion. "People," he would say, "are more surely led by the tongue than by the sword." More obstinate cases, including the People of the House ('Alids and Hashimites, Hashim being the Prophet's great-grandfather), were won over by gifts. "War," he would explain, "would cost infinitely more." Apparently the Prophet had resorted to the same technique in dealing with those "whose hearts were to be reconciled" (sur. 9:60). Umayyad relatives he treated with prudent precaution, a lesson learned from 'Uthman's experience. Poets— the journalists, painters, sculptors of the day who could make and unmake images—had their "tongues cut" by subsidies. A poet could be a satirist, corresponding to a blackmailer of our day. In such cases the caliph would say, "I don't bother with words so long as they do not lead into action." But his attitude toward poetry was not altogether negative. He tried to use poets to promote unity and instill patriotism among his people, whose tribalism and individualism did not pass away with passage from Bedouinism to urbanism. Thus with a leash of gold did the new master tie troublemakers to his person. He practiced opportunism, expediency and other Machiavellian principles long before there was a Machiavelli. His philosophy of rule as formulated by him reads:

> I apply not my lash where my tongue suffices, nor my sword where my whip is enough. And if there be one hair binding me to my fellow men I let it not break. If they pull I loosen, and if they loosen I pull." [1]

[1] Philip K. Hitti, *History of Syria, Including Lebanon and Palestine*, 2nd ed. (London and New York, 1957), p. 438.

This formulation became known in Arab history as "Mu'awiyah's hair."

For his treatment of Christian subjects we have to go to Moslem Spain for a parallel. Mu'awiyah must have appreciated the debt he owed to the Syrian Christians. His favorite wife was Maysun, a Syro-Arab Christian of Yamanite origin. Her tribe was one of many which had migrated in pre-Islam from South Arabia to the western fringe of the Syrian Desert. Maysun scorned court life in Damascus and yearned for the freedom of the desert. This nostalgia found expression in the following verses attributed to her:

> A tent with rustling breezes cool
>   Delights me more than palace high,
> And more the cloak of simple wool
>   Than robes in which I learned to sigh. . . .
>
> And more than purr of friendly cat
>   I love the watch-dog's bark to hear;
> And more than any blubber fat
>   I love a Bedouin cavalier.[1]

Her husband, who had a bulging belly and did not miss the contemptuous reference, took the dame at her word and sent her back whence she came. But he designated her son Yazid as his successor. His governors approved. The innovation was an improvement over the old procedure of seniority. It tended to insure more stability and continuity. Mu'awiyah's court poet was a Jacobite Christian, al-Akhtal. He appeared before the caliph with a cross dangling from his neck. Maronites—of whom we hear for the first time in Arab history—and Jacobites brought their religious disputes before the caliph. Mu'awiyah's physician, ibn-Uthal, was likewise a Christian. He was rewarded by an appointment as financial administrator of the district of Hims—an unprecedented event in early Moslem annals. The caliph's policy toward Christians bore political rewards.

At last Mu'awiyah was free to take up the cudgels against the "eternal enemy," al-Rum (Romans). These campaigns consti-

1 Reynold A. Nicholson, *A Literary History of the Arabs,* 2nd ed. (Cambridge, 1930), p. 195.

tuted the second wave of Moslem expansion; the first, having been initiated by abu-Bakr, had reached its climax under 'Umar and terminated with the civil wars of 556–561.

In the north nature had raised the lofty Taurus and Anti-Taurus as a frontier between the two hostile territories. The narrow thirty-eight-mile pass across the Taurus, known as the Cilician Gates, militated against the massive movement of troops. Tarsus, St. Paul's birthplace, guarded the southern entrance to the pass and served as a base for major campaigns against the "land of the Romans." Minor raids were carried out every summer as a matter of routine to keep the army in good trim. The practice was followed by Mu'awiyah's successors. The immediate objective, as in the case of the traditional Bedouin razzias, was booty, though the dim spectacle of imperial Byzantium four hundred and fifty miles away might have beckoned from beyond the distant horizon. Anatolia's cold climate presented a serious deterrent to the sons of the desert.

Not until 668 did an Arab army reach Constantinople. For the first time Moslem warring eyes opened upon the mighty and proud capital of Christendom. It was late in the year. The rigorous winter, combined with smallpox and famine, decimated the army, necessitating reinforcement. It was rushed under Yazid, whose father was presumably grooming him for the caliphate. The young prince had thus far been given to a life of ease and pleasure. Under its new leader the army advanced from Chalcedon (Byzantium's Asiatic suburb), where it wintered, and laid siege to the capital. Early in summer the attempt was given up as hopeless. According to the legendary account of the siege Yazid covered himself with honor and fame. As the pendulum of victory swung from one side to the other, alternate shouts of jubilation were heard from two Byzantine tents. One was occupied by the emperor's daughter, the other by Jabalah ibn-al-Ayham's daughter. The prospects of seizing the former princess spurred Yazid to extraordinary activity. Even more dramatic was the story of the aged Ayyub al-Ansari, Muhammad's first host at Medina. His presence was sought more for the blessing it might bring than for fighting. In the course of the siege Ayyub died of dysentery and was buried outside the city walls. His supposed tomb became a shrine for Christian Greeks. Centuries later, when the Ottoman

Turks laid siege to the city, the tomb was discovered thanks to
miraculous rays of light. A mosque was built on the site. Thus the
Medinese gentleman became a saint to three nations.

In 674 the mighty arm of the caliph in Damascus stretched
across Byzantine territory for the second time and reached the
capital itself. This time it was a joint land-sea campaign. The
fleet succeeded in establishing a base at Cyzicus (Tur-Kapidaği),
a peninsula projecting from Asia Minor to the Sea of Marmara.
The base served also as winter headquarters for the army. For
seven years the struggle continued. Arabic and Greek accounts
are confused and difficult to reconcile. But the net result was
clear: Constantinople was saved. Credit should be given to its
powerful fortifications and to use of Greek fire, a highly combus-
tible compound which could burn on and under water. The "secret weapon" inflicted irreparable damage on the Arab flotilla, the
remains of which were wrecked on the return journey (early
680).

Equally unsuccessful were later attacks from Damascus and
Baghdad on the citadel of Christendom. Centuries had to pass
before it yielded (1453) to the last champions of Islam, the Ottoman Turks.

More productive of results was the southwestern thrust through
Byzantine North Africa. The hero of these campaigns was 'Uqbah
ibn-Nafi' a nephew of 'Amr ibn-al-'As. 'Uqbah received his first
appointment in 663 from his uncle. He conquered Barqah
(Barca), pushed through Libya and in 670 founded al-Qayrawan
(Kairouan) a hundred and twelve miles south of modern Tunis
and ancient Carthage. Ibn-Khaldun quotes the general as saying,
"I intend to build a town as a depot of arms (*qayrawan*) for
Islam to endure to the end of time." From this military base Arab
troops, reinforced by native Berbers, chased the Byzantines out of
a large part of North Africa. Tradition claims that 'Uqbah advanced and advanced until his horse was stopped by the waters of
the Atlantic. In a few decades the new conquerors were able to
do, by way of Islamizing and Arabicizing the area, more than the
earlier conquerors had been able to achieve in centuries by way of
Romanizing or Hellenizing it. The Hamitic Berbers felt closer of
kin and in culture to the Semitic Arabs than to the Indo-Europe-
ans. Then too the earlier Semitic-Phoenician wave of conquest

and colonization must have left relics. The new Semitic colony borrowed columns for its mosque from the ruins of the ancient Semitic one in Carthage, and on a small scale duplicated the career of its illustrious predecessor. For more than a century it served as the seat of the caliphal viceroyalty and capital of Moslem Africa. From it the expeditions that netted Morocco and Spain originated. It developed into a flourishing religious, cultural and commercial emporium. To Western Moslems al-Qayrawan became the fourth holiest city after Mecca, Medina and Jerusalem—the fourth gate to Paradise.

'Uqbah fell in battle (683) near Baskarah (Biskra) in northeast Algeria. His tomb-mosque, considered the oldest architectural monument of African Islam, is a national shrine, referred to as Sidi (my lord) 'Uqbah. Like other great warriors who fell in the path of Allah, the martyred 'Uqbah has been sanctified in folk religion.

In the eastern half of the empire the situation called for pacification and consolidation rather than expansion. The entire area from the Oxus and the Indus to the Persian Gulf—it may be recalled—had been nominally brought by 'Umar and 'Uthman within the fold of Islam. But the territory was difficult to govern if not to hold. Iraq was imbued with Shi'ism. Persia, proud of its tradition of self-rule, was not happy under the new establishment. Tribute and other Islamic restraints were generally resented. Both countries were rich in nomadic population, notorious for its uncontrollability. Farther east lay the vast terrain of Turkish-speaking peoples, settlers and wanderers. But Mu'awiyah's viceroy was the man for the task. With sharp wits, iron will and strong arm he endeavored not only to hold the loose realm together but to push its frontier farther east. His court at Basrah, whence he ruled semi-independently, had the aura of a royal Persian court. At its gate stood 500 mounted guards. His public appearances were heralded by lictors. An armed police force of 1,000 patrolled the turbulent centers. The net of spies was widespread. Woe to him or her who failed to pass the political test: cursing the memory of 'Ali! Even discounting the number of those beheaded, as given by Shi'ite sources, the number must have been enormous.

During the civil strife of 656 to 661 several towns on the eastern

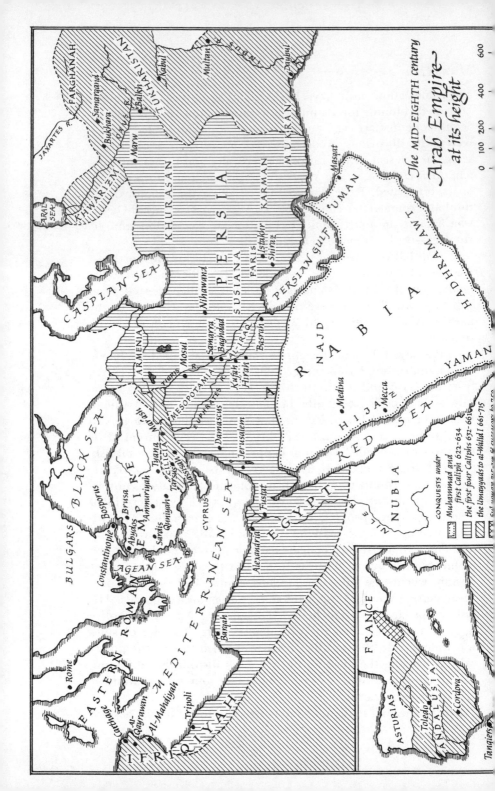

The MID-EIGHTH century
Arab Empire
at its height

0   100   200   400   600

CONQUESTS UNDER
Muḥammad and first Caliph 622-634
the first four Caliphs 632-661
the Umayyads to al-Walīd I 661-715
al-Walīd I and his successors to 750

FARGHANAH
JAXARTES R.
Samarqand
Bukhara
OXUS R.
TUKHARISTAN
Balkh
Kabul
KHWARIZM
ARAL SEA
Marw
KHURASAN
Multan
S I N D
Daybul

CASPIAN SEA
P E R S I A
MUKRAN
Nihawand
SUSIANA
KARMAN
Masqat
ʿUMAN
FARIS
Iṣṭakhr
Shiraz
PERSIAN GULF

ARMENIA
Mosul
Samarra
Baghdad
AL-ʿIRAQ
TIGRIS R.
MESOPOTAMIA
Kufah
Hirah
EUPHRATES R.
Baṣrah
NAJD
A R A B I A
HADHRAMAWT

BLACK SEA
BULGARS
Constantinople
Bosporus
Brusa
Abydos
Al-Mamuriyah
Sardis
EASTERN
ROMAN
Marʿash
Tyana
CILICIA
Tarsus
AEGEAN SEA
Quniyah
Mopsuestia
CYPRUS
E M P I R E
Damascus
Jerusalem
HIJAZ
Medina
Mecca
RED SEA
YAMAN

Rome
M E D I T E R R A N E A N   S E A
Carthage
Al-
Qayrawan
Al-Mahdiyah
Tripoli
Barqah
Alexandria
Fusṭaṭ
E G Y P T
NUBIA
NILE R.
IFRIQIYAH

FRANCE
ASTURIAS
Toledo
ANDALUSIA
Cordova
Tangiers

periphery of Islam cast off their nominal allegiance and had to be re-overrun. No sooner had Mu'awiyah become the undisputed master of the situation than his lieutenants started military operations. In 661 Marw, future capital of Moslem Khurasan, the area east of Persia, was attacked. In the same year Hirat (now in Afghanistan) was stormed. Two years later the walls of Kabul were breached by catapults and Balkh (Gr. Baktra) on the south side of the Oxus was seized. In 674, the year after Ziyad's death, his son penetrated into Transoxiana, captured Bukhara and pushed into Samarqand, now in Uzbek Soviet Socialist Republic. The last three cities were flourishing Buddhist centers with a thin Hellenistic veneer from Alexander the Great's day. These and other cities of central Asia developed into brilliant centers of Islamic religion and Arab culture. In the area a closer contact was established with a new racial clement, the Turkish, related to the Mongolist. And when later the arm holding the sword of Islam became paralyzed, it was these Turks who wielded it effectively.

Under Mu'awiyah's Umayyad successors much of the area had to be reconquered, settled and expanded. The expansion on the western wing of the empire was more spectacular. By 732, the centennial of the death of the Prophet, his followers had reached Tours in northwestern France. The word of the caliph in Damascus was law from southwestern Europe, through North Africa, into western and central Asia—an extent unattained by the Roman Empire at its highest point.

IV

To most Arab historians the hero of this story was no hero. The tradition transmitted by them was largely Shi'ite or 'Abbasid Sunnite. Only a trickle of the Syrian tradition, favorable to the house of Umayyah, has seeped down through the literary layers. 'Abbasid hostility, we shall learn later, was no less deadly to the Umayyad cause than the Shi'ite. Sunnite historians, of course, do not share the Shi'ite view of the illegitimacy of Mu'awiyah's caliphate, but they admit its changed character. It was a *mulk,* a royalty. Mu'awiyah was a *malik,* a despicable title then limited to such non-Arab potentates as the Byzantine emperor or the Persian Chosroes. Among other mundane innovations Mu'awiyah was cri-

ticized for erecting a throne (*sarir al-mulk*) in his palace, and a
bower (*maqsurah*) in his mosque whence he delivered his speeches
while seated. His explanation that due to a bulging stomach he
found it difficult to keep standing was not satisfactory. Another
favorite butt of sharp criticism was the nomination of his son, an
incorrigible drunkard, as his successor. Yazid was the first drunkard among the caliphs but by no means the last. Historians labeled
him Yazid al-Khumur (the Yazid of wines).[1]

In characterizing Mu'awiyah, biographers generally emphasize
his *hilm*, a combination of tolerance, magnanimity and self-
control. In the above sketch several cases were cited which illus-
trate these features in his character, his style in conducting state
affairs (*duha*), the *finesse politique* of which he was a master. In
his *hilm* and *duha* he left a model which many of his successors
endeavored to emulate but none were able to duplicate.

Mu'awiyah, the great innovator, first of the four political geniuses of Islam, architect of the Arab empire, founder of the dynasty under which Syria enjoyed its most glorious era and the
world of Islam attained its widest expansion, ranks third—after
Muhammed and 'Umar—among makers of Arab history.

[1] Of the modern historians who rehabilitated Mu'awiyah, mention may be
made of Henri Lammens, *Études sur le règne du calife omayyade Mo'āwia
Ier* (Beirut, Lebanon, 1908); *Études sur le siècle des Omayyades* (Beirut, 1930).

'Abd-al-Rahman 1:
Maker of History
on European Soil

I will not indulge in any distraction, be it of the sight or of the heart, until Spain is within my grasp.

'Abd-al-Rahman I

THE secret orders issued in 750 from Iraq were unmistakable: The house of Umayyah must be exterminated. Their originator was a new caliph, abu-al-'Abbas, victor over the last Umayyad Marwan II, destroyer of the ninety-year-old Umayyad dynasty, founder of a new caliphate and winner of the title al-Saffah (bloodshedder). Abu-al-'Abbas had headed a coalition of relatives closer to the Prophet than the Umayyads, of Shi'ites, eager for an opportunity to avenge themselves on the Umayyads, and of malcontents alienated by unworthy successors of the great Mu'awiyah. 'Abbasid agents and spies scoured the area, tracking down every possible quarry. As the surface became unsafe, refugees—to use the words of ibn-Khaldun—"sought shelter in the bowels of the earth." Even the long-dead were not to escape. Tombs were violated, corpses crucified, remains thrown out. The body of Caliph Hisham (724–43), after Mu'awiyah and 'Abd-al-Malik the third and last statesman of the dynasty, was exhumed, lashed eighty times and burned to ashes. Gone was Mu'awiyah's *hilm* and with it his *finesse politique*.

A new decree was issued admitting excesses and promising amnesty to all surviving Umayyads who presented themselves in a certain place at a certain date. Between seventy and eighty responded. They were invited to a banquet outside of Jaffa. No sooner had the guests started to eat than the hosts fell upon them and mowed them down one after the other. Over the still-warm bodies of the dead and the dying, the executioners spread their leathern covers to enjoy the rest of the meal. Groaning provided the music.

One scion of the fallen house escaped the snare. Nineteen-year-old 'Abd-al-Rahman, grandson of Hisham, rather than accepting the invitation, fled to an estate of his on the left bank of the upper Euphrates. In his company were a younger brother, two sisters, and his four-year-old son Sulayman. One day as 'Abd-al-Rahman lay in a darkened room nursing an ailing eye, Sulayman dashed in, excited and wailing. He had caught sight of horsemen with a black banner like those he had seen when his uncle Yahya was slaughtered. (Black was supposedly the color of Muhammed's flag; green was the Shi'ite color.) There was no doubt; someone had betrayed the refugees. Entrusting his son to his sisters and bidding them to send his Greek-born freedman to a rendezvous he named, 'Abd-al-Rahman led his thirteen-year-old brother by the hand and plunged into the Euphrates. The swift current and deep water discouraged the boy, especially as he heard from behind, "Come back. We mean no harm." The elder brother gained the other bank. He looked back and forever regretted it. There was his brother's head rolling on the ground. The pursuers took it as a trophy, leaving the body to rot.[1]

The fugitive prince trudged through the Syrian Desert from north to south. In Palestine he was joined by Badr, bringing cash and jewelry. The two crossed Sinai and started on the long odyssey through North Africa. The price on his head was implicit and someone came near receiving it from the governor general of al-Qayrawan, 'Ubaydullah al-Fihri. The governor evidently wanted to take advantage of the caliphal change and achieve his own independence. 'Abd-al-Rahman's identity was difficult to hide. From his Berber mother, originally captive from the Nafzah tribe, he inherited red hair and blue eyes. Biographers add that

---

[1] The entire dramatic story, told in the first person, appears in an early anonymous chronicle, *Akhbar Majmu'ah*, ed. and tr. Emilio Lafuente y Alcantara (Madrid, 1867), pp. 50–54, and is repeated by ibn-al-Athir, *al-Kamil fi al-Ta'rikh*, ed. Carolus J. Tornberg, vol. V (Leyden, 1871), p. 577, and by others.

his long hair hung down in two curls over his temples and that he was blind in one eye and deficient in sense of smell.

The expectation of being welcomed by his maternal uncles no doubt buoyed his spirit, but the dream of power and grandeur awaiting him in Spain, conquered by his ancestors (711–18), must have so filled his head and heart as to leave no room for fear or fatigue. Legend asserts that his family were convinced that he was destined to a caliphal career in the "west." A physiognomist cited in evidence certain signs in the face and neck. His grandfather Hisham, in whose house he was brought up following his father's death, trained him for that high office. The grandfather had even assigned him a lot in his Spanish holdings for building a palace. A beautiful eighteen-year-old Visigothic princess, Sarah al-Qutiyah (to use her Arabic nickname), had journeyed to Hisham's court to appeal a legal case and had told the lad that his new property adjoined hers in Cordova.

I

After five years of wandering the tramp landed in the territory of his uncles, on the Moroccan shore of the Mediterranean. Thence he caught his first sight of the land of his dream—a dream that was to end in a nightmare. The whole Iberian Peninsula was seething with unrest. Hither South Arabians (Yamanites) had carried their pre-Islamic feud with North Arabians (the Qaysites). The Qaysites were solid Sunnites; the Yamanites were impregnated with Shi'ite doctrines. The Berbers were against both parties. They were neither Sunnites nor Shi'ites but generally Kharijites. The Kharijites, we learned, were those who rose against 'Ali for acquiescing in arbitration, and one of them murdered him. Moreover the Yamanites resented the fact that the equality promised by Islam was not realized in their case, socially or economically. Their main grievance was that while they constituted the bulk of the invading army in Spain, the Arabs appropriated the smiling plains for themselves, leaving them the inhospitable areas. Each of these parties had within itself rival tribes under chieftains jockeying for power. All were people newly transplanted into a radically different area; they had not yet sent their roots deep, nor had they established a modus vivendi with the native population. Their governors may have distinguished themselves on the battlefield, but not in administration. In the years 732 to 755 no less than twenty-three of them had succeeded one another.

'Abd-al-Rahman's approach to the messy situation was through the Syrians, distinguished by their loyalty to the Umayyad cause, and of the Syrians through the four or five hundred clients (freedmen, *mawali,* sing. *mawla*) of his house. The Arab institution of clientage had its own code. It bound the descendants of a freedman to the descendants of the man who had manumitted him by a quasi-sacred artificial kinship that carried the obligation of mutual aid in time of need. Some nine thousand Syrians, mostly cavalrymen, had entered Spain in 741, in 'Abd-al-Rahman's grandfather's caliphate, under Balj ibn-Bishr al-Qushari. Balj established himself as governor general at Cordova. The division of Damascus was settled in the district of Elvira, that of Hims in Seville and that of Palestine in Medina Sidonia. South Spain, in its climate, topography and agricultural products, reminded them of the old homeland. It was to the leaders of some of these military divisions that the claimant addressed his message and sent it with Badr.

> It is amongst you, the clients of my house, that I fain would dwell, for I am convinced that ye would prove my faithful friends. But, alas, I dare not pay a visit to Spain, for the Emir of that country, like the Emir of Africa, would lie in wait for me; he would regard me as an enemy, a pretender. And in truth, have not I, grandson of the Khalif Hisham, a right to the Emirate? Since, then, I cannot enter Spain as a private individual, as a claiment only will I come. But I will not embark until I receive your assurance that you will aid me to the best of your power and that you will look upon my cause as your own.[1]

Of course, he did not end without assuring them of the exalted positions awaiting them in case of success.

'Abd-al-Rahman, who was not particularly religious but did fulfill his ritualistic obligations, caught sight one day, after his evening prayer, of a man jumping into the sea before his vessel had anchored. Yes, it was Badr, running towards him and shout-

---

[1] Reinhart Dozy, *Spanish Islam: A History of the Moslems in Spain,* tr. Francis G. Stokes (London, 1913), pp. 167–68.

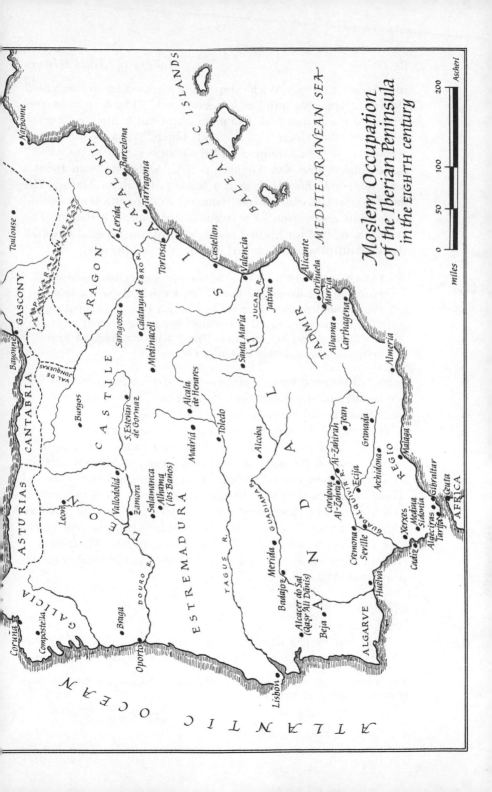

Moslem Occupation
of the Iberian Peninsula
in the EIGHTH century

ing, "Glad tidings." With him was a deputation of the client chiefs carrying five hundred pieces of gold. The first to be presented to the prince was Tammam abu-Ghalib (the "completer, father of the victor"). "A good omen," remarked 'Abd-al-Rahman. "We shall conquer and the conquest will be complete."

No time to lose. On August 14, 755, 'Abd-al-Rahman twenty-four years old, disembarked at a small port east of Malaga. His mentor was 'Ubaydullah ibn-'Uthman, chief of the Damascus division and a grandson of a freedman of Caliph 'Uthman. The guest was offered for his first night, as a token of special hospitality, a beautiful young slave girl, but he rejected the offer.

> Indeed, this maid is pleasing to the eye and gratifying to the heart. But if I were to be fair to her, I would do myself injustice and undermine the ambition to which I have dedicated my life. On the other hand, if I neglect her in the pursuit of my goal, I would do her injustice. Under both conditions I have no use for her. Take her back to her owner.[1]

It was all summed up in a pithy saying attributed to him: "I will not indulge in any distraction, be it of the sight or of the heart, until Spain is within my grasp."

The news of the arrival of a survival of the royal family spread like wild fire. One delegation after another came to offer its allegiance. Around the nucleus of clients gathered Yamanites, Qaysites and Berbers moved perhaps more by selfish desires than dynastic loyalty. Seville was the first large city to open its gates in welcome to the pretender (March 756). In Seville 'Abd-al-Rahman renewed his boyhood friendship with princess Sarah, now married to an Arab. She left a progeny of Moslems and Christians of whom one (Christian) Mary was the mother of the illustrious 'Abd-al-Rahman III.

II

Spain was then a dependency of Africa, of which the capital was al-Qayrawan, founded by 'Uqbah ibn-Nafi'. Spain's governor

[1] Al-Maqqari, *Nafh al-Tib min Ghusn al-Andalus al-Ratib,* ed. Reinhart Dozy *et al.* (Leyden, 1858–61), vol. II, p. 29.

was Yusuf al-Fihri, a descendant of 'Uqbah. His capital was Cordova. Al-Fihri lacked the vision and intelligence to adjust himself or his subjects to the new homeland, but nonetheless cherished ambitions of autonomy under his independent cousin in al-Qayrawan. His general of the army and son-in-law al-Sumayl ibn-Hatim, after some hesitation, followed his chief. The governor offered the newcomer (Ar. *al-dakhil,* the epithet given by historians to 'Abd-al-Rahman) the hand of his daughter in marriage and the governorship of two districts. But the young Umayyad was after a bigger prize.

As 'Abd-al-Rahman at the head of his recruits started his march against Cordova, abu-al-Sabbah al-Yahsubi of Seville, chief of many Yamanite followers, noted that he had no banner. Lifting his green turban, he fastened it to his lance. Honored and cherished, the impromptu device served as the Umayyad palladium for generations.

At last the two opposing armies stood facing each other across the Guadalquivir (From Ar. al-Wadi al-Kabir, the great river) outside of Cordova. By a deceitful stratagem, the invader induced the defender to let him cross over under pretext of peace. He then fell upon his unsuspecting victims and won a decisive victory. The date was May 15, 756.

Al-Fihri and al-Sumayl escaped with their lives. The victor had difficulty in restraining the bloody and marauding passions of his followers. He proclaimed general amnesty and ordered consideration for the rights of private property. Two of al-Fihri's sons were held as hostages. "Cousin," implored their terrified and tearful mother, with her two daughters standing by, "be good to us as God has been good to you." 'Abd-al-Rahman ordered honorable treatment for the harem under security and managed to restore some of their pillaged valuables. One of the daughters offered him a slave girl who became the mother of his son and successor Hisham.

Nominally 'Abd-al-Rahman was now the amir, the master, of Moslem Spain. In fact years had to pass before the country was actually within his grasp. His two chief foes, al-Fihri in Toledo and al-Sumayl in Jean, specialized in spreading sedition and dissention. Al-Fihri was finally decapitated and his head was exhibited on Cordova's bridge. Al-Sumayl was strangled to death in Cordova's jail.

Even after al-Fihri's death Fihrites continued to challenge the new regime. Rebellious heads popped up in different districts. Some of them were intimate friends and associates of the amir. Others were close relatives who hurried to Spain in the wake of his victory. Especially troublesome were Berbers and Yamanites alienated since he ordered a halt to the pillage of Cordova. No sooner was one head crushed than, Hydra-like, another succeeded it.

A new challenge to the new authority came from abroad. Reports of the spectacular success of the intruder were not slow in reaching Iraq. There al-Mansur, brother-successor of abu- al-'Abbas and founder of Baghdad, was not prepared to see the west wing of the caliphate amputated without a fight. He offered the governor of Africa, al-'Ala' ibn-Mughith, all necessary reinforcement, appointed him over Spain and ordered him to proceed against it. Al-'Ala' landed in Southern Spain (763) and unfurled the black banner. Shi'ites, pro-'Abbasids, self-seeking shaykhs and foot-loose tribesmen eager for booty rallied around it. 'Abd-al-Rahman chose to take his stand at Carmona north of Seville, reputed for its impregnability. A two-month blockade was enough to convince the amir that time was against him. He resolved on an audacious sally. He picked seven hundred of the bravest in his garrison, led them to the city gate, where a great fire was blazing, and flung the scabbard of his sword into it exclaiming: "Let us throw our scabbards into the flame and swear to fall like soldiers if victory cannot be ours. We conquer or die."

So impetuous was the ensuing charge that, it is affirmed, seven thousand of the enemy were slaughtered. The amputated heads of al-'Ala' and other leaders—each with an identification label attached to its ear—were preserved in salt, wrapped in the caliph's diploma of appointment and the black banner, and packed in a sack. The sack was entrusted to a Cordovan merchant with business to transact in al-Qayrawan en route to Mecca. Al-Mansur was there on a pilgrimage. The sack was left, under cover of night, on the way the caliph would take in the morning. As the gruesome contents were uncovered al-Mansur exclaimed: "Thank God for putting the sea between us and this devil of a foe." [1]

1 Maqqari, vol. I, pp. 213, 215.

On a later occasion, we are told, al-Mansur posed the following question to his courtiers: "Who do you think deserves to be called the falcon of the Quraysh?" The answer with one accord was expectedly "None but yourself, commander of the believers." But the caliph disclaimed such honor. Nor did he agree that Mu'awiyah or 'Abd-al-Malik could be worthy of it, for these two men, he argued, built on earlier foundations, they did not start from scratch. Finally al-Mansur answered his own question:

> The falcon of the Quraysh is none other than 'Abd-al-Rahman ibn-Mu'awiyah. It was he who, after long wanderings in the deserts of Asia and Africa and without an army, money or friends, had the audacity to seek a career beyond the seas in lands unknown to him. With nothing to rely upon but wits and industry, he crushed his foes, exterminated rebels, united a realm parceled out amongst petty rulers, secured its frontiers against Christian neighbors and established a solid and durable kingdom. No man before him ever did such deeds.[1]

Al-Mansur apparently learned his lesson but his successors did not. Their emissaries and secret agents did not cease to sow seeds of sedition and discord. His grandson Harun al-Rashid, who as crown prince had reached the Bosporus and concluded a humiliating treaty with Byzantium, looked for new laurels farther west. He entered into treaty relations with Charlemagne, the great king of the Franks and emperor of the Romans. Charlemagne was a natural enemy of his southern Umayyad neighbor, as Harun was the natural enemy of his Byzantine rival. In 777 a formidable confederacy of disaffected Arab chiefs in the north, headed by Fihrites, went as far as inviting this mighty enemy of Islam to come to their aid, implying acknowledgment of his suzerainty. Charlemagne's overriding ambition was to unite all Europe under his scepter. He led his army in person across the Pyrenees and advanced toward the leading rebel city, Saragossa. On second thought its people closed its gates in the face of this foe in the guise of a friend. New disturbances at home necessitated immedi-

---

[1] The original has a variety of texts, cf. Maqqari, vol. I, p. 213; ibn-'Idhari, *Al-Bayan al-Mughrib fi Akhbar al-Maghrib*, ed. R. Dozy (Leyden, 1849), vol. II, pp. 54, 61–62; Dozy, *Spanish Islam*, p. 207. The essence was expressed by 'Abd-al-Rahman himself in metric form.

ate withdrawal. On its "dolorous route" of retreat through the defiles of the mountain his army was attacked in the rear by Basques and other mountaineers who inflicted disastrous losses. The army leader Roland was one of those who fell. His defense, historical and legendary, has been immortalized in the *Chanson de Roland,* a gem of early French literature and an epic of medieval times.

'Abd-al-Rahman came out victorious without striking a blow. But now the time came. He seized Saragossa and had its rebel leader beaten to death, but only after his arms and legs had been severed. No serious challenge was made after this, the thirty-second year after the submission of Cordova. Throughout, 'Abd-al-Rahman led his troops in person, and at no battlefield did he suffer a major reverse. The lord of al-Andalus (from Vandals), to use the Arabic word for the Iberian Peninsula, was now in fact as in name its lord. Chroniclers assure us that at the time of Charlemagne's invasion 'Abd-al-Rahman was preparing a naval expedition to wrest Syria from 'Abbasid hands.

III

'Abd-al-Rahman's accomplishments in the area of peace may not have been commensurate with those in the area of war, but they were not of mean dimensions. Far from being a number— twenty-fourth—in a series of ephemeral amirs deriving their authority from al-Qayrawan or Damascus, he was the sovereign head of a state. For this state he laid down a governmental structure that endured, with certain modifications under 'Abd-al-Rahman III, for more than two and a half centuries. It endured in the face of centrifugul Arab-Moslem forces operating inside, and Christian pressure from inside and outside. Beyond the northern frontier at the foot of the mountain lurked the kinglets of Aragon, Navarre, Leon and Castile, preparing and praying for *la reconquista.*

The governmental institutions evolved by 'Abd-al-Rahman followed the model of Damascus. All authority—civil, military and judicial—was centered in the person of the amir. He could and did delegate authority. In the performance of his high office the amir was assisted by a chamberlain (*hajib*), the first of whom was his comrade at arms Tammam abu-Ghalib. The vizirial institution, an 'Abbasid rather than Umayyad, was not introduced until the time of 'Abd-al-Rahman III (d. 961). Under the chamberlain were secretaries (sing. *katib*) in charge of finance, army, interior and other bureaus. A consultative council comprised members of the nobility, the religious hierarchy and high palace officials. 'Ubaydullah ibn-'Uthman, another early supporter, was its first head. 'Ubaydullah served also as governor of the capital in the amir's absence. Abu-al-Sabbah was appointed governor of Seville. The legend on the amir's seal said, IN GOD HE TRUSTS.

The Visigothic provincial divisions were generally maintained but increased to six. Each district had its own governor (*wali*) and judge (*qadi*). Certain important cities had their own governors. The judge of Cordova is frequently referred to as "judge of judges," indicating a supreme position. The judge was, of course, one learned in the Koran and teadision. Criminal and police cases were under the jurisdiction of a special officer.

The army 'Abd-al-Rahman found in Spain was still operating according to the antiquated Arab tribal system. Each tribal group, Arab or Berber, was established in a land grant under its own shaykh who in wartime became its commander. In due course the amir raised and trained a standing army of mercenaries, recruited largely from Berber Africa. It reached 40,000 in number. Its mounted division used mules, more plentiful and steadier than horses. 'Abd-al-Rahman also had a Negro bodyguard recruited fresh from Africa. Its first commander was a Negro rebel whom the amir had pardoned. The army guarded the northern marches and dealt ruthlessly with domestic uprisings. Its loyalty to the amir was as intense as his subjects' hatred of them. They remind us of the Ottoman Janissaries.

But that left three vast frontiers of the realm open to attack by sea. 'Abd-al-Rahman laid the basis of the first naval unit in Moslem Spain. It was built after the Byzantine model and based at Almeria. 'Abd-al-Rahman appointed his first chamberlain, Tammam, as its head. Tammam thus became the first Moslem admiral in Europe. Under 'Abd-al-Rahman III the Arab navy became the most powerful one in the western Mediterranian.

The treatment of Spanish Christians did not differ from that of their coreligionists elsewhere. It originated in the Koran, was elaborated in the hadith and interpreted in books on jurisprudence (*fiqh*). As dhimmis Christians and Jews were entitled to certain rights—chief among which was state protection, and subject to certain obligations—featuring tribute (*jizyah*). The koranic revelation (9:29) reads:

> Fight, from among those who were given the Book, the ones who do not believe in God or the last day, who do not forbid what God and His Messenger have forbidden and do not practice the religion of truth, until they pay the jizyah out of hand and in a state of humiliation.

Only adult males in full possession of their physical and mental faculties and able to pay were subject to taxation. Children, women, slaves, monks, those disabled or afflicted with chronic diseases were generally exempt. The amount due could be paid in money or in kind. It was graduated from 1 to 4 dinars (12 to 48 dirhams) depending upon the financial ability of the payer. This poll tax was additional to the land tax (*kharaj*). Kharaj usually followed the existing system at the time of conquest and averaged one fifth of the yield. The jizyah, of course, terminated in case of conversion. The landed properties of lords who fled at the conquest were confiscated and parceled out among the warriors, but the serfs were left on the land and required to pay four fifths of the produce.

As in other conquered territories native Christians and Jews were left under the jurisdiction of their ecclesiastical heads. Cases involving Moslems were heard in Moslem courts. Most Western scholars[1] think that the change from the Visigothic to the Moslem rule did not worsen the condition of the indigenous population. In fact it ameliorated at least that of the servile class and of the Jews. The Jews were at times subjected to persecution by the Visigoths. The Christian subjects, too, were alienated from their rulers. These Goths were originally teutonic barbarians and, before becoming Catholics, they were Arians, heretics in the eyes of the Church. The conquest loosened the hold of the nobility and clergy upon the underprivileged class. 'Abd-al-Rahman allowed

[1] Led by the Dutchman Reinhart Dozy and by the Frenchman É. Lévi-Provençal, *Histoire de l'Espagne musulmane*, vol. I, (Paris, 1944).

Christians to repair their old churches and build new ones. He did not enforce on them any other disability imposed by his pious predecessor 'Umar II (717–20). Certain Spanish scholars lament the break in the Christian tradition, as Islamic rule sandwiched in between early medieval and modern times. The fact remains, however, that Spain under Islam reached economic and cultural heights unattained before, and its capital vied with Constantinople and Baghdad as a world center of grandeur, affluence and enlightenment. Arab writers styled Cordova the "bride of al-Andalus" and an Anglo-Saxon nun called it the "jewel of the world."

The Cordova 'Abd-al-Rahman left was different from the one he found. To it flocked Moslems from North Africa and western Asia seeking their fortunes. With or without invitation Umayyad fugitives and relatives sought its security. It was the fashion then for the head of state to surround himself with members of his immediate family and to assign some of them to key posts in the realm. The lone eagle of the Quraysh was now afforded that opportunity. "Next to sovereignty," commented the amir, "the greatest blessing God granted me is the ability to provide my kinsmen a home and to benefit by them." Especially welcome was his son Sulayman, the four-year-old boy whose keen observation had saved his father's life. It was good riddance from the 'Abbasid viewpoint. But the boy's two aunts would not risk the sea voyage. The capital's population was further augmented by Neo-Moslems (sing. *muwallad*) whose numbers swelled as the days went by. The country folk, as elsewhere, maintained their ancestral way of life. In 'Abd-al-Rahman's lifetime the bulk of the country's population must have become Moslem.

It thus became necessary to enlarge Cordova's congregational place of worship. This was done at the expense of the adjoining Christian church. Three years before his death 'Abd-al-Rahman embarked upon a more ambitious plan: rebuilding and expanding the mosque and making it worthy of his capital and comparable to Christian cathedrals. The building was encircled by a wall as thick as that of a fortress, enriched by a spacious outer hall and decorated by a forest of stately columns. In one year, we are told, he spent on it about 100,000 dinars. The Mosque of Cordova became the Kaabah of western Islam. Transformed into a cathedral at the time of the reconquest, it survives to the present under the name "La Mezquita," and next to Alhambra attracts the largest number of tourists.

In addition to the great mosque chroniclers credit 'Abd-al-Rahman with other religious and secular structures in the capital. The half-century-old fortifications of the city were renovated in 766. The bridge over the Guadalquivir was enlarged. The amir also improved the aqueduct, not only to meet the increasing need of the city but to enable it to withstand siege and drought. For his own use he built a new government house (*dar al-imarah*) near the grand mosque to replace the old structure in use since Visigothic days. Two miles outside the capital he established an attractive country home and surrounded it with a garden rich in exotic flowers and trees. He named it al-Rusafah after that of his grandfather Hisham on the Euphrates, where he was brought up. It was customary for Umayyad caliphs to build country villas for hunting and relaxation and to satisfy their nostalgia for desert life. To a lonely palm tree in his garden, said to be the first imported from Syria, 'Abd-al-Rahman addressed the following tender verses:

> O Palm, thou art a stranger in the West,
> Far from thy Orient home, like me unblest.
> Weep! But thou canst not, dumb, dejected tree,
> Thou art not made to sympathize with me.
> Ah, thou wouldst weep, if thou hadst tears to pour,
> For thy companions on Eurphrates' shore;
> But yonder tall groves thou rememberest not,
> As I, in hating foes, have my old friends forgot.[1]

Poetry, like oratory, was considered a *sine qua non* for a chief of state and the amir was a master of both. But it is an exaggeration to ascribe to him the introduction of the palm of his realm. The palm was introduced by the Phoenicians, who used seed. The Arabs propagated new varieties from offshoots, and did introduce rice, apricots, peaches, pomegranates, oranges (the bitter or Seville variety), sugar cane, saffron and other plants and fruits attested by their Portuguese and Spanish names. This re-

[1] Nicholson, *A Literary History of the Arabs*, p. 418.

sulted in the increase of the agricultural resources of the land. Arab contribution to industry was no less remarkable. The art of inlaying metals with gold and silver was imported from Damascus. It flourished in several Spanish cities and spread into France and other European countries, leaving a linguistic heritage in such words as damascene, damaskeen. Tourists can still buy, from Toledo, knives and scissors on the medieval Damascus model.

The hero of our story started the capital of Spanish Islam on its way to glory; its apogee was attained under his third namesake and bibliophile successor al-Hakam (961–76). In 929, seven years after his accession to the amirate, 'Abd-al-Rahman III took the logical step and declared himself *amir al-mu'minin* (commander of the believers). The 'Abbasid caliphate had then reached a low level. The new Umayyad caliphate lasted until 1031. Shortly before his death the first 'Abd-al-Rahman, following Mu'awiyah's example, designated his son Hisham as his successor. He thereby bypassed Sulayman, Hisham's senior by eleven years. Like Yazid, Hisham was the son of a Christian mother. The introduction of the hereditary principle contributed to the state's stability and continuity. On his first anniversary of the amirate 'Abd-al-Rahman cited the name of the 'Abbasid caliph in the Friday sermon. This caliphal fiction was also maintained on the early coins, as the few extant samples indicate.

IV

'Abd-al-Rahman began his political career in the tradition of Mu'awiyah's hilm, but ended it in that of the 'Abbasid al-Saffah. We recall here his magnanimous conduct at Cordova's conquest. He then tried to win over his two deadliest enemies, al-Fihri and al-Sumayl. Later experience, with them and others, soured him, however. Next to beheading, crucifixion became his favorite style of punishment. He became as uncompromising with his friends as he was ruthless with his foes. His name meant "servant of the Merciful," but if he did worship any such deity he did not emulate it. Before long he developed an infallibility complex. Those who disagreed became disagreeable and took the first step toward becoming suspect. Unlike in his earlier days, when he roamed in his capital's streets mingling with his subjects, he now became morose and solitary behind thick walls and bodyguards' bayonets. The wine of life turned to vinegar in his veins.

Once a venerable old theologian dared defy the autocrat. He declined the post of judge of Cordova, for he would not serve under a governor who put his power above the law. The governor began to twirl his mustache, signal of a rising tempest. The courtiers held their breath, expecting a sentence of death to fly from his lips. "But God," to use a chronicler's words, "turned aside his evil thought." "Get out," shouted he, "and accursed be those who recommended you." Those who recommended him were 'Abd-al-Rahman's two sons, Sulayman and Hisham.

One after the other of his confidants fell from grace. The first was abu-al-Sabbah, who began his association by losing his turban and now ended it by losing his head. When the amir dismissed him from the Seville governorship, abu-al-Sabbah headed an uprising of Yamanite malcontents. The aged 'Ubaydullah, to whom 'Abd-al-Rahman owed his throne, came near meeting the same fate. But 'Abd-al-Rahman thought of a more effective punishment: "I shall simply ignore him, treating him with cruel indifference." Nor did his faithful and useful freedman Badr end his career unscathed. He was not as servile as he used to be to the master. His property was confiscated and he was banished to a frontier town. But the deepest cuts of all were those inflicted on the amir's emotions by blood relatives. The first came from two Umayyad princes who hatched a plot but were betrayed and beheaded. More painful was the blow inflicted by a nephew, Mughirah ibn-al-Walid. Mughirah conspired with a son of al-Sumayl and was likewise beheaded at his uncle's command. In a melancholy fit the tormented ruler unburdened himself thus:

> How disappointing have my kinsfolk been! I struggled hard and long, at the risk of my life, until with God's aid I attained my goal. Under the shadow of my sword they entered my realm. Therein I provided them with a haven of security. With them I shared the manifold blessings and gifts that God bestowed on me. But then what did they do but turn against me? In their haughtiness they sought my destruction. But God has punished their ingratitude by laying bare before me their machinations. It was a question of their lives or mine. Their suspicion of me, the innocent, made me suspect the innocent among them.

I feel most wretched on account of my brother al-Walid. By killing his son I left him without a progeny. How can my eye meet his? [1]

Then, turning to a courtier, he handed him 5,000 dinars, ordering him to go to al-Walid, apologize for his brother, hand him the money and request him to go anywhere beyond the frontiers of Spain.

On September 30, 788, the unhappy amir died and was buried in his capital city.

'Abd-al-Rahman, the outcast of Syria, vagabond of North Africa and pretender of southern Spain, founder of the second glorious Umayyad dynasty and the match of the two mightiest rulers of the West and the East, was the first Arab to write his name indelibly in the annals of European history.

[1] Maqqari, vol. II, p. 32, and others.

Al-Ma'mun: Radical Caliph and Intellectual Awakener of Islam

> As for him of the judges who fails in your
> presence to profess the creation of the
> Koran and its non-eternal character—in
> conformity with the commander of the
> faithful's belief—he should be promptly
> dismissed from his office as one in whom
> the commander of the faithful has no
> faith.
>
> —Al-Ma'mun

NUMEROUS caliphs excelled al-Ma'mun in military exploits, a number in statesmanship and administrative ability, but none equaled him in his rationalism and patronage of exotic learning. The intellectual movement he fathered in Baghdad, involving translation of Greek and Syriac works, was the earliest in Islamic history and one of the most momentous in the history of thought. As the sea of medieval Islam engulfed an extensive part of the civilized world, the figure of this caliph stood out, against a background of caliph-defenders of the faith, as an islet, isolated and unperturbed. The Orthodox caliphs of Medina were too close to the Prophet physically and mentally to be anything but orthodox. The Umayyad caliphs of Damascus had rapport with Byzantine government and culture, but their preoccupation was military, and their period remained one of intellectual incubation. It was left to this seventh 'Abbasid caliph—in a city where Syrian, Persian and Greek cultures meet and interplay—to write the unique chapter he did in Islam the religion and Islam the culture.

I

The year 786 witnessed the installation of the most celebrated of all caliphs, Harun al-Rashid, and the birth of his two sons, the future caliphs Muhammad—known by his honorific title al-Amin (the trustworthy) and 'Abdullah—known as al-Ma'mun (the trusted one). The father surpassed the second son in fiction but not in history. His name, thanks to anecdotists and taletellers in the *Arabian Nights,* has become a part of the heritage of the civilized world.

When barely five years old al-Amin was designated as successor to the high office, though he was six months younger than al-Ma'mun. Al-Amin's mother was the talented and beautiful Zubaydah, granddaughter of Caliph al-Mansur and sharer with her cousin-husband of the glamor and distinction that later generations bestowed upon the memory of his court. Al-Ma'mun was the son of a Persian slave girl, Marajil. Al-Amin was the only 'Abbasid caliph born of two Qurayshite parents.

As the two boys grew the father must have noted the superior mental and moral qualities of the "son of the Persian woman" and had second thoughts on the succession. Not so the Arabian mother. Her influence was reinforced by that of her brothers. "Let us subject the two sons to a test," argued the caliph one day, "by asking each what he would do if he were a caliph." Impulsively the heir apparent told the messenger, "I would bestow on you a fief and enrich you with gifts." The cool and calculating al-Ma'mun ordered an inkstand and wrote, "How dare you address such a question involving the life of the commander of the believers? May we all lay down our lives for his!"

Harun in 799 designated al-Ma'mun as his second successor. Aware of the perennial problem of succession that had plagued Islam since the Prophet's death, the caliph subsequently drew up two documents: one, for al-Amin's signature, would make him forfeit his right to the throne should he contest his half-brother's right to succeed him; the other, for al-Ma'mun's signature, contained his solemn pledge of loyalty to his half-brother. The two documents, properly signed and witnessed were deposited at the Kaabah on the occasion of the caliph's pilgrimage (802). At about that time the caliph appointed one of the two teen-agers, al-Ma'mun, as governor over the eastern province from Khurasan to the Indus, and made the other his assistant in Baghdad. Al-Ma'mun took up his residence at Marw. The empire could then be said to have been administratively divided.

The death of the caliph in March 809 at Tus, while on a puni-tive expedition, opened the way for the fraternal struggle—a struggle which the father had taken unusual measures to avert. On the surface it was a contest between a frivolous, wine-women-and-song-loving man in power and an intelligent, ambitious would-be successor. Both men were in reality dominated by their viziers, one by al-Fadl ibn-al-Rabi' and the other by al-Fadl ibn-Sahl. The first Fadl, al-Amin's mentor, was descended from a Syr-ian slave manumitted by Caliph 'Uthman, but he was more Arab than Arabian. The other Fadl was a Persian fire-worshiper who had lately adopted Islam. Both Fadls were masters in the diplo-matic techniques of the day. Ibn-Sahl's definition of what happi-ness meant to him was significant: "Happiness consists in being able to issue orders at will, with the full assurance that they will be executed." His opposite number would have heartily agreed.

But the contest was more than one between personalities on the caliphal or vizirial level. While primarily a dynastic dispute, it involved issues with nationalistic, religious, political, social and economic aspects, interlocked and overlapping. It became a con-test between Neo-Moslems, mostly Persians with a rich and proud legacy of culture and national life, and early Moslems, nucleated in Arabians. The contention involved on one hand Shi'ites—largely Persians, Arab 'Alids and Yamanites, and on the other hand Sunnites, centered in Qaysites (North Arabians). Al-Amin represented the Arabian-Qaysite-Sunnite camp, al-Ma'mun the Neo-Moslem, Shi'ite-Persian-Yamanite camp.

From his deathbed at Tus, Harun had ordered his men to pass under the command of al-Ma'mun, in whose province the rebellion had broken out. But al-Amin ordered them back home. His vizir, who was in Tus, advised the generals to "return to the service of the powers that be rather than join the powers that might or might not be." On the advice of ibn-Sahl this first provocation was bypassed by al-Ma'mun. He was not yet ready for a showdown. The governor paid homage to the caliph, cited his name in the Friday prayers and sent him the expected gifts, rich textiles and mineral products of Khurasan. But he remained in full control of the provincial treasury, the army, and the judiciary. To the farsighted ibn-Sahl the provocation was a forewarning hastening forearming. The explosive elements were all there: a playboy in control, a more competent successor awaiting his turn, and two unscrupulous counselors with unlimited ambitions for their masters and consequently for themselves. Al-Ma'mun had already set a network of spies extending as far as his brother's court, while the brother had been lavishly spending money from the state treasury to win friends for himself and enemies for the other party.

The spark was provided in 810, when the caliph, at the instigation of ibn-al-Rabi', decreed that his infant son Musa be mentioned, next to him, in the Friday prayer. Although the decree did not delete al-Ma'mun's name, the intent was unmistakable. Earlier al-Amin had sent an embassy to his brother requesting his acquiescence. The envoys were received in state and the answer was courteous but unequivocal: The addition would be a contravention of their father's sacred will. In the meantime ibn-al-Rabi' had sent for the copies of the wills at the Kaabah and given them the scrap-of-paper treatment. The only course open for the caliph was to depose his brother and muster the armed forces against him.

Some 40,000 troops, mostly Iraqi and Syrian Arabs led by an incompetent general, 'Ali ibn-'Isa, started the eastward march. At al-Rayy (near Teheran) they were met (May 811) by 4,000 Khurasanians and Persians commanded by the redoubtable general Tahir ibn-al-Husayn, whose mother tongue was Persian. The caliph's army was utterly routed and its general slaughtered. Tahir is said to have used his sword with both hands so effectively that the governor entitled him "he with the two right hands" (*dhu-al-yaminayn*). But so confident were the Baghdad authorities of victory that when a courier from the battlefield arrived with the tragic news, he found the caliph fishing with his favorite slave

Kawthar in the Tigris. Al-Amin, chroniclers assure us, would not
be interrupted, because his companion had caught two fish and
he none.

The battle of al-Rayy marked the beginning of the end of al-
Amin's regime. He soon found himself facing not only a victorious enemy from the east but new ones in his immediate territory.
The most dangerous was an 'Alid in the capital. In 812 Tahir's
army laid siege to Baghdad. In September of the following year
all resistance ceased and the caliph sued for peace. As he fled,
Tahir's men caught him on the Tigris, where he kept a fleet of
barges for his extravagant night ballets, and assassinated him. In
recording his obituary the celebrated Iraqi historian ibn-al-Athir
writes, "We find nothing in his biography praiseworthy to record"—an appropriate epitaph.

The death of al-Amin left al-Ma'mun as the sole but not undisputed ruler of the empire. It was six years before he made his
entry into the capital. For obvious reasons he was not a favorite
in the western half of the caliphate. A rash of uprisings covered
the face of the Arab world. One of the most serious was that of an
'Alid pretender in Kufah, ibn-Tabataba, who went as far as striking coins in his name (815). The rebellion in Iraq was crushed by
a general whom al-Ma'mun, at the instigation of his jealous vizir,
shamefully rewarded by throwing into prison where he died. But
the movement spread eastward and assumed more dangerous proportions. The caliph was somehow persuaded that the knotty
'Abbasid-'Alid conflict could not be settled in the Gordian style,
but by compromise. To this end he summoned from Medina to
Marw a descendant of the caliph 'Ali, 'Ali al-Radi by name, fourteen years his senior, and appointed him heir apparent—a radical
step that shocked and infuriated Sunnites everywhere. The caliph
apparent appeared dressed in green, the 'Alid color, and the
caliph ordered that throughout the empire green flags and uniforms replace the black of the 'Abbasids. Al-Radi was more noted
for piety than for political acumen. In July 817 Baghdadis hastily proclaimed caliph Ibrahim ibn-al-Mahdi an uncle of al-
Ma'mun. While on a tour with al-Ma'mun, al-Radi met sudden
death, which Shi'ites claimed was brought about by poison in a
drink of pomegranate juice for the caliph's convenience. His

burial place near Harun al-Rashid's in a village outside Tus became a venerated shrine (*mashhad*), giving its name to the city
which grew around it. Meshed is still the most frequented place
of pilgrimage in Shi'ite Persia.

The sudden death of al-Radi, followed by the assassination of
al-Fadl ibn-Sahl by discontented Arabs, eased the situation at
Baghdad. The incompetence of Ibrahim was becoming more apparent. One after the other of the pretender's generals deserted
him. In August 819 al-Ma'mun made his triumphal entry into the
caliphal capital. He lost no time restoring the black colors.

With the seizure of Baghdad peace did not prevail. Babak,
head of a dissident politico-religious group called Khurrami
(after a Persian town), continued terrorizing the eastern area.
Supported by Armenians and possibly Byzantines, the movement
was not crushed until the reign of al-Mu'tasim, brother-successor
of al-Ma'mun. Another insurgent group which was not subdued
until then was a strange Indian tribe, al-Zutt, which had occupied
the lower Euphrates marshes, lived on the salt industry and grew
so powerful as to levy tolls on the shipping and even cut off supplies to Baghad. They were finally attacked by a general of al-
Mu'tasim and dispersed, some finding their way as gypsies into
Europe via Asia Minor. In Egypt the old Yamani-Qaysite conflict
flared up in 825 and the subsequent fires were not extinguished
until al-Musta'sim's reign. The situation became complicated by
the part played by Copts. Then Spanish Moslems, banished by
'Abd-al-Rahman III's successor, disembarked at Alexandria, seized
the city and had to be dislodged by force.

New problems were created for the caliph by his close friends.
His former trusted general Tahir ibn-al-Husayn, then governor of
Khurasan, took advantage of his distance from the capital to re-
nounce his fealty. The governor ordered (822) substituting in the
public prayer for "the victory of the reigning caliph" "the victory
of religion (*al-din*)." Tahir passed on the realm to his son, starting
a quasi-independent state, the first of its kind. It presaged the
beginning of the empire's disintegration at its eastern fringe.

II

The Baghdad al-Ma'mun entered (819) was not the Baghdad he knew. A large part of it lay in ruins. Gone was the "round city" started (762) by his great-grandfather al-Mansur and, ironically, styled by him "the city of peace." Surrounded by a double brick wall, a deep moat and an inner wall rising ninety feet, the city had taken four years to build at a cost of 4,888,000 dirhams. Al-Ma'mun chose for residence the palace of his father's vizir Ja'far al-Barmaki on the east side of the river. But it was not long before Baghdad resumed the march of progress initiated by Harun but interrupted by al-Amin. The reigns of the illustrious father and more illustrious son are universally considered the golden age in the five centuries of the 'Abbasid caliphate, indeed of the entire Arab caliphate. Al-Ma'mun's capital soon rose to eminence as a commercial, industrial and intellectual center, a worthy successor of a series of metropolises beginning with Ur and Babylon and ending with Ctesiphon. Its advantageous position on the Tigris, close to the Euphrates and not far from the Persian Gulf, rendered all parts of the then charted world accessible by sea if not by land. The city meantime resumed its role as the scene of the extravaganza commemorated in the *Thousand and One Nights*.

To the markets of Baghdad now began to flow—more than before—taxes in kind and cash from the many provinces, some of which also sent their products for sale. From Egypt came high-class linen fabrics; from Syria metalwork; from Lebanon glassware; from Bahrain pearls; from Yaman frankincense and spices; from Persia carpets, brocades and embroideries; from Khurasan highly prized gold, silver and marble works. A late historian has left us an itemized list of the annual taxes in kind offered by the provinces and districts. The list includes the number of robes, suits and rugs, of mounts, cattle and slaves as well as the exact quantities of wheat, barley, dates, olive oil, honey, sugar and rose water. He additionally lists in detail the amounts of dirhams and dinars received, which reached the staggering total figure of 27,037,000 dinars.

From other than provinces India shipped spices, minerals, dyes;

central Asia rubies, fabrics, slaves; China porcelain, silk, musk; Russia and Scandinavia honey, furs, white slaves; and east Africa, ivory, gold dust and black slaves. Soon the Baghdad merchants found themselves handling not only domestic agricultural and industrial products but exotic ones too. They waxed wealthy. They began to play a leading part in community life. A group of industrialists added to their native techniques those of Persia, long noted for its advanced industry. The personal contact al-Ma'mun had with that country and Khurasan must have contributed to the extension of the bounds of trade and industry, which thus assumed international dimensions unknown before. Hordes of coins lately unearthed in countries as far north as Finland and Russia attest the brisk world-wide trade activity of this general era. The memorable adventures of Sindbad the Sailor of *Arabian Nights* fame have an undoubted basis in actual Arab merchants' reports. Craftsmen and traders had their shops in markets (sing. *suq*) of their own, as some of them still have today. The monotony of Baghdad streets was broken from time to time by a parade celebrating a wedding, a circumcision, or the memorizing of the Koran by a student.

Basrah, founded by Caliph 'Umar (636), seconded Baghdad's efforts at achieving commercial eminence. It had commenced its ascent under Harun. Its favorable location at the Euphrates-Tigris juncture (head of Shatt al-'Arab), closer to the Persian Gulf, gave it special advantages. Besides, it stood amidst a fertile region growing rice, corn, millet, barley and wheat. It is still the main port for the export of dates which bear its name. Fabulous stories are told about the fortunes accumulated by Baghdadi and Basran magnates and tycoons—the Carnegies and Rockefellers of the era. A Basran maritime merchant had an annual income of 1,000,000 dirhams. Another, a miller who could hardly read and write, could afford 1,000 dinars a day as alms to the poor.

Basrah had a rival in Siraf on the eastern shore of the Persian Gulf. Its maritime merchants carried pearls, silks, striped cloth and Indian spices as far as the Malay Peninsula and Canton, which they reached in a month's journey. And how they thrived! Records claim that some were worth 4,000,000 dinars each and many lived in 30,000-dinar homes. The Sirafis became known for luxurious and voluptuous living. With the commencement of the decline of the empire, shortly after al-Ma'mun, the two ports started on a downward course.

As for the common man—the farm laborer in outlying districts, the unskilled manual worker in cities, the sources are silent on his lot. He was the forgotten man. We may be sure, however, his share in this top-level prosperity was disproportionate to his needs. He presumably remained underpaid, underfed and living under unsanitary conditions.

The process of social integration between Arabians and non-Arabians, begun early in 'Abbasid days, was accelerated under al-Ma'mun. The early tribal organization was almost obliterated. The gap between old and new Moslems was bridged. Intermarriage, polygamy, concubinage and slavery served as arches. Gone was the early military Arabian aristocracy nucleated in the Quraysh and insisting on pedigree as the sole qualification for admission. The new class of businessmen, teachers, writers, scholars, physicians—recruited mainly from Neo-Moslems—inched its way to new heights under al-Ma'mun. The economic change seriously affected the social and political structures.

Other than business, politics and warfare offered opportunities for "getting rich quick." So massive was the wealth accumulated by vizirs that caliphs, beginning with Harun, found it in the interest of the state—at least the heads of the state—to confiscate their properties. When this caliph destroyed the Barmakids, he reportedly seized, in addition to their palaces, villas and villages, no less than 3,378,500 dinars. When al-Ma'mun's general Tahir died, 1,300 unused *dabiqi* trousers (sing, *sirwal*) were found in his wardrobe. "Dabiq" was the name of an Egyptian town the world-renowned fabrics of which were imitated in Persia. Tahir's son and successor on one occasion paid 200,000 dirhams for ransoming his men captured by Turks in central Asia. Equally huge must have been the fortune of al-Hasan ibn-Sahl, al-Ma'mun's minister of finance and later governor of Wasit, a fortune acquired after his conversion in 812. Neither Tahir nor al-Hasan, it will be recalled, was of Arabian descent.

Al-Hasan had a daughter named Buran, who at the age of ten was betrothed to the caliph. The celebrations were not held until 825, eight years later. The scene was her father's villa outside of

Wasit at the juncture of a canal with the Tigris. The festivities continued for seventeen days on such a lavish and gorgeous scale that later historians like al-Tabari, al-Mas'udi and ibn-al-Athir took pains to report its detailed expenditures. The ladies of the imperial household attended dressed in their wedding attire. They were headed by the caliph's stepmother, Zubaydah, who for long had set the fashion for the smart set in Baghdad. Zubaydah was the first to ornament her shoes with precious stones. At her table she would tolerate no vessels not made of gold or silver and studded with gems. The poets, the reporters of the day, were of course invited to sing the beauty of the harem and memorialize the occasion. A two-hundred-rotl candle of ambergris, fixed in a candlestick of gold in the bride's apartment, turned the nights into days. At the final ceremony, while the royal couple sat on a golden mat studded with sapphires, the bride's grandmother showered them from a gold tray with a thousand pearls of unique size. As the princes and high dignitaries departed, the governor gave them robes of honor and showered them with balls of musk each hiding a ticket naming an estate, a slave, a team of horses or some other gift. The rest were given gold or silver coins or eggs of amber. To recoup his father-in-law's expenses, the caliph granted him a year's revenue from two Persian districts. By her beauty and wit the young queen exercised domestic as well as political influence on her husband for the remaining eight years of his life. The wife survived her husband by nearly fifty years, long enough to witness the commencement of the empire's decline from the height of its glory.

But the glory of al-Ma'mun's age did not lie solely in such fields. It lay in the impetus the caliph gave to learning and intellectual activity. The movement developed into one of the most momentous in Islam if not in history of thought.

III

The new orientation began with translation. Translation had an early start. It was initiated by al-Mansur, to whose court an Indian traveling scholar had introduced two manuscripts, one on mathematics and the other on astronomy. The caliph ordered the books translated. The one on astronomy—*Siddhanta* (Ar. *Sind-*

hind)—was done by Muhammad ibn-Ibrahim al-Fazari. It served
as a model for later works and laid the basis for the scientific study
of the stars. Pre-Islamic interest in the stars stemmed from the
need to determine directions in a roadless desert and from the
belief that heavenly bodies were influential in human affairs and
could provide foreknowledge of terrestrial happenings. Al-Mansur had his astrologers, and so did Harun and al-Ma'mun. Islam
added still another practical aspect, the determination of the direction in which legal prayer should be conducted. Al-Fazari took
his place among the earliest astronomers in Islam.

The Indian mathematical treatise was rendered into Arabic
about the same time as the astronomical. The Siamese twins of
astronomy and mathematics were never separated. The two treatises introduced the Arabic numerals, called by the Arabs Hindi.
Until then the letters of the alphabet were used in the East as in
the West for counting. The new device made possible the development of arithmetic, astronomy and other mathematical sciences. In the numeral system the little circle or dot called *sifr* in
Arabic (whence cipher, zero) is of capital importance. It enables
us to "keep the rows," to borrow the Arabic expression, to keep
each figure in its place, i.e., in the series of powers of ten, units,
tens, hundreds and so forth, whenever one of these powers is not
represented. The zero was known in the Arab East at least two
and a half centuries before it was used in the West.

If India supplied the first impulse to scientific study in Islam,
Persia provided the early literary prose model. Al-Mansur had a
secretary, 'Abdullah ibn-al-Muqaffa', a convert from Zoroastrianism, to whom he entrusted the translation of Persian works. From
ibn-al-Muqaffa''s pen we have the earliest Arabic literary work
extant. It is a delightful collection of fables in which animals are
personified and carry on dialogues discussing their experiences
for the benefit of the reader. The narrator, a Hindu philosopher
named Bidpai, corresponds to Aesop of the East. His fables (Ar.
Kalilah wa-Dimnah) had their ultimate origin in the Sanskrit
Panchatantra, the great epic of the Hindus. So facile in language
and elegant in style was the Arabic rendition that it took its position as a classic in Arabic literature, a position it still holds. Its
learned writer had a tragic ending. Suspecting him of tampering
with the language of a political document and of practicing in

secret the faith he abjured, al-Mansur ordered (757) his limbs cut off one by one and thrown into a blazing furnace.

The movement initiated under al-Mansur was accelerated under his grandson Harun. Harun's efforts in this field were seconded by those of his Persian Barmakid courtiers. Greek as a source for transmitting thought had been tapped before but now the flow was also considerably enriched.

Hellenization, in the sense of adoption of Greek language, thoughts and ideas, had been going on in the area since the days of Alexander and the Seleucids. At the time of the Arab conquest the intellectual legacy of Greece formed the most precious treasure at hand. Of all existing foreign influences the Hellenistic was the most potent. By now Greek was considered an earmark of a cultivated Syriac-speaking man, as French or English is today in the case of an Arabic-speaking man of the same area. Syrians therefore were the logical transmitters of Greek thought to their new masters. Harran (Carrhae), Edessa (al-Ruha) in northeastern Syria and Nisibis (Nasibin) farther east were centers radiating Hellenistic learning. Harran was a seat of heathen Syrians. Antioch was one of the many ancient Greek colonies; so was Alexandria, where Oriental and Occidental philosophies met.

In the numberless colonies of Syria and Mesopotamia not only ecclesiastical but also scientific and philosophic studies were cultivated. In those Christological controversies which constituted the intellectual preoccupation of clerical scholars, the basic issues were metaphysical and psychological. For the battle of words Orthodox, Arians, Nestorians and Jacobites found in the Aristotelian and Neo-Platonic armory ready ammunition. Polemicists resorted to Greek logic to buttress their argumentation. Especially valuable in this connection were Aristotle's great work on metaphysics and Porphyry's *Isagoge,* which to Syrians and Arabs became a recognized manual of logic preparatory to Aristotle's *Organon.* Porphyry ("clad in royal purple"), a founder of Neo-Platonism, was born in Syria and given the name Melik (king). The *Isagoge* and the *Organon,* which in Arabic included Aristotle's *Rhetoric* and *Poetics,* took their place side by side with Arabic grammar as the core of humanistic studies.

Syrian translators into Arabic could then use already existing Syriac versions or the original Greek. Some of those who flourished under Harun and al-Ma'mun tapped both sources. Such was al-Hajjaj ibn-Matar (d. after 833) of the Harranian school. Al-Hajjaj prepared (828) an Arabic version from the Syriac of Ptolemy's *Almagest*. This work by the famed Alexandrian scientist of the mid-second Christian century sums up what was known to the ancients of theories and observations of astronomy and geography. The original Greek has survived in its Arabic rendition, bearing the title meaning "greatest (composition)," with the Arabic definite article prefixed. Al-Hajjaj is credited with making the earliest translation of Euclid's *Elements* in two versions, one for Harun and one for Harun's son. Euclid flourished also in Alexandria some four centuries and a half before Ptolemy; the *Elements* laid the basis of the science of geometry and remained in vogue till modern times.

A more notable translator of this period was Yuhanna (Yahya) ibn-Masawayh (Lat. "Mesuë," d. 857). Yuhanna was a physician by profession. He translated for Harun medical and philosophical works pillaged by the caliph in the course of a military campaign into Asia Minor. This was not the only experience of its kind for early 'Abbasid caliphs. Nor was the medical-philosophical combination in ibn-Masawayh unique. To the medieval Arab what we now consider different sciences looked like aspects of one and the same thing. A linguistic relic has survived in *hakim* (literally "wise"), used for both physician and philosopher. Nor was the dichotomy between the natural sciences and the humanities so much in evidence. Al-Ma'mun is said to have held weekly sessions in his palace for scholars to discuss and reconcile their differences.

Next to astronomy, medicine was now the science in demand. Ibn-Masawayh had for teacher another Christian Syrian physician, Jibril (Gabriel) ibn-Bakhtishu', court physician of Harun and al-Ma'mun. The Bakhtishu' family had six or seven generations of distinguished physicians. Its founder was a professor at the school of Jundi-Shapur. The teachers in this Persian school were largely Syrians using their language as a medium of instruction.

Of the two great caliphal patrons of learning, Harun's son was the greater. His father had more interest in poetry, music and song; these brought more glamor to the court. Al-Ma'mun had a personal reason for concentrating on philosophy and science. He sought therefrom support for his unorthodox views.

The caliph must have felt alienated from his society. Starting as a non-conformist, he ended as a religious radical. He was conditioned by his mother and wife, tutor, counselors and vizirs—all non-Arabians. The major part of his mature life was spent in Khurasan and Persia. For a time his restless spirit sought satisfaction in Shi'ism but failed to find it. Now in his capital he found congenial atmosphere in a radical, schismatic school of thought termed al-Mu'tazilah (seceders). The Mu'tazilah rebelled against the doctrine of the eternal character of the Koran on the ground that it conflicted with the more basic doctrine of the oneness of God. How could we, they argued, maintain that God is the only eternal being, creator of all things, and then set alongside Him an uncreated word? They prided themselves on being the "people of unity and justice."

The Mu'tazilah had for intellectual ancestry the Qadarite school of late Umayyad days. Qadarite theologians taught that man had power (*qadar*) over his deeds, a direct challenge to the almightiness of God, repeatedly preached in the Koran. One of the most beautiful and favorite verses (sur. 3:25) reads: "O God, possessor of kingly might! Thou givest might to whom Thou willst and withdrawest might from whom Thou willst. Thou exaltest whom Thou willst and abasest whom Thou willst. In Thy hand is all Good, for verily over all things Thou hast power." Other verses in the Koran (e.g., 27:77; 57:22) teach that whatever befalls man, whatever happens in heaven or on earth, is brought about by Him and recorded in a clear book (*kitab,* whence *maktub,* decreed). These sectarians could not reconcile such doctrines with man's moral obligation and responsibility. God, they argued, is not only almighty but also just, and a just God does not punish a wrongdoer for a decreed deed. Such issues had for long agitated the minds of Christian theologians. In Damascus the impact began to tell on Islam. In that city for the first time reason (*'aql*) was brought to act and react upon revealed dogma. In Medina theologians worked in a non-sophisticated society. St. John of Damascus (Joannes Damascenus, d. *ca.* 748) may be cited as a principal agent in transmitting Christian lore and Greek thought. Among his works is a dialogue with a "Saracen" dealing with Christ's divinity and the freedom of human will. The book was intended as a manual for the guidance of Christians in their debates with Moslems.

In 827 al-Ma'mun took a most radical step; he raised the Mu'tazilah creed to a state religion. In a momentous proclamation to his provicial governors he declared his belief in the "creation (*khalq*) of the Koran" and made this doctrine the touchstone of the new orthodoxy. This was followed by an edict that no judge who did not subscribe to the novel dogma could hold his office or be appointed as judge. The significant part of the edict reads:

> Summon all judges under your command. Read them this message from the commander of the faithful. Then subject each to the test to determine whether his answers reveal his belief in the creation of the Koran. As for him of them who fails in your presence to profess the creation of the Koran and its non-eternal character—in conformity with the commander of the faithful's belief—he should be promptly dismissed from his office as one in whom the commander of the faithful has no faith.[1]

By way of implementation the caliph instituted an inquisitional tribunal, the first in Islam. Ironically the movement for free thought became a deadly instrument for suppressing thought.

The inquisition (*mihnah*) continued under al-Ma'mun's brother-successor al-Mu'tasim (833–42) but was abolished in 848 by al-Mu'tasim's son al-Mutawakkil. Its list of victims was headed by the "imam of Baghdad" Ahmad ibn-Hanbal, founder of the fourth and last rite of Sunnite Islam. In his puritanical conservatism ibn-Hanbal stood as a bulwark against Mu'tazilite innovations. Chained by al-Ma'mun and for two years jailed and scourged under al-Mu'tasim, he nevertheless stubbornly refused to recant. Not an iota of modification in the traditional view would he admit. The 860,000 men and women mourners who reportedly followed his coffin in 855 bore witness to the massive admiration for this champion of orthodoxy. The many more who

[1] Al-Tabari, *Ta'rikh al-Rusul w-al-Muluk*, ed. M. J. de Goeje (Leyden, 1881), ser. III, pp. 115–16.

have since visited his shrine in Baghdad testify to his abiding influence. Today the Wahhabis of Saudi Arabia constitute the bulk of his rite's followers.

Al-Ma'mun implemented his concern for Greek learning by sending special emissaries for the acquisition of manuscripts from Constantinople and Sicily. Emperor Theophilus at first hesitated to cooperate because he thought the learning that made the Roman name illustrious should not be wasted on a barbarian. Ibn-Masawayh and Hunayn ibn-Ishaq headed such missions in quest of new material. The caliph institutionalized the learned activity by building (830) in his capital Bayt al-Hikmah, a combination of academy, library and translation bureau. Next to it he built the first observatory. The concept was no doubt inspired by Syrian and Persian academies. The first head of the Baghdad institution was young Hunayn (L. Johannitius) ibn-Ishaq (809–79), a student of ibn-Masawayh and ibn-Bakhtishu' and superior to both in brilliancy and achievement. Hunayn is said to have received five hundred dinars a month plus the weight in gold of every book he translated.

In his work the shaykh of translators was assisted by his son Ishaq and his sister's son Hubaysh ibn-al-Hasan. The father was more proficient in Greek and Syriac, the young collaborators in Arabic. Hunayn evidently made the first draft into Syriac, in case it was not already there; the other two carried it over into Arabic. The industry of this school yielded the Arabicization of part or all the works of Hippocrates father of medicine; Galen, for centuries after his death (*ca.* A.D. 200) the supreme authority in medical science; Archimedes (d. 212 B.C.), the most celebrated mathematician of antiquity; Apollonius of Perga, another Greek mathematician of the third pre-Christian century; Euclid, the master geometrician, as well as Aristotle's *Categories* (*Maqulat*), *Physics* (*Tabi'iyat*), *Metaphysics* (*Ilahiyat*) and *Magna Moralia* (*Khulqiyat*) and Plato's *Timaeus* (*Timawus*) and *Republic* (*Siyasah*). Some of these works had been done earlier, but the new editions were an improvement.

In his life as translator and physician ibn-Hunayn represented the best in the East Syrian (Nestorian) Church. Asked by his patron al-Mutawakkil to concoct a poison for an enemy, he flatly refused and was committed to jail for a year. Sitting with a sword nearby, the caliph summoned the scholar and requested him to obey the order at the risk of forfeiting his life, but Hunayn once more refused. The curious caliph asked for an explanation, claiming that he was simply testing his physician's integrity, and this was Hunayn's reply:

> My religion and my profession prevent my compliance. My religion decrees we should do good even to our enemies, how much more to our friends. And my profession is instituted for the benefit of humanity and limited to relief and cure. As a physician I am under oath never to administer a deadly medicine.[1]

Arab interest in Greek learning seems to have stopped at the borderline of literature. Greek drama and epic poetry held no attraction for the Moslem reader. Their close association with foreign gods and mythology made them repulsive. A Maronite Christian translated for Harun's father a part of Homer's Iliad, but it did not survive. The century of translation ended shortly after al-Ma'mun's death. By then Arab readers—whose ancestors at the conquest of Ctesiphon did not think there was a number above ten hundred—had available the finest product of early European mind; and while Arab rulers were delving into Greek philosophy, Charlemagne's lords were still dabbling in the art of writing their names.

Transmission of thought plays no less significant a role in the development of culture than origination of thought. If the Ten Commandments, the Sermon on the Mount, the first surah of the Koran; if Homer, Dante and Shakespeare were not transmitted, what would they have availed anyone beyond a limited place and time? But the Arabs of the ninth century were not only translators and transmitters. Their reservoir of knowledge had many outlets, as it had inlets, and much of what they passed on was enriched by their original contributions. The Bidpai fables, lost in Persian, survived in their Arabic rendition to become a source

[1] Ibn-al-'Ibri, *Mukhtasar Ta'rikh al-Duwal,* ed. Antun Salihani (Beirut, 1890), pp. 251–52.

of new versions in no less than forty languages from Iceland to Malaysia. Al-Khwarizmi's tables (*zij*), revised in Moslem Spain, were translated into Latin in Toledo and served as the model for later astronomical tables in the West as well as in the East. From the pen of ibn-Masawayh we have a medical treatise on fevers which was translated into Hebrew and Latin. To Hunayn ibn-Ishaq is ascribed the earliest extant book on ophthalmology. Al-Ma'mun's astonomers, headed by the sons of Musa ibn-Shakir, conducted on the plain near Palmyra a most delicate operation to determine the length of a terrestrial degree. They found it to be $56\frac{2}{3}$ Arabic miles, exceeding the accurate figure by less than 3,000 feet.

But the greatest scientific mind of the age was al-Khwarizmi. Besides his astonomical activity including membership in the team of banu-Shakir, he composed the oldest work on arithmetic and wrote *Hisab al-Jabr w-al-Muqabalah* (calculation of integration and equation), the first book on algebra. Translated into Latin in twelfth century Toledo, this work was used for four centuries as a textbook in European universities. Together with al-Khwarizmi's astonomical works it was responsible for introducing into Europe the Arabic numerals called after the author algorisms. Thanks to the intellectual productivity of this and other Arab scholars, Baghdad took its place as the scientific capital of the world, paralleling Athens as its philosophic, Rome as its juridical and Jerusalem as its religious capitals.

Arab translators and researchers mediated oriental learning and Greek philosophy to the West. The Spanish Moslem ibn-Rushd (Averroes, 1126–98, who will be studied later) was the last link in the chain that dragged Aristotle through the back door into the continent of his birth.

Al-Ma'mun's preoccupation with matters of the mind did not prevent his taking the field against the Byzantines when necessary. Such occasion arose in 830 and 833. An August day in 833 found him outside his military camp in Tarsus, sitting with his younger brother abu-Ishaq and another companion on the bank of a nearby mountain stream. Weary and hot, they dangled their feet into the cool flow. "What is it we now need to make ours a perfect day?" asked the caliph. The companion, who tells the story,[1] replied, "You, commander of the faithful, know best." "Only a dishful of fresh choice dates," remarked al-Ma'mun. No sooner said than a mule loaded with the very fruit was heard approaching. The three ate to the full, leaving little room for the crystal-clear water. But no sooner had they risen than they felt stricken with burning fever. The caliph's case worsened. His rescript to the governors of the provinces designating abu-Ishaq, now al-Mu'tasim, as his successor was already drawn. His last will and testament was now written and signed in the presence of dignitaries and judges. In it he enjoined upon his successor justice in administration, devotion to religion and enforcement of the Koran creation dogma. He concluded with detailed instructions on the funeral, last prayers and burial place, directing that no weepers or mourners accompany his coffin. There he was buried, aged forty-eight, after a reign of twenty-two years, five months and twenty-three days.

Son of a foreign slave woman, winner in the struggle for the caliphate against a pure-blooded Arabian, radical in an era of conservatism, promoter of a most momentous movement in the history of thought, sharer with his people of the classical heritage of the West, al-Ma'mun lifted his people from the tradition-oriented phase of culture—through the imitative—to the creative and made his capital an intellectual center of the world.

[1] Tabari, ser. III, pp. 1133–40, records the story of his death and includes his rescript and will. The only comprehensive biography of al-Ma'mun is Ahmad F. Rifa'i, *'Asr al-Ma'mun,* 3 vols. (Cairo, 1927), in Arabic.

'Ubaydullah al-Mahdi
Founder of the Fatimid Empire
in Africa

But Satan made them slip. And I there-
fore purged them with the sword.
—'Ubaydullah al-Mahdi

IT was time. For two and a half centuries Shi'ite followers of 'Ali
had labored to seize the supreme power in Islam for one of his
and Fatimah's descendants, but failed. Their battles were unsuccessful but not always unheroic. In their prayers they invoked
Allah's blessings on 'Ali, His friend, and on 'Ali's progeny, the
divinely guided imams (spiritual leaders), as they invoked His
curses on the Umayyad and 'Abbasid usurpers; but prayers
proved to be ineffective. They plotted and conspired; they battled; they chased after that headship of Islam, once for five years
(656–651) held by their founder, but it was as elusive as the mi-
rages of their desert. The caliphs of Damascus and Baghdad
spared no Shi'ite pretender. 'Ali's eldest son Husayn was slaughtered (680), as we have learned, by Mu'awiyah's successor. Four of
the ten imam descendants of Husayn were either certainly or possibly poisoned by 'Abbasid agents: one in Medina, two in Baghdad and one in Tus (Persia).

When the 'Alids allied themselves with the banu-'Abbas
against banu-Umayyah in hope that the caliphate would be restored to the "family of the house" (*ahl al-bayt*), the 'Alids discovered to their disillusionment that the 'Abbasids considered
themselves as close to the house of the Prophet as they were. At

one time, when al-Ma'mun by a freakish move appointed an imam as heir apparent, fortune seemed to smile on them but it was a lightning smile. Throughout their long night of dark struggle against the established order, the Shi'ites were sustained by the charisma of Muhammad's prophethood flowing through his progeny, by the *mystique* of 'Ali's personality and by the passion induced by Husayn's martyrdom. And ironically when at last (909) the seemingly lost cause won a victory, it was through an enigmatic person of undetermined parentage and origin in whose arteries many historians believe there was not a single drop of 'Alid or Arabian blood. Even his first name has not been established. He entitled himself 'Ubaydullah (little slave of God) al-Mahdi (909–34) and became the founder of the first and only great Arab shi'ite dynasty.

But 'Ubaydullah did not represent the majority sect of the Shi'ite community. Its members styled themselves Twelvers. He belonged to a splinter group known as Seveners or Isma'ilis. The Twelvers believed in twelve imams in the line of Husayn, ending in Muhammad al-Muntazar (the expected one). When in 878 the ten-year-old Muhammad was in Samarra (north of Baghdad), he entered a cellar whence he never returned to his mother waiting outside. A cathedral mosque now stands on the site. Muhammad's followers explained his absence as a temporary state of occultation (*ghaybah*) from which he will return at the opportune moment. As such he remains immune from death. Though hidden (*maktum, mustatir*), the imam continues to be master of the age (*qa'im al-zaman*). "He who dies without knowing his imam," Shi'ites assert, "suffers the death of an unbeliever." At his reappearance as *mahdi* (divinely guided) he will restore true Islam, conquer the entire world and usher in a millennium of peace and prosperity. The end of the world will follow. Clearly the basic element in Mahdiism—as in Messianism—is the longing of a suppressed, frustrated minority for relief, and the personification of that longing.

The imamate then occupies a central position in Shi'ite creed. Unlike the Sunnite caliphate, it is primarily a spiritual office limited to the 'Ali-Fatimah line and surrounded by an aura of divinity. Of course the imam performs also all caliphal temporal functions. Until today the imam-mahdi dogma forms the main line of demarcation between Sunnah and Shi'ah. Fear of extinction under pressure from an overwhelming Sunnite majority prompted other extraordinary doctrines in the minority sects. One of them was temporary marriage (*mut'ah*), an especially convenient device for travelers, salesmen and others away from home. Another was dissimulation (*taqiyah*), dispensation from the requirements of religion under compulsion or threat of injury. It meant that when a believer found himself in a perilous position, he not only might but was obliged to profess outwardly the form of the prevailing religion as a measure of protection for himself and his community. But the Shi'ah survived in its two major branches, Twelvers and Seveners. Shi'ite communities thrive today in Persia, Iraq and Yaman. Small settlements are sprinkled over the entire face of the Moslem land. In Syria and Lebanon they go by the name Matawilah (those with allegiance [to 'Ali]).

Most Arabians were especially receptive to Shi'ism. It furnished their nationalistic aspirations with an outlet. The 'Alid cause became a common ground for the politically, socially and economically dissatisfied, particularly among Neo-Moslems. In dissident Islam, intellectuals found a more congenial atmosphere for the exercise of their activity. Orthodoxy enforced a measure of conformity that was to them uncomfortable. To the Sunnah deviation in the direction of innovation (*bid'ah*) was tantamount to a heresy. That is why we find such a number of scientists, philosophers, bellestrists in Shi'ite or heterodox camps. The great physician ibn-Sina (Avicenna), to be studied later, was an Isma'ili.

An early offshoot of Isma'ilism was founded by an Iraqi ox-driver, Hamdan Qarmat, and developed communistic tendencies relating to property and wives. By the turn of the tenth century the Qarmatis, Bolsheviks of Islam, had established an autonomous state on the western shore of the Persian Gulf. From there they conducted marauding raids to Mecca, Baghdad and cities in Khurasan. The second great offshoot was the Assassin (Ar. *hashshashin*, *hashish*-addicts) order, founded in Alamut, Persia. The Agha Khans, currently spiritual heads of the Isma'ilis, claim descent from the founder of the order ibn-al-Sabbah. Other surviving Isma'ili offshoots are the Nusayris of al-Ladhiqiyah (Latakia), Syria, and the Druzes of Lebanon and Syria.

Twelvers and Seveners agreed on the first six imams. The Seveners accepted the sixth imam's eldest son, Isma'il (d. 760), as his father's successor, but the Twelvers bypassed him in favor of his brother Musa. Isma'il was seen drunk and predeceased his father. His followers denied that he had been disinherited. They also denied his father's authority to change the initial designation. They further argued that as imam Isma'il was above the law. Isma'il's fifteen-year-old son, Muhammad al-Maktum (concealed), was so surnamed because he disappeared from his headquarters in the city of his birth, Medina. He evidently fled the wrath of Harun al-Rashid, hid near al-Rayy (Persia) and was no more. His descendants dispersed east and west, but the imams among them hid in a small Syrian town, Salamyah (now Salamiyah, between Hims and Hamah). To the Isma'ilis the number seven assumed a

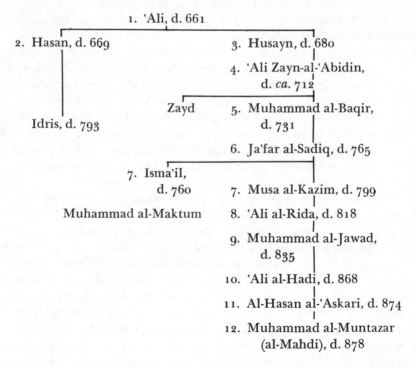

1. 'Ali, d. 661

2. Hasan, d. 669   3. Husayn, d. 680

                                     4. 'Ali Zayn-al-'Abidin,
                                        d. *ca.* 712

                        Zayd   5. Muhammad al-Baqir,
       Idris, d. 793   d. 731

                                     6. Ja'far al-Sadiq, d. 765

            7. Isma'il,
               d. 760   7. Musa al-Kazim, d. 799

       Muhammad al-Maktum   8. 'Ali al-Rida, d. 818

                                     9. Muhammad al-Jawad,
                                        d. 835

                                    10. 'Ali al-Hadi, d. 868

                                    11. Al-Hasan al-'Askari, d. 874

                                    12. Muhammad al-Muntazar
                                        (al-Mahdi), d. 878

The Relationship of the Seven and the Twelve Imams

religious dimension, as it did in the Pythagorean system of old. They "periodicated" cosmic and historical happenings by this number.

In the course of its development Isma'ilism acquired from Neo-Platonism ill-digested philosophical and cosmogonical accretions, adding esoteric gnostic doctrines. This made of it a philosophical-political-religious school of thought. The steps of emanation were seven headed by God, followed by the universal mind (*'aql*) and the universal soul (*nafs*). The world was favored with seven legislative prophets beginning with Adam, continuing through 'Isa (Jesus) and Muhammad and ending with Muhammad al-Maktum (the hidden). In between each two prophets seven silent (*samit*) prophets are inserted. Such were Ishmael and 'Ali. According to the esoteric doctrine, the words of the Koran have an inner (*batini*) meaning of which the apparent (*zahir*) is but a veil. Gnostics, Jews and Christians had developed the idea long before Islam. The Song of Songs is still interpreted allegorically. Esotericism was intended to keep the truth from the uninitiated and leave it open only to the few. In the hands of unscrupulous leaders the doctrine lends itself singularly to exploitation.

By way of practical implementation, Isma'ilis organized the most subtle and effective politico-religious propaganda the world of Islam ever experienced. The missionary (*da'i*) was chosen, screened and trained with care and under strict discipline. He had to have a passion for anonymity and secrecy, special talent for polemics and philosophic argumentation as well as an ability to act politically when the decisive moment came. Under oath of secrecy the novice was initiated in the esoteric doctrine, a procedure involving seven to nine hierarchical 'stages. To each region one propagandist was sent in disguise. The manipulator of the entire propaganda machine was a high official (*hujjah*), the closest to the mahdi and his mouthpiece. And when the mahdi is concealed his hujjah assumes greater significance.

This esoteric Isma'ili system was perfected by one 'Abdullah ibn-Maymun, of obscure Zoroastrian origin. 'Abdullah's father, Maymun al-Qaddah (the oculist), was evidently closely associated with Muhammad al-Maktum, and initiated the propaganda method as he practiced his profession in al-Ahwaz. 'Abdullah op-

erated first from al-Ahwaz and then from Basrah, both uncom-
fortably close to Baghdad, before moving to Salamyah. Salamyah
became and remained Isma'ili headquarters. In it 'Abdullah took
his post as the hujjah of concealed imams. From there he and his
successors trained and sent secret missionaries with instructions to
start by playing on the disaffection of would-be followers, arous-
ing their skepticism and finally pointing out to them the forth-
coming appearance of the deliverer in the person of the mahdi.
'Abdullah took full advantage of the situation in which he found
himself—manipulating an extraordinary secret powerful machine
in the name of a hidden imam—for the advancement of his personal political ends. He died in 874 after designating his son
Ahmad as his successor in the hope that someone in his line
would ultimately seize the supreme power. Thus did the son of a
humble Persian oculist conceive the audacious plan of uniting
conquerors and conquered in a secret fraternity that would use
religion as an instrument to destroy the Arab caliphate and give
his descendants the throne—a project as fantastic in its conception as it was swift in its execution. For it was this project that
culminated in the victory of 'Ubaydullah and the birth of the
Fatimid dynasty.

                                   I

    Of all the obscure personages in Arab history none is more ob-
scure than 'Ubaydullah. He and his followers claimed descent
from the seventh imam Isma'il. Others trace his descent to 'Abdullah son of Maymun al-Qaddah. Modern scholars are in equal
disagreement. A controversy raging for a thousand years has not
yet been fully resolved.
    The self-styled 'Ubaydullah was born in Salamyah about 873.
That much is certain. Those who support the legitimacy of his
Fatimid origin trace it through Muhammad al-Maktum ibn-
Isma'il, who had disappeared more than a hundred years earlier.
Their case is weakened by not agreeing on one single pedigree. At
least eight varying ones are offered. 'Ubaydullah himself, according to one source, presents a still different one. The pro-legiti-
mists are not all Shi'ites. They include two notable Sunnites, ibn-
al-Athir and ibn-Khaldun. The majority of Sunnite authors,

however, deny or suspect the Fatimid genealogy and hold that
the so-called 'Ubaydullah al-Mahdi was an impostor, who was
really Sa'id, great-grandson of none other than 'Abdullah ibn-
Maymun al-Qaddah. They insist on calling his dynasty 'Ubaydi-
yah. The charge that 'Ubaydullah was of Jewish parentage can
readily be dismissed as one often levelled against controversial
unorthodox figures. Against the anti-legitimist case is often
pressed the interesting, but not damaging, argument that not
until the year 1011, when the 'Abbasid caliph issued a curious
manifesto signed by notables and judges—Sunnite and Shi'ite—
was the question of Fatimid legitimacy raised. By then the Fatimids in Cairo had stripped Baghdad of all its African and a large
part of its western Asian possessions and were posing a threat to
the heart of the orthodox caliphate.[1]

Of the early life of 'Ubaydullah as little is known as might be
expected. The first we hear significantly of him is in 902, when he
left Salamyah carrying his treasures, accompanied by his wife,
their son al-Qasim and attendants, headed through Palestine toward Egypt. The move was in response to messages from an
Isma'ili missionary in North Africa, abu-'Abdullah al-Shi'i. By
this time Isma'ilism had penetrated Yaman and Egypt, and in its
Qarmati form had spread over eastern Arabia and parts of western Persia. But the Qarmatis were now in open revolt against the
Salamyah hujjahs for usurping the imamate functions. Originally
a Twelver, al-Shi'i was born in San'a, Yaman, and was richly endowed with those qualifications that make a successful Isma'ili
propagandist. He started his work with the Berber pilgrims to
Mecca in the early 890's. So charmed were they by his personality
and impressed by his piety and learning that they urged him to
join their caravan returning home.

The North Africa to which al-Shi'i addressed himself was politically fragmented into independent and semi-independent states,
interspersed with tribal units owing no allegiance beyond their
local shaykhs. This fragmentation was rendered possible by the
weakening of the central power in Baghdad. Religiously the area

---

[1] The most extensive modern research on the Fatimids has been done by
Hasan Ibrahim Hasan, Ta'rikh al-Dawlah al-Fatimiyah, 3rd ed. (Cairo, 1964);
on 'Ubaydullah, by Hasan and Taha Ahmad Sharaf, 'Ubaydullah al-Mahdi
(Cairo, 1947).

was shared by Sunnites, Shi'ites and Kharijites. The ruling class was mainly Semitic Arab, the ruled Hamitic Berber. Obviously such a situation was not conducive to social stability or healthy economy. The eastern part, dominated by Egypt, was under the Tulunid dynasty (868–905), which used Fustat as its capital. Its founder was the son of a Turkish slave received as a present by the caliph and sent in 868 to Egypt as deputy governor. There he refused to pay tribute, incorporated Syria into his realm and established the first independent state in the valley of the Nile. The Tulunids were Sunnites; they acknowledged the religious authority of the caliph, symbolized by citing his name in the Friday congregational prayers. The dynasty started a series of independent Egyptian states that lasted until the Ottoman conquest (1517). As a rule these states held Hijaz as well as Syria.

Central North Africa, headed by Ifriqiyah (Africa Minor, roughly Tunisia, western Libya and eastern Algeria), was now under the Aghlabids (800–909) with al-Qayrawan as capital. The Aghlabids repeated the Tulunid performance. They went further, however, and ceased to inscribe the caliph's name on their coinage as a token of spiritual suzerainty, despite the fact that they were Arabs and Sunnites. Their founder, ibn-al-Aghlab (800–811), was originally sent by Harun al-Rashid as governor over the area. His dynasty built a sizable fleet, extended its sway into Sicily and for more than a century dominated the mid-Mediterranean. Under their rule the hitherto Latin-speaking, Christianity-professing population began to assume an Arabic-Moslem aspect.

Western North Africa (al-Maghrib, largely Morocco) had emerged earlier (788) as an independent territory and so remained until 974. The founder, Idris (788–93), was a descendant of 'Ali. He headed one of those unsuccessful insurrections in Medina and fled to the extreme west. The Idrisids used Fas (Fez) as a principal capital. They were, of course, Shi'ites, but their Berber Sunnite subjects were ever ready to espouse a schismatic cause.

Singlehandedly, with the gospel of Isma'ilism buried deep in his chest, the man from San'a set out to convert Africa. His ambition was no less daring than that of the man of Tarsus who, in response to the voice from Macedonia, crossed over to conquer Europe for Christ. Al-Shi'i's approach was through the contact previously made with the Kitamah tribesmen at Mecca. The Kitamah occupied the area in what is today northeast Algeria, then nominally under Aghlabid control. To their west and south lay the territory of the Sanhajah and Zanatah tribes. The reception given him was as warm as the response to his message was quick. The appealing feature of the new teaching was the approaching sudden appearance of the deliverer and the conquest of the world by his followers. To bring the message nearer home, al-Shi'i and his disciples circulated a prophecy from a "book of ancient records" that "the sun of Mahdiism shall rise in the *maghrib* (west)." But the Kitamah deserved a more personal consideration. So he pulled out from the same book of jugglery another linguistic legerdemain: "Verily, the Mahdi shall appear in a land far away from his to be supported by a people of righteousness, a people with a name derived from *kitman* (secrecy)." The Mahdi, they were assured, can perform miracles, even raise the dead. For this promised man, al-Shi'i posed as a precursor, a voice in the desert: Prepare the way. The rich harvest readily reaped suggests that seeds had been sown by earlier missionaries.

By the turn of the century al-Shi'i was ready to lay down the gospel and girdle the sword. His Kitami assistants became his lieutenants, and the believers army recruits. Making of religion a handmaid of politics was no novelty in Islam. The preacher-turned-warrior was now in a position to challenge the mightiest state in the continent, a hundred-year-old state with well-oiled military machinery including a navy. Hence the need for the presence of 'Ubaydullah as a morale booster.

'Ubaydullah entered Egypt disguised as a merchant. But it was not long before 'Abbasid spies were on his track. His Egyptian host assured the inquiring officer that he did indeed entertain a "noble Hashimi merchant, known for his learning, wealth and beneficence; but his guest had returned to Arabia." Hashim, we recall, was the Prophet's grandfather. Cautiously and slowly the fugitive party moved westward, narrowly escaping the dragnet spread for it by 'Abbasid agents. Bribery no doubt played a part.

By the time it reached Tripoli the Aghlabid king Ziyadat-Allah III (903–9) had all necessary details to identify the group and its "merchant" head. 'Ubaydullah hit on a caravan going to Sijilmasah in the extreme south of Morocco and joined it, leaving hundreds of miles of barren land between him and his expectant followers. It does seem that al-Shi'i, who kept contact with him throughout the journey, had second thoughts involving selfish ambitions. He therefore preferred his chief's proximity over his presence. The governor of Sijilmasah, ibn-Midrar, was a Kharijite, whose sect was the oldest schism in Islam. Ibn-Midrar extended to his guest the courtesy and hospitality worthy of his noble descent. In his turn the guest was generous with his presents, and with his party was assigned a special wing of the palace. It was not long, however, before reports reached the governor about the identity of his guest. He threw him into a dungeon under heavy guard. Scourging extracted no confession. His son abu-al-Qasim was confined in another cell.

Al-Shi'i the warrior turned out to be no less successful than al-Shi'i the preacher. He mustered, according to ibn-al-Athir, 200,-000 horse and foot. Tribes who did not yield to persuasion yielded to coercion. One Aghlabid stronghold after the other fell. Messages of the cheerful news were relayed to the Sijilmasah prisoner. One was delivered by a secret agent in the guise of a butcher vending his meat. What was reported to be a giant of an Aghlabid proved to be a statue of clay. Meantime the uncheerful news was reaching Ziyadat-Allah, and he, on the advice of his jester, was dulling his senses by more song and more wine. In 909 the Isma'ili army stood at the gates of Raqqadah, the Aghlabid residential quarters nine miles south of al-Qayrawan. Al-Qayrawan, the mightiest stronghold on the continent, sent envoys offering submission. Ziyadat-Allah took to flight without putting up a fight. Egypt was his destination. With him ended the Aghlabid dynasty, last Sunnite bulwark in Africa.

For six days and nights the troops feasted on luxuries, enjoyed maidens and shared treasures on a scale unexperienced formerly. Al-Shi'i installed himself in the royal palace and behaved like a king. He struck new coinage bearing on the obverse, "I have attained the rank of Allah's hujjah" and on the reverse, "Allah's enemies have been dispersed." His seal carried the inscription, "Put thy trust in Allah, for thy stand is on clear truth" (sur. 27:81). His flag displayed, "All hosts will be routed; they will turn and flee" (sur. 54:45). On his horses' thighs was stamped, "Rule belongs to Allah." When he mounted, the herald shouted, "O horsemen of Allah, mount." In the Friday service no names were mentioned but those of Muhammad, Husayn and Fatimah. It was three months before al-Shi'i moved for the liberation of 'Ubaydullah, leaving his brother abu-al-'Abbas in charge. Was he in the meantime flirting with the idea of replacing him? And did he on third thought feel that the Frankenstein he had created had grown too powerful?

As al-Shi'i at the head of his horde traversed the area to the southeast border of Morocco, tribes and towns offered their submission. Sijilmasah put up a token resistance. Its governor did not escape the slaughter. According to the famed biographer ibn-Khallikan, when al-Shi'i entered 'Ubaydullah's cell, he found his dead body and a faithful Jewish slave whom he substituted for the Mahdi; but the report lacks evidence. This was indeed a banner day for the Fatimid cause. The long period of concealment for the imam ended. Dressed in ceremonial robes of silk, with turbans to match, and set on horses, the Mahdi and his son were conducted to a special tent, with the triumphant leader walking before them crying: "This is your lord, to whose obediences I have invited you." Tears of joy at times interrupted his cry. At the tent "a throne of heaven" was ready for the new lord. A forty-day period of celebration and rest at Sijilmasah followed.

II

Early in 909 the victorious party made its ceremonial entry into Raqqadah. Shaykhs of Arab and Berber tribes, leaders and officials hastened to offer their allegiance. Al-Mahdi ensconced his family in the Aghlabid palace. From the royal harem he chose those pleasing to him, offering others to his son. In the first Friday service his name, titled al-Mahdi and commander of the believers, was mentioned in all mosques of Raqqadah and al-Qayrawan, the

official capital. For the first time in history names of two antagonistic caliphs were cited on such occasions. An extreme Shi'ite
rival to the orthodox Sunnite caliphate was born. 'Ubaydullah's
son abu-al-Qasim was made heir apparent and surnamed al-
Qa'im. The Fatimid victory was in a sense the victory of non-
Arabs over Arabs, of Berbers over Arabians, of new Moslems over
old Moslems.

The new monarch stepped into the shoes of the old in other
than domestic affairs. Lacking in governmental experience and
handicapped by excessive Divine claims, he faced the gigantic task
of ruling a realm nominally extending from near Barqah to the
neighborhood of Fas. Pacification and consolidation were the two
preliminary steps. The double role of conspirator-adventurer he
had thus far played could hardly be considered a qualification.
Aghlabid institutions, technicians and minor officials were ready
for use. Isma'ilis were installed in key positions. To the provinces,
including Sicily, governors from the Kitamah were sent. The
judges had also to be believers. Wisely, the dissident ruler did not
insist on conversion, the bulk of the Arabs and townsmen being
Sunnites. After all, Isma'ilism was but a thin crust over layers of
Sunnah and other forms of Shi'ah. The religious aspect began to
recede into the background and the secular advanced to the
front. Gradually the 'Ubaydullah in the ruler entirely eclipsed
the Mahdi. After an ascendancy of more than two and a half
centuries, Isma'ilism in Africa hardly left a trace, whereas in Asia,
where it never enjoyed such a privilege, it survived in more than
one country. In one government institution, the military, 'Ubaydullah made certain that control remained in family hands.
Hence the appointment of his son as commander, assisted by generals trained in the Shi'i school. To al-Shi'i was given command of
military operations against disaffected tribes in the western region.

To the Sanhajah and the Zanatah, the two most powerful
Berber confederations of tribes in the area, the position of superiority given the Kitamah in the new regime was galling. The
Sanhajah were Sunnites. Their territory extended southwest of
Kitamah's through the desert to Senegal. The males among their
descendants, the Tawariq (Tuareg) of southern Algeria, are distinguished by wearing veils covering the face below the eyes. The

Zanatah, mainly nomads living "in the manner of the Arabs,"
were impregnated with Kharijite doctrines.

That the novice ruler was a good judge of men is indicated by
the performance of the high officials he chose. His governors of
Tripoli, the gateway for eastward expansion, not only suppressed
separatist movements and held the line for the Fatimids, but they
assumed an aggressive posture toward Egypt. The country was
now in a state of political instability. The Sicilian governors were
similarly successful in effecting, peacefully or violently, transition
from the old order to the new. As in Aghlabid days the fleet was
used to harass the shores of southern Italy and neighboring islands, as well as to protect the North African coast against Byzantine attacks. Probably it was still partly manned by mercenary
Greeks.

Before long (910) 'Ubaydullah found himself facing problems
in his court that tested his ability to act decisively. They began
with the man on whose shoulders he had climbed to the throne.
Until yesteryear abu-'Abdullah al-Shi'i had been in name
(*'ubayd,* diminutive of *'abd,* slave of) and in fact playing the
leading role on the stage. He awoke one day with the feeling that
he was nobody. With his brother, he started a whispering campaign intended to throw suspicion · on the genuineness of al-
Mahdi. The apparent discrepancy between promise and performance lent credence to the rumors. A Kitamah shaykh had the
nerve to appear before al-Mahdi and ask for the "signs," the
expected miracles. The head of the old man was then and there
severed from his body. It was not difficult to ascertain the source
of the treasonable activity. Abu-'Abdullah and abu-al-'Abbas
were invited to a repast at the palace, waylaid and killed. As the
shining dagger was raised over the head of the unsuspecting victim, abu-'Abdullah heard muttered into his ears the words, "In
obedience to the command of him you ordered us to obey." One
strike sufficed. But abu-al-'Abbas took several. The bodies of the
two brothers were left on exhibit for hours before funeral prayers
were authorized. A good precedent for the act was the case of
Harun al-Rashid and his Barmaki vizirs. In the Fatimid no less
than in the 'Abbasid firmament, there could be no two suns. The
announcement of the execution read:

To the Shi'ites in the Orient, greetings.

You are no doubt aware of the high positions attained by
abu-'Abdullah and abu-al-'Abbas in Islam. But Satan made
them slip. And I therefore purged them with the sword. And
peace be unto you.[1]

The allusion is to surah 2:34, "But Satan made them [Adam and
Eve] slip." With the removal of abu-'Abdullah al-Shi'i from the
scene, the last vital link with Mahdiism was broken. The ghost
remained to be invoked to give the despot's deeds ethical respectability.

Simultaneously a third conspirator, abu-Zaki, was disposed of.
He was sent to Tripoli carrying a sealed order for his instant
execution—which he was told was an order for his appointment
as governor. The incumbent, whom the messenger addressed as
uncle as he presented his "credentials," carried out the order, reported it by carrier pigeon to Raqqadah, and confirmed the report
by sending home the victim's head. In the Fatimid book of hor-
rors there were many recipes.

The repercussions of the purge in Berberland were perhaps
more violent than 'Ubaydullah had anticipated. The Kitamah
were the first to translate their feelings into action. Some of them
claimed that abu-'Abdullah was still alive, urging them to fight—
this time against the man for whom they were once ordered to
fight. Others put up a new mahdi, an infant. A punitive expedition under al-Qa'im nipped the movement in the bud. Al-Qa'im
reduced the tribal settlement to ashes, and took the infant and
other prisoners to grace his triumphal return to the capital, where
he paraded them, then slaughtered them. As often happens, other
groups—dissatisfied for a variety of reasons—took advantage of
the disturbed situation. In Tripoli, in Sicily, in al-Qayrawan itself serious uprisings threatened the infant state. Amidst the disturbances 'Ubaydullah remained levelheaded. Mounting his
horse, he would ride courageously out into the streets to declare
that justice was now satisfied and that no further inquiry would
be made or punishment inflicted.

1 Ibn-'Idhari, vol. I, p. 164.

Another general, the Kitami 'Urubah ibn-Yusuf, to whom 'Ubaydullah had entrusted the execution of abu-'Abdullah, carried military operations into the heart of al-Maghrib. After a three-day siege Tahirt, Zanatah's capital, was captured (911), plundered and left with 8,000 of its population and defenders slain. The city had first been reduced two years earlier by abu-'Abdullah. It was now the seat of the banu-Rustim; these with the banu-Midrar of Sijilmasah were the most powerful Kharijite princes. The Kharijite sect was introduced by Arabian tribesmen fleeing from the wrath of Umayyad caliphs. It was neither Shi'ite nor Sunnite but antagonistic to both, and both considered it a heresy. Tahirt became the seat of 'Urubah as governor and the center for operations into the extreme west. 'Urubah met the fate of his victim abu-'Abdullah, but his successors carried on. In the north Ceuta (Sabtah) was reached. Only the Idrisid realm now stood in the way of reaching the Atlantic. The Idrisids, we recall, were Shi'ites but not of the Isma'ili variety. A large part of their realm was overrun; Fas, however, remained under an Idrisid prince. Progress was halted by the specter of a new giant from the north trying to straddle both sides of Gibraltar—the Umayyad 'Abd-al-Rahman III.

This namesake of the 'Abd-al-Rahman we studied earlier, and his rival for the distinction of being the greatest of the line, ascended the Cordova throne shortly after 'Ubaydullah (912). In 929, taking advantage of the decline of and distance from Baghdad, he proclaimed himself caliph. Thereby was the Moslem world divided into three major antagonistic caliphates—a unique phenomenon in its history. The only direction in which the rising empire could expand was southward, dragging itself into a clash with the Fatimid empire. There the Umayyads used the Sunnite Sanhajah as the spearhead of subversion and insurrection. 'Ubaydullah's sight was from the outset oriented in the opposite direction. Egypt was the rich prize. Beyond it lay enemy number one.

The Nile valley was then in a brief interval of precarious 'Abbasid sway between the fall of the Tulunid dynasty (905) and the rise of the Ikhshidid (935). The country was under the remote control of a caliph who was himself under the immediate control of the chief of his palace guard, a Turkish eunuch. Feeling insecure against internal and external enemies, 'Ubaydullah in 912 undertook the building and fortification of a new capital, al-Mahdiyah, on a peninsula sixteen miles southeast of al-Qayrawan. Yaqut among other geographers describes in detail its high walls, wide enough for two horsemen abreast, with two doors of solid metal, each a thousand kantars in weight, opening to a tunnel that could hold five hundred horsemen. Then there were the deep moats, the shipyard that could accommodate two hundred boats under cover and the rock-hewn harbor with a capacity of thirty ships. Al-Mahdiyah must have developed into the mightiest stronghold in North Africa. It survived to the Ottoman era as a center of Tunisian piracy. The new town was poised like a dagger pointed at the heart of Egypt.

In the summer of 914 the first attempt at Egypt was made by a land force commanded by al-Qa'im. The invaders captured Barqah, seized Alexandria, plundered it and pressed southward to al-Fayyum. In the following year the Egyptian army, reinforced from Baghdad, compelled their evacuation, but 'Ubaydullah was nonetheless convinced that the conquest lay within the sphere of possibility. Two years later the second attempt was made. This time it was supported by an eighty-five-ship fleet. A naval victory at Alexandria and a land victory at al-Fayyum left Upper Egypt at the mercy of the invaders. Evidently they found among the natives many sympathizers, if not actual supporters. Egypt had long been the butt of Isma'ili propaganda, first from Salamyah and then from al-Qayrawan. Local rivalries and jealousies must also have given the invaders an opportunity for subversion. In the technique of subversion and the use of money for corruption, Fatimids were past masters. Four years of occupation (917–21) gave the 'Abbasids time to hit back. In a battle not far from the great pyramids, the new recruits inflicted a decisive defeat on the occupying forces. About the same time a twenty-five-ship task force, manned by experienced Greeks from Tarsus and other Byzantine towns, destroyed the enemy task force. The Fatimids had to wait almost half a century before they could claim Egypt as their own.

Statewise 'Ubaydullah built better than he knew. The four chaotic decades of his and his predecessor's rule were marked with dynastic collapse, insurrections, civil wars, earthquakes and famine. From unpromising material, in one of the least developed areas in the world of Islam, peopled by some of the most turbulent tribesmen and townsmen, the father of the Fatimid dynasty brought forth a state mighty and durable, stable and orderly. His successors ruled a realm the size of which no Pharaoh or Ptolemy had ever ruled. They gave the valley of the Nile one of the most prosperous periods in its long history. 'Ubaydullah's son and grandson made of the central and western Mediterranean a Fatimid lake. Their fleet harried the southern coasts of Italy, France and even Moslem Spain. One admiral raided Genoa. Another sent back to al-Mahdiyah live fish from the Atlantic in a jar. But the highwater mark was the conquest of Egypt in 969. This was accomplished by 'Ubaydullah's great-grandson al-Mu'izz. The country was then under a boyking of the Ikhshidid dynasty, whose Turkish founder Muhammed al-Ikhshid (935–46) duplicated ibn-Tulun's performance. Sent by Baghdad as governor, al-Ikhshid incorporated Palestine, southern Syria and Hijaz. He ruled independently, maintaining the citation of the caliph's name in the congregational service. Al-Mu'izz' conquering general, Jawhar, originally a Sicilian slave, built near the old capital (Fustat) a new one, Cairo (al-Qahirah). He provided it with a mosque-university, al-Azhar, the oldest of its kind extant. The city he built is today the most populous in Africa.

Under al-Mu'izz' son al-'Aziz (975–96) the empire reached its zenith. The Fatimid caliph's name was cited in the weekly sermons from Mosul (al-Mawsil) on the Tigris to the Atlantic and from Aleppo to the Sudan. So confident was al-'Aziz of ultimate victory over his rival that he invested two million dinars in a guest house for his future Baghdad prisoners. Al-'Aziz' son al-Hakim (996–1021) established a remarkable educational institution, Dar al-Hikmah (house of wisdom), modeled after that of al-Ma'mun. The Fatimids' interest in education stemmed from concern for propagating extreme Shi'ite views. Al-Hakim's attempt to destroy the Holy Sepulcher indirectly contributed to the Cru-

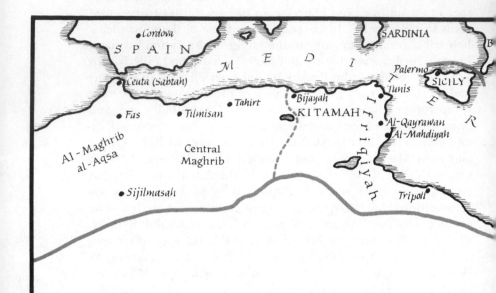

SARDINIA

Cordova

S P A I N

M   E   D   I

Ceuta (Sabtah)

Palermo

Tunis

SICILY

B

Fas

Tilmisan

Tahirt

Bijayah

KITAMAH

Al-Qayrawan

Al-Mahdiyah

T

E

R

Al - Maghrib
al - Aqsa

Central
Maghrib

I f r i q i y a h

Sijilmasah

Tripoli

The Fatimid Caliphate
at its height, ca. 990

| 0 | 100 | 200 | 300 | 400 | 500 |

miles

Ascherl

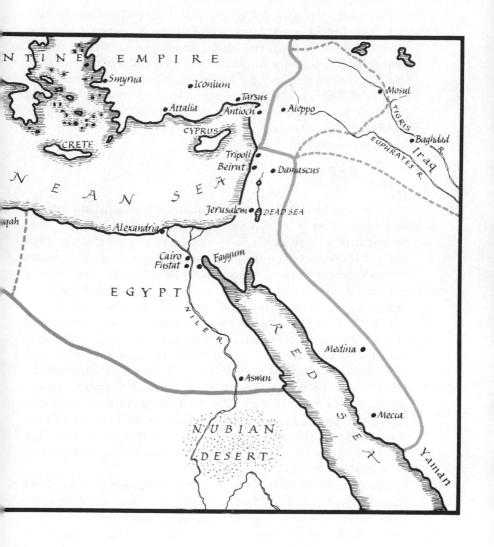

sades. But this caliph is better known for having initiated Druzism, represented today by thousands of devotees in southern Lebanon and the Syrian district of Hawran.

The dynasty fathered by 'Ubaydullah followed in its course the cycle inscribed by other Moslem dynasties: an energetic founder, succeeded by able men, reaching a small plateau with a zenith, then going down under incompetent power holders precipitously to the nadir. In this case the nadir was hit under the fourteenth caliph, al-'Adid (1160–71). When the renowned Salah-al-Din (Saladin), to whom the next chapter is devoted, deposed al-'Adid and restored the 'Abbasid names in the prayers, no Egyptian rose in defense of the Fatimid rule.

III

At the age of sixty-one 'Ubaydullah died (934) in the city he had built, after a twenty-five-year reign. His last years were shrouded in secrecy as his early years had been. From the high walls of his residential quarters we cannot eavesdrop; nor can we through their solid doors peep into his domestic life. We know of only one wife—mother of al-Qa'im—who accompanied him from Syria. She was his first cousin. Of his concubines we hear of only one, La'ib, who was killed in the Qarmati attack on Salamyah at about the time of 'Ubaydullah's departure. Al-Qa'im is the only son of whom we are sure. We read of two daughters who were presumably in the party from Syria. With regard to 'Ubaydullah's physical features we are equally in the dark. His Isma'ili biographers hold no doubt that the Mahdi's face—as foretold—radiated light like a bright star (*kawkab*); no one in his presence but felt the awe of his personality. His strength was that of ten men. Any tall men by his side would look short, and any big man would seem small.

About his inner traits, however, there can be no doubt. They shine through any recital of his achievement with more certitude than his face does. He was certainly of the stuff of which unscrupulous leaders of men are made: energy, persistence, fearlessness, resolution. Gratitude had no place in his make-up. The force that motivated him was passion for power, power as an end justifying all means.

A man of undetermined parentage and of probable non-Arab origin, member of a minor heterodox sect, 'Ubaydullah al-Mahdi succeeded in capturing the scepter of 'Ali after fifteen generations of 'Alids had tried and failed, and established in a backward turbulent area the third-greatest and the second-longest-lived Arab empire.

Salah-al-Din:
Hero of the Anti-Crusades

*As soon as Allah the most high enables me
to wrest the rest of the maritime plain, I
plan to divide the realm among my aides,
give them instructions, bid them farewell
and cross the seas, pursuing the enemy to
their islands. There I shall destroy the last
one on the surface of the earth of those
who do not believe in Allah—or else I die.*
—Salah-al-Din

ACTION and reaction between the Near East and the West began early and lasted long. They can hardly be said yet to have ceased.

The first series was initiated by Darius and Xerxes attacking the Greek homeland. The visit was repaid by Alexander the Great, whose successors were followed by the Romans, Western and Eastern. The second was launched by Islam, with a religious overtone, ending the thousand years of Western ascendancy in the area, and threatening Europe in its rear by Arabs in Spain, in its belly by other Arabs in Sicily and in its front by Saljuqs aiming at Constantinople. The Crusades, undertaken by men with crosses sewed on their clothes, were in a sense the reaction.

Any significant acquisitions by the invaders were made in the initial stage, 1097–1144. By that half century the principalities of Edessa (al-Ruha, Urfa), Antioch, Tripoli and more importantly the Latin Kingdom of Jerusalem had been established. The achievement was due more to the weakness of the opposition than the ability of the invaders. The area had been fragmented among Saljuqs, Turks, Arabs, under sultans, princes, chieftains, mostly concerned in personal affairs with no dedication to a common cause. The beginning of the end was inaugurated not by an Arab from the affected area, nor by a representative of the two neighboring caliphates of Baghdad and Cairo, but by a blue-eyed Turkish amir of Mosul, Zangi. His were the first of the hammer blows under which the exotic states were to disintegrate. The initial blow fell on Edessa (1144), the first to rise in the area and the first to fall. Zangi's son Nur-al-Din (the light of the faith) rode the tide as it turned in favor of Islam. He wrested Damascus from Saljuq hands (1154) and ruled a kingdom extending through Aleppo to Mosul. The state was virtually independent under 'Abbasid nominal suzerainty. The capture of Damascus removed the last barrier between Nurid and Latin domains.

Salah-al-Din followed Nur-al-Din as champion of the cause. Third in the series of anti-Crusading heroes, to which the Mamluk Baybars should be added, Salah was by all criteria the greatest. His superiority in peace and in war, as a man and as a hero, was acknowledged by friend and foe. The passage of time has dimmed the memory of several Moslem heroes; research has tarnished the names of others, but in Salah's case time and research have added honor to the memory and luster to the name. In recent years his ghost has been invoked in the Arab struggle against the mandatory powers, and Egyptians had no more flattering compliment to pay their nationalist leader than to compare him to this hero of Crusading days. To the many modern Arab biographers Salah is the "immortal hero" (*al-batal al-khalid*), to a French biographer *Le plus pur héros de l'Islam*. His tomb by the Umayyad Mosque (Damascus) has become the object of an increasing stream of visitors.

I

Yusuf (Joseph), better known by his title Salah-al-Din (Saladin, rectitude of the faith), was born in 1138 to a Kurdish family at Takrit, a fortress on the Tigris between Mosul and Samarra. His father Najm-al-Din Ayyub (star of the faith, Job) was the citadel's military commandant; his uncle Asad-al-Din (lion of the faith) Shirkuh was likewise a military man. Shortly after Salah's birth the family moved (1139) to Baalbak, over which the father was appointed by Zangi as governor and citadel commandant. The citadel (*qal'ah*) was the converted great temple built by the Syrian dynasty of Rome in the third century. The town was so rich in water and gardens as to bear comparison to Damascus. Five years later, when Nur-al-Din occupied Damascus, he chose Ayyub as its governor and Shirkuh as a general of his army. Both became very close to the ruler.

In 1164 a displaced vizir of the Fatimid caliphate, Shawar by name, appeared in the Damascus court and appealed for aid, offering a third of the country's revenue less military expenses. Welcoming the opportunity to gain a foothold in a dissident and decadent empire—with self-seeking vizirs contending for control over the child-caliph al-'Adid—and to strengthen his position against Jerusalem, the Sunnite king responded. He dispatched Shirkuh at the head of an expeditionary force. Shirkuh prevailed on his twenty-six-year-old nephew—despite his "great reluctance" —to go on his staff. The march against Egypt turned out to be a treble affair, and on the third occasion the future grand warrior of Islam expressed even more aversion to war than on the earlier two. But in obedience to the king's command he went, "feeling as if going to his slaughter." Salah might have remained an X in the mathematics of history with a non-Europeanized name. The reluctance of the young man, we are generally assured, was due to his absorption in theological studies. But from a statement of his official biographer ibn-Shaddad we infer that it was due to absorption in wine and good time. Through the obscurity that shrouds his life till then the searchlights of history yield but glimpses. It is safe to assume that he pursued the classical course of studies, based on the Koran, hadith, Arabic language, rhetoric and poetry. A scion of a prominent family, he presumably indulged in hunting, riding, chess and polo playing.

Shirkuh fulfilled his immediate mission and returned home with his nephew bearing the conviction that Egypt was vulnerable. Three years later, when the perfidious Shawar allied himself with Amalric I of Jerusalem, Nur sent Shirkuh and Salah against Egypt for the second time. Amalric (Fr. Amauray) was the second native-born king of Jerusalem and one of the few able heads of the kingdom. He realized the politico-geographical importance of Egypt to his realm and valued its prosperity. The contest for the Fatimid heritage between Damascus and Jerusalem began. The first round ended in a tie. At the battle of al-Baban (the two gates, ten miles south of al-Minya) in April 1167, Salah had his first baptism in fire. The joint Franco-Egyptian host was routed. So pleased was Shirkuh with his nephew's performance that he ordered him to proceed at the head of a contingent against Alexandria. This was his first independent command. Here again he acquitted himself well. But he was finally pressed hard by the Franks with their siege artillery and a collaborating fleet, and his uncle had to conclude a peace treaty, exchange prisoners and withdraw from the country. Both sides claimed victory.

Amalric hastened to Cairo, ostensibly to collect tribute. He must have been more convinced than ever of the vital importance of the country to the security of Crusading Palestine. A joint Egypt-Syria would almost encircle the Latin Kingdom, and from its ports it could interdict recruits and supplies from the West— the lifeline of the kingdom. Al-'Adid now himself sent a message to Nur imploring his aid. Nur entrusted the mission to the same men. This time (1168) the Lion of Islam was determined to fasten his claws in his prey. Shawar was murdered. Early in January 1169 Shirkuh seized the vizirate for himself and, on his death barely two months later, bequeathed it to his nephew. In a pantomime scene al-'Adid bestowed on Salah the vizirial robe and the title al-Malik al-Nasir (the supporter-king).

Salah had first himself to support. His double position as lieutenant of a Sunnite Syrian king and prime minister of an Egyptian Shi'ite caliph was fraught with difficulties. The Sudanese palace guard, ready to serve the highest bidder among self-seeking vizirs jockeying for power, saw in him a different newcomer. Some of his older comrades-at-arms failed to embrace him as he was promoted. He satisfied several of these with gifts and fiefs and sent others back to Damascus. From Damascus he summoned his father and the rest of the family. His father was made treasurer. His starting point was the military. The Egyptian forces comprised, besides the 30,000 Sudanese footmen, a number of white cavalry officered by Egyptians. The new vizir lost no time building up his own army of Syrians, Kurds and loyal Egyptians commanded by his brothers. The vast majority of Egyptians, it will be recalled, were Sunnites to whom Fatimids were heretical usurpers.

The time came to act decisively when a messenger of the eunuch major-domo of the guard was caught en route to Amalric. A vigilant guard at the border noticed him carrying a pair of sandals with double soles, where the message was secreted. The major-domo was beheaded, and as his men mutinied they were pursued throughout Cairo; their quarter was reduced to ashes and the site converted into a garden. The caliph's palace was put under a new guard headed by a white eunuch, Qaraqush. In the course of the following five years, Salah's brothers pursued the remnant to Upper Egypt, even to Nubia. Northern Sudan was added to the growing realm. In the meantime Salah started reorganizing the fleet with aid from Constantinople and from Italian cities. Naval support to land forces attacking Crusading ports could be invaluable.

Nor was the implementation of psychological warfare neglected. Isma'ili judges and professors were replaced, new schools for indoctrination were founded and machinery for spying and propagandizing was set. Provincial governorships were, of course, given only to relatives or trusted friends, and minor fiefs were so distributed among different ethnic groups in his entourage as to keep a balance.

In the summer of 1171 a serious illness of the captive-caliph al-'Adid gave his vizir the signal to take against him the final action long urged by Damascus and behind Damascus Baghdad. On the second Friday of September a preacher in the congregational mosque prayed aloud:

> O God, make great Thy faith; make strong its pillars. Cause
> unbelief to tremble by the preservation of Thy servant and the
> son of Thy servant al-Mustadi'-bi-Allah.

The worshipers could not believe their ears. Al-Mustadi' was the 'Abbasid caliph in Baghdad. The preacher continued:

> O God, grant him victory and grant victory to his army,
> O Thou Lord of our faith and of the world present and the
>   world to come,

> O Lord of all beings in the universe,
> O God, grant victory to all forces of Moslems and all armies
>   of the worshipers of Thee and Thee alone.
> O God, frustrate the infidels and polytheists,
>   Thy enemies, enemies of the faith.[1]

Three days later al-'Adid died unaware of the change in his status. The instructions to the entourage read: "If he recovers he will know the truth soon enough; if not, let him die in peace." Salah put the Fatimid family under strict surveillance and separated the two sexes to insure the destruction of the line. So peaceful was the radical operation that in the words of ibn-al-Athir "there was not so much as the butting of two goats."

Baghdad was jubilant. The celebration lasted for days. Al-Mustadi' sent Nur-al-Din robes of honor and with the robe for Salah he sent the black flag, 'Abbasid emblem. Salah's flag was yellow. The vizir became in fact a sultan, not officially but popularly. Cyrenaica and Hijaz were adjuncts of Egypt. The guardianship of al-Haramayn (the two Holy Cities) made the new star rising in Cairo shine with greater luster. Hijaz' neighbor Yaman, impregnated with Shi'ism, was added to the realm by Turan-Shah, Salah's elder brother. The boundary line in Cyrenaica was pushed to Tripoli.

The Egypt inherited by Salah was weak politically but not economically. Next to Iraq it was probably the richest and most prosperous country in the Near East. Its main source of revenue was the transit East-West trade, particularly between India and the three Italian republic-cities—Genoa, Pisa and Venice. The opulence was reflected in the caliph's palace, for generations the wonder of tourists and envoys. According to Arab historians the palace had four thousand chambers with a golden gate that opened to a golden hall, and a gorgeous pavilion where the caliph had his golden throne. Then there was the emerald hall with beautiful pillars of marble. The furniture and ornaments were of ebony and ivory studded with precious stones. Silk, tapestry and brocades were embroidered with gold. Fatimid jewels became proverbial in Arabic literature and their extant specimens in the Arab Museum at Cairo justify their reputation.

[1] Cf. Stanley Lane-Poole, *Saladin and the Fall of the Kingdom of Jerusalem* (London, 1888; reprint Beirut, 1964), pp. 108–9.

Entrance to the caliphal residence led through devious dark tunnels, guarded by Negroes, into spacious courts open to the sky, and arcades with gilded ceilings amidst zoological and botanical gardens of unsurpassed beauty. William of Tyre, the leading Latin historian of the early Crusades, has given us a graphic account of the presentation of Amalric's envoys to al-'Adid. William was native born, knew Arabic and was attached to Amalric's court. He must have received the information firsthand from the head envoy:

> They approached and were admitted to the inner part of the palace. Here the sultan [Shawar] showed the usual reverence to his lord, according to custom; twice he prostrated himself on the ground and humbly offered as to a divinity due worship and a kind of abject adoration. Then for a third time bowing to the ground, he laid down the sword which he wore suspended from his neck. Thereupon the curtains embroidered with pearls and gold, which hung down and hid the throne, were drawn aside with marvellous rapidity, and the caliph was revealed with face unveiled. Seated on a throne of gold, surrounded by some of his privy counsellors and eunuchs, he presented an appearance more than regal.
>
> With all reverence, the sultan approached him and, humbly imprinting a kiss upon the foot of the seated monarch, stated the reason for the envoys' visit.[1]

Ibn-al-Athir gives us an idea of the fabulous treasures found in al-'Adid's palace:

> Qaraqush brought before Salah-al-Din al-'Adid's treasures he had put under his custody prior to al-'Adid's death. So immense were they that they could not be counted. Among them were precious pendants and other strange jewelry the like of which can be found nowhere. There were also gems unique in kind and size. One mountain-size ruby was seventeen dirhams or miskals [2,400 carats]. There can be no doubt about it; I saw it with my eyes and weighed it myself. The pearls also had no peer. Among the emeralds was one four fingers long.[2]

[1] William of Tyre, *A History of Deeds Done beyond the Sea*, tr. Emily A. Babcock and A. C. Krey (New York, 1943), vol. II, pp. 320–21.
[2] Ibn-al-Athir, *Kamil al-Tawarikh*, ed. C. J. Tornberg, vol. XI (Uppsala, 1851), p. 242.

Salah distributed the treasures among his officers, sent Nur his share and kept nothing for himself—an unheard-of procedure that was not only generosity but good statesmanship. Certain treasures were sold for the state treasury. It took ten years to dispose of them all. The library of 120,000 manuscripts was given mostly to his secretary and trusted counselor al-Qadi al-Fadil. The sultan maintained his residence in the vizir's house. There he lived abstemiously in contrast to his uncle, who died after two months from overeating.

Salah the sultan was a different man from Salah the fresh recruit. "He then," reports ibn-Shaddad, "gave up for ever wine and all pleasures of this world and dedicated himself to serious affairs and hard work." In the opinion of William of Tyre the new sultan was "a man of keen and vigorous mind, valiant in battle and generous beyond measure." His reputation spread far and wide and Moslems everywhere began to see in him a new leader.

Soon the relations with Damascus became strained. An immediate cause was Nur's dissatisfaction with the share received from Egypt's revenue. Salah facilitated the task of an auditor sent from Damascus to check. He continued the mention of Nur's name, together with the caliph's, in the Friday prayers and to insert it on the new coins. Behind the dissatisfaction was probably the feeling that the viceroy was getting too powerful for the sovereign. As a matter of fact Salah was now more powerful economically and militarily. His trade treaty with Pisa, followed by similar ones with Genoa and Venice, increased that source of wealth to his country and to some extent detracted from the flow to Palestine. As if to test his vassal, Nur in 1173 instructed him to attack al-Karak (Crac des Moabites), a Crusading fortress at the southeastern extremity of the Dead Sea on the caravan route. Salah proceeded to the outposts of the fortress when the news reached him that Nur was approaching with his army. Suspecting a trap, he hastily beat a retreat, offering his father's illness as an excuse.

Nur's death the following year precluded the need for a showdown, but the succession of his eleven-year-old son, al-Malik al-Salih, introduced new problems. Salah acknowledged al-Salih's

suzerainty, ordered his name to be recited in the prayer and en-
graved on the coins. But a cousin of the king declared his independence in Mosul and proceeded to annex Edessa and neighboring districts in northern Syria. Al-Salih's officers wrangled for his
control. They appeased Jerusalem by paying tribute, and removed their charge to Aleppo. There its eunuch governor Gumushtagin threw his rivals into jail and arrogated to himself the
viceregency. Disorder spread and fragmentation threatened the
entire kingdom. Salah faced a dilemma: loyalty to the house
which brought him up or dedication to a higher cause—Islamic
solidarity against Christian aggression. He argued that he, as the
highest ranking officer in the Nurid army and viceroy in Egypt,
had a prior claim on the regency. He could have gone further and
claimed to be the only one competent to carry out the policies of
the departed monarch, and to that extent to be his spiritual heir.
But to his competitors such language was unintelligible. They
saw in him but another general seeking self-aggrandizement at
the expense of others.

But time was of the essence and Salah did not hesitate long. At
the head of seven hundred picked horsemen he dashed through
the desert, unnoticed by Crusader garrisons to the west, and on
October 24, 1174, entered the Syrian capital unopposed. He took
up his residence in the citadel. Damascenes high and low hurried
to welcome him as the protector of their king. Later he married
Nur's widow, a practice common and politically advantageous in
such circumstances. Leaving his brother Tughtagin (Sayf [sword
of-] al-Islam) in charge, he set out with fresh recruits from Damascus, crossed Eastern Lebanon and turned north through the
fertile Biqa' plateau. Baalbak, scene of his childhood days, was
bypassed. Hims (the Emesa of the Romans), birthplace of the
mother of the Syrian dynasty on the throne of the Caesars, offered
no resistance, but its castle did. Salah left a contingent to isolate
the garrison and followed the route north along the Orontes,
dotted with water wheels (sing. Ar. *na'urah,* noria) whose mur-
murous, monotonous noise has not ceased since Roman days. Like
its sister to the south and other Syrian cities, Hamah was surrounded by a wall and guarded by a castle. The city was more
hospitable and surrendered in its entirety. Both of these towns
were in name dependencies of Aleppo but acted independently.

The temporary Syrian capital was the main goal of the invader. In the last two days of a cold December he pitched his camp outside the city wall and started its siege.

Gumushtagin had his lines of defense all set. Under his tutelage the puppet king paraded the streets on horseback passionately imploring his people not to deliver him to the enemy coming in the guise of a deliverer. The role played was made more effective by tears running down the cheeks of the king as he spoke. Gumushtagin meanwhile enlisted the interests of two natural enemies of the invader, Rashid-al-Din Sinan of Misyaf (Masyaf, Masyad), master of the redoubtable Assassin order of Syria, and Raymond III, count of Tripoli. The Assassins had their forts in the Ladhiqiyah mountain; hence the chief's title *shaykh al-jabal,* the Crusaders' *le vieux de la montagne.* The fort of Misyaf lay on the eastern slope of the Nusayri mountain. The Iraqi-born Sinan was sent by Alamut, Persian headquarters of the order, to promote its interests in Syria. For thirty years beginning 1163 he played a role in the politics of Syria and Egypt and was treated as a quasi-sovereign power. The Assassins, it will be recalled, were Isma'ilis to whom the destroyer of the Fatimid imamate was an archenemy. The Syrian branch was especially active at this time and spared neither Christians nor Moslems. Among their notable victims were Raymond II, count of Tripoli (*ca.* 1152), and king-elect of Jerusalem Conrad of Montferrat, to be mentioned later. Nur-al-Din once discovered an Assassin dagger under his pillow. The most distinguished Moslem victim of the Persian branch was the enlightened Saljuq vizir Nizam-al-Mulk, founder of the Nizamiyah academy in which the illustrious theologian al-Ghazzali (see next chapter) held a chair.

Both Sinan and Raymond were ready, in consideration of cash, to make of their natural enemy an actual one. Sinan sent his professional men (sing. *fida'i,* self-sacrificer), who gained admission into Salah's tent and would have succeeded in fulfilling their mission but for the vigilance of his guard, who tore them to pieces. The Tripoli army marched against Hims in an attempt to cut off Salah's route. Prudence dictated withdrawal. Salah hastened back, reduced the Hims castle, occupied Baalbak and returned to Hamah to meet a combined Aleppo-Mosul host in his pursuit.

Ghazi, king of Mosul, acted on the Arabic dictum, "my brother

and I against our cousin; my cousin and I against a stranger,"
and sent troops to defend al-Salih. Salah took an advantageous
position on two hills outside Hamah (Qurun [horns of] Hamah)
in the hope that that would compensate for the disparity in numbers. It did. He had another advantage in commanding veteran
troops against relatively raw material. The rout (April 1175) was
complete. The victory sealed the fate of Syria. The name of al-
Malik al-Salih was deleted from the prayers and the coins, but he
was retained in charge of Aleppo. The name of al-Malik al-Nasir
Salah-al-Din Yusuf ibn-Ayyub was substituted for that of al-Salih
after the caliph's name. The caliph sent to Salah, at his request, a
diploma of investiture over Egypt, Nubia, al-Maghrib, western
Arabia, Palestine and central Syria. He thereby gave away what
was not his to give but what was flattering for him to do.

As the sultan was besieging 'Azaz north of Aleppo, he entered
his tent for rest one day and suddenly felt a blow on his head. But
for the cap of mail still under his turban his skull would have
been crushed. The guard rushed to the rescue and three of Sinan's desperadoes appeared, one after the other, as if from nowhere. They were finally overwhelmed. As it turned out the three
had contrived to enlist in the bodyguard. Salah, we are told, was
terrified as never before on a battlefield. Evidently Gumushtagin
was intent on accomplishing by treachery what he could not do
openly. All booty from the campaign was distributed among the
troops.

On his return to the vicinity Aleppo the sultan was met by the
young sister of al-Salih, whom he received respectfully. The little
girl asked for the return of the fort of 'Azaz. Her wish was granted
and, loaded with presents, she was sent safely back home. On July
29 he exacted from al-Salih a treaty recognizing his sovereignty
over all the territory he had conquered. Al-Salih remained amir
of Aleppo, which Salah did not enter until 1183.

Salah was now free to deal with the Assassins. In mid-summer
of that year he moved against their domain, where they maintained nine castles. It was devastated except for their headquarters Misyaf. The castle perched on an almost inaccessible peak
commanding a desolate ravine. Siege artillery and storming par
ties made no dent in its rocky structures. Its fortitude was rein-

forced by the training and blind devotion of its defenders. Salah's memory of the two attempts on his life haunted him. He found it difficult to sleep at night and suffered from nightmares. Ashes strewed around his tent to detect secret footsteps, guards with special lights, and frequent changes of watchmen did not seem to allay his fears. He finally agreed to raise the blockade while Sinan pledged him immunity from further attacks. The contest between the conqueror of Egypt-Syria and the Old Man of the Mountain ended in a tie. A century had to pass before a successor of Salah, Baybars, could crush the Syrian order.

II

Salah could now claim two great achievements. The destruction of the Fatimid caliphate was to a degree a case of greatness thrust upon him. The conquest of Syria was entirely to his credit. The union of the two realms was an indispensable step toward the realization of the third and greatest achievement, now the central aim of his life. His entire past career seemed but a prelude to the future performance.

When precisely this daydreaming of crushing Christian Jerusalem between the two jaws of the Cairo-Damascus cracker began to haunt his military head cannot be ascertained. The idea must have been long in the air. Nur-al-Din had it in an incipient form. He could concentrate on the Crusaders, but after Edessa his father had to fight Moslem states. In the vizirial investiture signed by al-'Adid (1169) we read:

> As for the jihad, you are surely the suckling of its breast, the child of its adoption. Make therefore yourself at home on horses' backs, and let tents be your dwelling place. Only in the darkness of war dust will your superior qualities shine and your achievements be recorded. Girdle your spears; plunge into the sea of swords; free yourself of all impediments in the path of Allah, and let valleys overflow with the foe's blood and hills form with heads. Persist till Allah grants victory, which the commander of the believers hopes lies in store for you, a victory worthy of your high post.[1]

[1] Abu-Shamah, *Kitab al-Rawdatayn fi Akhbar al-Dawlatayn,* ed. Muhammad H. M. Ahmad and Muhammad M. Ziyadah, vol. I (Cairo, 1962), p. 409.

The composition was that of Salah's secretary, al-Qadi al-Fadil, whose ornate, bombastic style became known in Arabic literature by his name (*al-insha' al-Fadili*).

To the Moslems Jerusalem (Bayt al-Maqdis, al-Quds, the house of holiness) was after Mecca and Medina the third holiest city. It was the stopping place of Muhammad on his nocturnal journey heavenward. Once the ultimate goal of the Crusaders, it now became the main goal of the Moslems. The spirit animating the Crusading movement and the motivation behind the jihad were similarly religious. The objectives of both were the same: seizure of Jerusalem. The two contending parties were in each other's eyes alike: infidels.

Salah was now in a position to turn his attention to Palestine. Its southern part was more accessible from Egypt. It was anyway time to visit his headquarters there after two years' absence. Leaving his brother Turan-Shah, conqueror of Yaman, in command, he made his way quietly and uneventfully, entering Cairo in 1176. He tarried there attending to routine administrative business, repairing the city walls and planning the construction of a citadel. For site he chose a spur of al-Muqattam, where Qal'at al-Jabal (the citadel of the mountain) still stands like a sentinel over the most populous metropolis of Africa. The mighty stronghold completed 1183–1184 (A.H. 579, as the writing on one of its portals says) served a warning on all in the city who dared raise their heads in rebellion, as well as on those outside who ventured to attack the sultan's capital.

The situation in Palestine was inviting. In violation of the truce treaty, Jerusalem was undertaking raids northward beyond Aleppo, leaving Palestine without adequate defense. The Moslems had yet to learn that a Christian treaty or pledge with an "infidel" could be invalidated on a bishop's authorization. The Jerusalem throne was now held by Amalric's sixteen-year-old son, Baldwin IV, a leper and so surnamed. Besides, his right arm was rendered immobile by a nail driven as a test of stoic fortitude, a favorite practice of knights. Baldwin inherited all his father's realm but none of his qualities. But his Moslem adversary was not yet ready for decisive engagements. Salah's military operations were undertaken with deliberation and after consultation with his amirs. Meantime he engaged in minor battles to keep his troops in good trim, the prospects of booty before their eyes. On November 10, 1177, he entered southern Palestine.

Ascalon ('Asqalan) was a key city between the two enemy domains. Salah had no difficulty in capturing it and plundering the territory around it. It was a promenade for his men, numbering 26,000, and they made full use of it. Following the coastal route, the invaders left Jerusalem behind and pushed on to al-Ramlah. By then the Franks had assembled their forces from Jerusalem, headed by Templars, from Sidon under an able warrior Reginald, and from al-Karak, led by its adventurous Reginald of Chatillon. The military order of Templars (Knights of the Temple) owed its name to the Temple of Solomon in Jerusalem, where it was founded (1118) to protect pilgrims and fight with other Crusaders. A brother religio-military order was that of the Hospitalers (Knights of St. John of Jerusalem), originally organized to provide hostel service for pilgrims. On the Ramlah battlefield also appeared the bishop of Bethlehem carrying the "true cross" and instilling enthusiasm in the fighters. Somehow Salah was caught unawares outside al-Ramlah and isolated from the main body of his army. His bodyguard was almost annihilated and he himself escaped by a hair's breadth. Mounting a swift camel, he fled under cover of night; behind him raced the remnant of his troops, leaving the wounded behind. This day of al-Ramlah (November 25) was one of the most humiliating in his military career.

The following year Baldwin began building a fort at a passage over the Jordan called Jacob's Ford (Banat Ya'qub), where tradition locates the site of Jacob's wrestling with the angel. The passage connected the Jerusalem domain with that of Damascus and opened upon the plain of Baniyas, rich in water from the main source of the Jordan and luxuriant in vegetation. On its products of wheat, rice and cotton, Damascus partly depended for its supply. Salah viewed the fort building with alarm. He offered Baldwin 10,000 gold pieces, but the king would not desist. Saladin started recouped his military losses at al-Ramlah by new troops from Cairo and Damascus.

On August 25, 1179, began the siege of the Jacob's Ford castle. Its Templar defenders fought valiantly in expectation of relief. Its thirteen-foot-wide walls of solid masonry resisted for five days sappers' undermining activity. Deep holes were dug outside the walls and wood was kept burning for days; other holes were filled with water. A breach was finally made and the fort stormed. Many of the occupants were slaughtered and their bodies thrown over the wall; seven hundred were taken prisoners. Despite the August sun and the corpses' stench the victorious commander waited to see the last vestige of Baldwin's folly dismantled. The spot where Moslem tradition located Jacob's place of lamentation over the loss of his son Joseph and named Bayt al-Ahzan (house of sorrows) became a house of sorrows for Christians.

Immediately after that Baldwin, whose disease was worsening, asked for a two-year truce, which Salah with his realm threatened with drought and famine accepted. Early in 1181 Salah returned to Egypt. The death of the inoffensive al-Malik al-Salih in Aleppo in December of that year raised new issues. Salah wrote repeatedly to the new caliph al-Nasir, claiming that his diploma of investiture entitled him to the inheritance of Aleppo and that even Mosul itself was necessary for the successful persecution of the jihad against the forces of unbelief. But although al-Nasir was perhaps the ablest of the last 'Abbasids, there was nothing he could do.

On arrival in his Syrian capital (May 1182) the sultan learned that 'Imad-al-Din, brother of 'Izz-al-Din then king of Mosul, had already entered upon the heritage of his cousin in Aleppo. Al-Salih on his deathbed had exacted from his officers an oath of fealty to his Mosul relatives. Salah was convinced more than ever that without Aleppo and Mosul he could win battles but lose the war.

Salah avoided a head-on clash with Aleppo (Halab). The north Syrian capital, a hotbed of Zangism, was more populous, more affluent and better defended than Damascus or any other sister town. It was crowned with a citadel for centuries considered impregnable. The citadel formed the crest of a mount with sides so polished as to render them unclimbable. The invader realized that beginning with the conquest of upper Mesopotamia was the surer way. He had been negotiating with provincial governors there and had received an invitation from at least one.

Crossing the Euphrates, (September 1182) he found himself early in November at the gates of Mosul. One city after the other from Edessa to Nasibin on the Tigris fell before him, some for bribes, others from fear, still others because of discontent. But Mosul was different. Salah's demand was: Mosul or Aleppo. 'Izz-al-Din's reply was: neither. Salah began the siege of Mosul November 10. A month of fruitless effort was enough to convince the Damascus army that the Zangid capital, with its double rampart defended by sturdy well-equipped fighters, its arsenals crammed with ammunition and war engines and its storehouses packed with provisions, had no weak spot left in its defense armor. Different tactics were resorted to: devastating the surrounding area.

Aleppo's turn came. June 11, 1183, found the victorious sultan knocking at its gates. They opened. Both governor and governed were in a different mood. 'Imad-al-Din was transferred to Sinjar and dependencies, his former domain. The Aleppines opened their arms and hearts to their new king, one whose military exploits, acts of chivalry, magnanimity, equity and generosity have been reverberating over the entire world of Islam.

The modus vivendi with 'Imad was followed by one with his brother 'Izz-al-Din. 'Izz' suzerainty over Mosul and vicinity was acknowledged, while he in turn pledged military support against the common foe. The sultan of Egypt and Syria could now add to his title upper Mesopotamia, to all of which he preferred "sultan of Islam and the Moslems."

III

With a past history of success, high aspirations and commitment to a goal, the sultan of Islam and the Moslems faced the future with confidence. That could not be said of his adversary. The enemy territory now consisted of two principalities—Tripoli and Antioch—and one kingdom—Jerusalem—held together vaguely and loosely by feudal ties. The three states occupied a narrow four-hundred-mile coastal strip against a background of solid Islam. The two principalities acknowledged the primacy, or supremacy, of the kingdom. After all, the kingdom was considerably larger, extending from Beirut to al-'Arish (on the Sinaitic border), and richer, lying on important trade routes. Besides, the name of Jerusalem, like that of Rome, carried prestige. In all three a feudal hierarchy of princes, barons and counts ruled. For defense they depended—as in their lands of origin—on feudal levy, augmented here by the two military orders.

In the population the European element was but a thin crust over layers of Moslems and Christians: Armenians and Jacobites in the north, Maronites, Greek Catholics (Melkites) and Greek Orthodox in the center and south. For renewed security the Franks depended upon newcomers, mainly pilgrims. But pilgrims generally considered their vows fulfilled on reaching Jerusalem and turned back home. As birds of passage pilgrims had little to contribute to security or stability. Then there were the Genoese, Venetians and Pisans, mostly merchants with pecuniary interest. Those of them who settled were given special quarters with personal privileges. The early Crusading spirit in Europe with its cult of the warrior had by now become discredited. Newly developed commercial interests and a different outlook on life prevailed. To our modern mind the entire undertaking looks irrational; so may seem to future generations the current communist-capitalist conflict. From the outset exotic and artificial, the states now found themselves almost marooned. As the encircling Moslem area became united, they became disunited and decadent.

Jerusalem was unfortunate in its royalty, mostly mediocrities. Tripoli was better served but its potential was limited by its size. After the retirement (1183) of Baldwin IV because of the effects of leprosy, the royal line faced problems of succession. Baldwin's brother-in-law Guy of Lusignan seized the crown three years later. Raymond III of Tripoli was regent and contested the right of succession. He signed a treaty with Salah against his new liege lord, visited his strange ally in Damascus and, some alleged, embraced Islam. In all the Crusading states dissension was rife; more than one feudal lord acted independently of his seigniory. Frequently Crusaders entered into alliances with Moslems against fellow Crusaders. Symptoms of the malaise from which Moslem rulers suffered at the advent of the Crusaders, and to which they succumbed, were now manifest in the conqueror's body politic.

A persistent source of irritation was al-Karak. Its French lord, Reginald (Raynald, Renaud) of Chatillon, whose marriage gave him its possession, lived—in the opinion of Western authors—in greater luxury than the kings of Europe. This was made possible by intercepting and pillaging merchants' and pilgrims' caravans passing by the walls of his castle, in violation of treaty obligation. Piracy by his fleet from Aylah (at the head of the Red Sea) along the coast of Africa and Arabia added to his coffers. The man was as unscrupulous as he was audacious. He made a landing on the holy soil of Hijaz with the aim of seizing the body of the Prophet and exhibiting it in his castle for a fee.

Salah made four abortive attempts on the stronghold. In the course of one he received a surprising gift of a wedding cake from a Karak officer and his bride celebrating their marriage. The sultan issued immediate orders that the nuptial tower not be molested. In 1187 a caravan headed by the sultan's sister was captured. To injury Reginald added insult by telling his victims, "Let your Muhammed protect you." The sultan swore for the second time (the first after the raid on Hijaz) to separate the head of the treacherous treaty-breaker from his body with his own hand.

The long-deferred hour of a showdown came. The march from Damascus began on a Friday—Salah's favorite day—June 26, 1187. The sultan's host comprised 12,000 horsemen, mustered from Cairo, Damascus, Aleppo and Mosul, all holders of fiefs and stipends, and 6,000 volunteers, largely footmen. Tiberias was the first objective. The town was surrounded and in six days captured. In the meantime King Guy had amassed 1,200 heavily armored knights, 3,500 lightly armed horsemen and 18,000 footmen at the spring of Saffuriyah north of Nazareth on the way to Tiberias. The full armor of a knight consisted of a leather jacket under chain mail, a heavy helmet, long sword, lance and shield. Between the two camps stood a volcanic hill amidst a waterless plain. The summits, Qurun Hittin (the horns of Hittin, Hattin), once the crater of a volcano, towered 1,700 feet above the Sea of Galilee. Tiberias' fall induced the enemy to foresake its favored position and proceed to the attack. This was precisely what the Moslems had been praying for.

Raymond, the only able soldier in the group, had patched up his differences with Guy and was leading the van, but strongly advised against the move, despite the fact that his wife was trapped in the Tiberias castle. "Treachery! cowardice!" charged Reginald, the master of the Templars and other royal consult-

ants. "Alas! Alas! Lord God," cried Raymond, "the war is over.
We are dead men. The kingdom is undone." The exhausted columns encamped (Friday, July 3) with horses drooping their
heads in quest of water, heavily armored knights wet with sweat
and footmen more anguished than both. Their water supply was
exhausted and the enemy stood between them and the five-mile-
distant water of the Galilee. Detachments had harassed them
along the dusty sunny road, while the main body sharpened their
weapons. The king pitched his tent on the hill to be better able
to control the operation. The camp spread along the slope to the
plain. But soon the situation got out of hand. To the burning
rays of the Saturday morning sun, the enemy added heat by burning bushes around the camp. Maddened by thirst and lured by
the sparkling fresh water of the sea, numberless footmen heedless
of orders rushed to find themselves encircled by bloodthirsty men.
They were mercilessly cut down. Deprived of their crossbowmen,
the knights became easy prey to light-armed riders on slender
agile Arabian steeds. Before the "Allahu akbar!" battle cry, the
cross held high by the bishop of Acre fell. It was seized and kept
as a treasured trophy.

A long row of chained prisoners, headed by Guy and Reginald,
stood at the door of the victor's tent. Raymond had sought safety
by flight; so did a few armed men. Others found it in abjuring
their religion. But for Templars and Hospitalers there was nothing but the sword. Guy shook in his boots. But the sultan seated
him near, ordered for him iced rose water to drink, and to allay
further his fear whispered in his ear, "A king does not kill a
king." As for Reginald, he merited a different treatment. Salah
killed him with his scimitar. He never violated a pledge. Why
should he now?

The loss was irreparable. If the Horns of Hamah netted Syria,
those of Hittin sealed the fate of Jerusalem and Palestine. For
years after, Hittin, the traditional site of the greatest sermon of
the Prince of Peace, was the scene of bleached skulls and bones—a
relic of the greatest Christian-Moslem carnage of the period.

Jerusalem, held too holy to be bombarded or stormed, was bypassed in favor of coast towns, denuded of their garrisons on behalf of the kingdom. The aim was to seal them off against new

recruits. In two months the victor's northward march netted him all the seaports, Tyre excepted. The city that once defied the great Macedonian for seven months and before him an Assyrian and a Neo-Babylonian, was not now to submit to an Arab. Its daring stand, after being on the point of surrender, was owed to a fresh arrival, Conrad of Montferrat, veteran of many European wars. Conrad infused new spirit into a disheartened community. Under his command Tyre's population was swelled by refugees from neighboring towns.

On September 20 Salah knocked at the doors of Jerusalem offering easy terms for capitulation, which were spurned. In a few days his mangonels effected a breach in the east wall and his eagle bedecked flag was hoisted on the Mount of Olives. The city surrendered (September 29) and its population was held for ransom as prisoners of war. The terms were ten dinars a man, five for a woman, one for a child and a round sum for the poor to be paid by the royal treasury. Those desiring to leave were given safe-conduct to their destination. At the conquest of the city associated with the ministry of Christ, a follower of Muhammad behaved in a more Christian manner than Christ's followers had in 1099, when—to borrow the words of their own historians—they waded in blood to their ankles. "If," in the opinion of Stanley Lane-Poole[1] "the taking of Jerusalem were the only fact known about Saladin, it were enough to prove him the most chivalrous and great-hearted conqueror of his own, and perhaps of any, age."

In commemoration of the victory the sultan enriched the city with hospitals and schools, mostly converted monasteries and knights' hostels. The nun's convent of St. Anne became the Sala-hiyah school, where a Greek Melkite seminary today stands. Like other schools built by Salah in Cairo and Damascus, these were seminaries intended to inculcate orthodoxy.

It was at about this time that the sultan confided to his secretary-biographer his plans to invade Europe (as quoted[2] as the introduction of this chapter). But Salah had no idea what was in store for him.

---

[1] *Saladin*, p. 234. This volume is the most lucid presentation of the subject.
[2] Ibn-Shaddad, *Al-Nawadir al-Sultaniyah w-al-Mahasin al-Yusufiyah* (Cairo, 1317), p. 17; cf. tr. *Saladin: or, What Befell Sultan Yusuf* (London, 1897), p. 26.

The fall of the holy city set off a wave of jubilation in the world of Islam as it did of lamentation in Christendom. A flare-up of the old Crusading spirit spread. Three crowned heads, the mightiest in Western Europe, took the cross: Frederick Barbarossa of Germany, Philip Augustus of France and Richard the Lionhearted. They agreed on Acre ('Akka) as the rendezvous. It was nearer to Palestine than Tyre and a better key to Jerusalem. Acre was then in Salah's possession and in anticipation he had sent for the ex-slave (*mamluk*) and major-domo of his guard who had built the Cairo citadel to strengthen the city's fortifications. Qaraqush was made its governor. On August 27, 1189, King Guy, freed from captivity by Salah and from his parole (presumably by a cleric), took a position near the city. The king had become a rallying center for old as well as newcomers, mostly French, British and Italian but including Danes, Frisians and members of other nationalities. With 21,000 recruits he threw a cordon around the city. A Pisan flotilla blockaded the harbor. Salah, accompanied by his brother al-'Adil and two sons al-Muzaffar and al-Afdal, hastened to the relief of the garrison. He started to besiege the besiegers. Neither siege was fully effective. Hearing about the imminent arrival of a numberless host from Europe, he dispatched his secretary-biographer ibn-Shaddad to Baghdad and an embassy to al-Muwahhid (Almohad), sultan in Morocco, but got no response. Having earlier disbanded his tried but tired veterans, he now commanded an ill-disciplined, hastily assembled heterogeneous groups of Arabs from Alexandria to Aleppo, Sinjar, Mosul and Diyar Bakr, and of Kurds and Turkomans from farther east together with mamluks of multiple nationality. They were primarily interested in booty, and only loosely united in obedience to the commander. As time dragged on and on, it became apparent that the Moslems had missed their chance. Salah had little appetite for prolonged sieges and his troops had less. Guy could not count on the wholehearted cooperation of Conrad, now a rival to the throne by virtue of his marriage to Amalric I's youngest daughter.

The first contingent to arrive from overseas was the German (October 1190), a bare thousand, remnant of a huge army. Its seventy-year-old leader, Frederick, had been drowned under his heavy armor in a Cilician river. He had chosen the land route. On June 8, 1191, Richard landed at the head of 8,000 knights. Philip had arrived two months earlier with a smaller unit; a larger unit had preceded him. The arrival of the greatest warrior in England, if not in all Europe, raised the entire morale. His engineers worked feverishly. They set up new and powerful siege-machines the like of which had never been seen before. The moats were deepened and the towers strengthened. The almost two-year-old struggle raged with more furor.

Around this small Palestinian town, lying on a tongue of land jutting out southward into the sea, more nationalities were now amassed in battle array than around any place before. The operation took its place among the major ones in medieval history. In saga Acre became the Troy of the Arabs. Legend and history collaborated to dramatize the military exploits of the two greatest heroes of the Orient and the Occident. One stone brought from Sicily and hurled from a sling slew a dozen 'Akkans at once. It was carried to Salah as an exhibit. On a newly contrived engine dubbed "the cat" Richard's men could scale the city walls like cats. One of his mangonels hurled rocks that could shake walls and land in the heart of the city. To smuggle provisions for the garrison, Salah used Moslem mariners from Beirut dressed in Frankish garb and accompanied by pigs, a taboo for Moslems. A Damascene forewent the sultan's reward in favor of Allah's for a destructive explosive he compounded. Pigeon carriers and swimmers were the only available means of communication. In reporting the case of a swimmer whose body was washed up on the sea shore and found with a belt full of gold, ibn-Shaddad remarks, "never before has it been known that someone received a trust in his lifetime and delivered it in his death."[1] A touching story illustrating the strange combination in Salah of gentleness with warring impacability was that of a French woman who found her way into the sultan's tent to plead the case of her baby carried off by his men. With "tears in his eyes," according to ibn-Shaddad, he ordered a thorough search. Mother and daughter were soon on their way back under guard to the enemy's lines.

By July 12 the city was reduced to the direst straits. The commander without his sovereign's consent sued for peace. The terms

[1] Ibn-Shaddad, p. 136.

of agreement included the return of the cross, release of the 1,600
Christian prisoners and the payment of 200,000 gold pieces as
ransom for all members of the garrison and for other purposes.
Because of a month's delay in the payment or the release of all
those in captivity, Richard ordered the 2,700 prisoners that he
held beheaded outside the city within sight of the Moslem camp.
Clearly Richard was the match of Salah in valor but not in character. The fall of Acre registered the greatest Christian victory of
the century and the greatest Moslem reverse. "The sultan grieved
like a mother for her lost child."

At Acre the king and the sultan were the principal actors. After
Acre they were the only ones. Philip hastened back home. He and
his English colleague were often at odds, Philip siding with Conrad, Richard with Guy. As a compromise Guy agreed to erect for
himself a new throne at Cyprus, which was seized by Richard on
his way to Palestine. Conrad was elected king. One April day in
1192, as he was walking on a street in Tyre, a stranger handed
him what looked like a letter. As he stretched out his hand two
men plunged their knives into his body. The assassins were members of that dreaded order. Rumors blamed the act on Salah,
others on Guy, without substantiation.

The two antagonists—Englishman and Arab—engaged in battles at times and in friendly exchanges, including gifts, at others.
The combat results were of no serious consequences. Jaffa ex-
changed hands twice in as many days. Richard was convinced that
the recapture of Jerusalem was a forlorn hope. Salah, no more
young and after five strenuous years on the battlefield his iron
determination not so sharp, realized that holding the entire coast
was hardly possible; so did his council. The sea was controlled by
the other side. As for his men, after two years of perilous service
they were developing a mutinous mood. Salah's nephew, governor
of a Mesopotamian province, had rebelled. As Richard pressed for
peace, Salah became more responsive. Salah's brother, al-'Adil,
surnamed Sayf-al-Din (sword of the faith, Latinized Saphardin),
was the intermediary. The king had struck up a friendship with
him, invited him to his tent and girded his son with the belt of
knighthood. Western sources assure us that Salah himself was
once knighted by a Crusading friend, but Arabic sources are judi-

ciously silent. Richard first came out with a strange proposal: marriage between his sister Joan and al-'Adil and a dowry of Acre, Jaffa, Ascalon and Jerusalem. Al-'Adil was agreeable, but the sultan and his council took it as a bad joke. On September 2, 1192, a three-year peace treaty was signed, giving the king the coast from Tyre to Jaffa and the interior to the sultan with the understanding that Christian pilgrims would not be molested. As Richard boarded ship in Acre he sent a message to his adversary promising to come back at the expiration of the truce period and restore Jerusalem to the Crown. To this the sultan replied that if he must lose the city, he would rather do it to such a man than to any other one.

Salah dismissed his troops and on November 4 entered Damascus amidst a wave of acclaim greater than ever before. Only one ambition remained, to undertake the long-deferred holy pilgrimage, a duty that had to await a much-needed rest. But the feverish attacks of malaria from which he had long suffered did not wait. On February 20, he went to bed. Physicians, in those pre-quinine days, treated him with barley water. On March 4 as a divine was repeating in his ear the words of the profession of faith, the sultan murmured "true." It was his last word, at age 55. The one Tyrian dinar and forty-seven dirhams found in his treasury were not enough to pay his funeral expenses. No other property personal or real did he have. But the kingdom he left extended from the Tigris to the Maghrib and southward to the Sudan.

Salah-al-Din's reign began in an area partitioned into several statelets and so again it became shortly after his end. The partition was among his sons, brothers and nephews. Soon al-'Adil gained sovereignty over Egypt and Syria. From him sprang a variety of Ayyubid branches. In 1250 the slave guards of the dynasty superseded their masters and held the area till the conquest of the Ottoman Turks (1517). It was on the shoulders of the fifth of those Mamluk dynasts, Baybars (1260–77), that the anti-Crusading mantle of Salah fell. He began practically where his distinguished predecessor ended and brought the anti-Crusading war close to a successful conclusion.

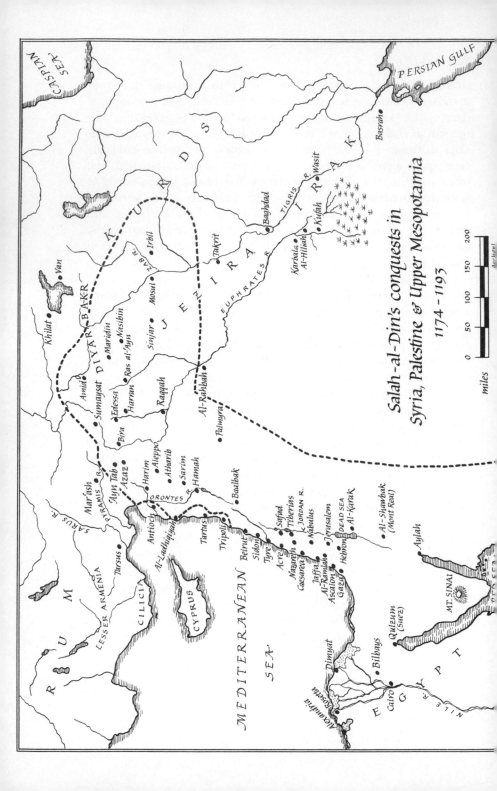

Salah-al-Din's conquests in
Syria, Palestine & Upper Mesopotamia
1174-1193

IV

Salah-al-Din was fortunate in having had two admiring friends and counselors, Baha'-al-Din ibn-Shaddad and 'Imad-al-Din al-Isfahani,[1] who left full-dress biographies of their hero. Of the two Imad-al-Din was the stylist; flowery diction was uppermost in his mind. A contemporary general historian, ibn-al-Athir, native of Mosul, fountainhead of Zangism, was not so flattering. From these and other sources we hardly get a glimpse of the sultan's home life. As a matter of fact his "dwelling place" was the military tent suggested in al-'Adid's diploma of investiture. We know only one wife by name, Nur-al-Din's widow whom he married in 1176, but Salah left seventeen sons and one young daughter. The physical picture left us is that of a medium-sized man of fair skin, finely-chiseled features and a trimmed beard, wearing a long-sleeved gown, a turban of rich cloth and a jeweled dagger at his waist. A Damascene poet, evidently dissatisfied with his subsidy, satirized him as a "sultan with a lame leg, blear-eyed secretary and an idiot of a minister." His manners were those of a gentleman, considerate, unostentatious, and abstemious in food. Any outbursts of uncontrolled temper or impatience have escaped recording. Power and gentleness, authority and magnanimity seem to have found in him a happy and rare combination. In searching for a word that sums up the totality of his character, "integrity" is the one that readily comes to mind, integrity as including a high sense of honor, lofty ideals and living up to the best in oneself. There is no Arabic word for integrity, which this Arab had in greater measure than any European peer of his time. His treatment of the two Crusading orders, however, would be difficult to square with this characterization. So would the order given his son to execute the illuministic Sufi al-Suhrawardi in Aleppo. But to him Templars and Hospitalers were the embodiment of the Crusading ethos intent on the destruction of the religion of which he was an extreme devotee. By this same extremism he felt justified in killing a fellow Moslem who committed a heresy. His toleration of acts did not extend to beliefs.

Dante, though bound by medieval Catholicism to send Salah to

[1] *Al-Fath al-Qussi fi al-Fath al-Qudsi,* ed. Carlo de Landberg (Leyden, 1888).

the inferno, was considerate; he consigned him to limbo. Of the modern novelists, Walter Scott with perceptiveness and accuracy portrayed in *The Talisman* Salah's generosity, justice, and nobility of character but offered to him, instead of to his brother, the hand of Richard's sister. Before Scott, Gotthold Lessing featured the Arab leader in his *Nathan der Weise,* a plea for religious and racial tolerance.

Salah-al-Din al-Ayyubi, flower of Arab chivalry, champion of orthodoxy, destroyer of a dissident caliphate, unifier of Egypt and Syria, he broke the backbone of the Crusader host and lived in Arab history as the hero par excellence.

Part 2
Intellectual

Al-Ghazzali:
Greatest Theologian of Islam

*Ever since I was under twenty (now I am
over fifty) . . . I have not ceased to investigate every dogma or belief I come
across. No Batini did I meet without desiring to investigate his esotericism; no
Zahiri, without wishing to acquire the gist
of his literalism; no philosopher, without
wanting to learn the essence of his philosophy; no dialectical theologian (mutakallim), without striving to ascertain the object of his dialectics and theology; no Sufi,
without longing to probe the secret of
his asceticism; no atheistic zindiq, without
groping for the causes of his atheism and
zindiqism. Such was the unquenchable
thirst of my soul for research from my
early youth—an instinct and a temperament implanted in me by God through no
choice of mine.*

—Al-Ghazzali

Makers of Arab history—of any history—are not only doers: warriors, architects of nations, builders of empires; they are also
thinkers: theologians, philosophers, scholars. In both cases they
are themselves the products of political, social, intellectual or
spiritual movements on the waves of which they ride to guide or
modify the courses taken. The flow of history acts upon them, and

they in return react upon it. With a theologian, al-Ghazzali, we introduce the second category.

The world of Islam in which the subject of our study found himself was a disturbed and confused world in both its doer and thinker sectors. Politically it was fragmented between Spanish Umayyad, North African Fatimid and 'Abbasid caliphs. Of these the 'Abbasid caliphs reigned but did not rule. Three years before al-Ghazzali was born, Baghdad had fallen into the hands of Saljuq Turks who, starting as nomads from central Asia, had over-run the entire eastern portion of the empire and established their sultanate in Baghdad. Before these Saljuqs, Persian war-lords, the Buwayhids, claiming descent from the Chosroes, had seized power and ruled in Baghdad for more than a century. The Saljuqs were Sunnites but the Buwayhids were Shi'ites; yet the caliph was retained in his religious headship. Intruders called Franks, never before heard of, were by then helping themselves to Saljuq and caliphal property in Asia Minor, Syria and Palestine. Gone was the imperial caliphate of Mu'awiyah, the word of whose successors in Damascus was law from central Asia to southwestern Europe. Dim was the memory of the patriarchal caliphate of 'Umar ibn-al-Khattab in Medina, established on the ruins of the Persian and a large section of the Byzantine empires. But not dim was the glory that was Baghdad a century and a half before under al-Ma'mun.

In its spiritual aspect the age in which al-Ghazzali set out to play his part was as disturbed and confused as it was in the politi-cal arena. Most prominent in this field were the theologians and jurists of varied shades of thought from the conservative who were satisfied with the Koran and hadith, to the "modern" who incorporated philosophical and rational elements into their knowledge. The latter became known as Mutakallims (sing. mutakallim, scholastic). The Mu'tazilite friends of al-Ma'mun had preceded the Mutakallims in the use of Greek philosophy and Aristotelian logic for argumentation. But the Mu'tazilites had Fatimid leanings; the Mutakallims were Sunnites. Opposite the Mutakallims were the Shi'ite Batinis, esoteric interpreters of religious literature discussed earlier under Isma'ilis. In contrast to the Batinis the Zahiris insisted on the literal interpretation of the scripture.

An entirely different school of thought with a radical approach to religion was represented by the Sufi. Sufism began as an ascetic movement and became mystical, believing that true knowledge of God is a form of gnosis achieved by the inner light of the individual soul, in contrast to knowledge by the intellect or acceptance of tradition. Lastly came the philosophers (sing. *faylasuf*) who, as the Arabic term indicates, were in the Greek tradition, particularly the Neo-Platonic. They did not have to know Greek, as the material was available in the translations of Hunayn ibn-Ishaq and others made in the days of al-Ma'mun. All these schools of thought were now in the arena contending for the Moslem mind.

Against this quasi-chaotic political and intellectual background is projected the historic figure of our man. His silhouette appears first dim and confused. But later it clears, and as it brightens light is shed on problems germane to the current fields of intellectual activity and arising from their interrelationship and interplay. His early confusion and spiritual pilgrimage makes this Moslem seeker after God a most engaging figure in the history of religious thought. His life and writings have been subject to more study by Westerners than probably any other figure in Arab history with the exception of Muhammad. One Protestant missionary considers him the Moslem nearest to being a Christian and recommends use of his writings as schoolbooks to lead Moslems to Christ. An American Orientalist, Duncan B. MacDonald, describes him as "the greatest, certainly the most sympathetic figure in the history of Islam." A German historian of Arab philosophy, T. J. de Boer, agrees. With the time came the man.

I

Abu-Hamid Muhammad al-Ghazzali was born in 1058 at Tus, Khurasan, not far from modern Meshed. This small town in northeastern Persia, now in ruins, was then a flourishing settlement with water, trees and mineral deposits in the neighboring

mountain. It could claim the honor of cradling other world celeb-
rities, such as the great epic poet Firdawsi and the wise vizir
Nizam-al-Mulk, al-Ghazzali's patron. In an uprising (1389)
against the Mongol conqueror Timur, nicknamed prince of de-
stroyers, the city was destroyed and never rebuilt. Its supply of
water was directed to its neighbor, Meshed, the Shi'ite sacred city
which had been encroaching for some time on Tus.

Al-Ghazzali's father like his grandfather was a wool spinner
(*ghazzal,* both *z*'s sounded in Arabic), whence his last name
comes. But "Ghazali" from Ghazalah, a nearby village, is the
more common form. The boy had a paternal scholar uncle, abu-
Hamid, whose title he bore. Poor, unlearned and devout, the father daily prayed for a learned son, but did not live to see his
prayer doubly answered. One of the two sons he left, Ahmad,
became a Sufi preacher of such power that the "wood of the
pulpit quivered" as he portrayed the punishment awaiting the
wicked.

The first scene of the orphaned boys' education was Tus, under
the care of a family friend entrusted with the modest legacy left
by the father. Being a Sufi the friend saw that his charges got
some Sufi instruction in addition to the usual elementary schooling. Then abu-Hamid studied at Jurjan two hundred and fifty
miles away near the southeast corner of the Caspian Sea. "Travel
in quest of learning," involving joining a caravan and getting
board and lodging freely at mosques, was then a recognized educational procedure for the mature ambitious student. But abu-
Hamid was then still in his teens and he wrote later that he "had
sought knowledge for other than God, but that knowledge refused to be for other than God." On his way back, highwaymen
robbed him of the little he had, mostly notebooks of lectures. As
he fervently pleaded for their recovery, the bandits' chief
scoffingly asked what kind of knowledge this could be if by losing
notebooks he became knowledgeless. That made the youth re-
solve to commit what he learned to memory and not only paper.

Naysabur, capital of the province, thirty miles southwest of
Tus, was his next place of study. Thither he was attracted by one
of the most learned men of the country, al-Juwayni. This theologian had the distinction of having lectured for years at the two
Holy Cities and won the title imam al-Haramayn. The imam was

soon to acquire another honor, of being the shaykh of al-Ghazzali. Al-Juwayni was a Mutakallim and held the chair of theology at the newly founded Nizamiyah which, like its many sisters founded by Nizam-al-Mulk, was so endowed as to provide free tuition, lodging and board. Here abu-Hamid spent eight years (1077–85), studying theology, philosophy, logic and natural science. Foreign languages were not in the academic curriculum of the day. The young man was bilingual like other scholars of his country, using Persian at home but studying, writing and thinking in Arabic, the "tongue of the angels" to Moslems everywhere. While studying he did part-time teaching as assistant to al-Juwayni and later independently. As a teacher he made his mark as an original, sharp-witted, stimulating expositor of theological and philosophical themes. He must have been conscious of his intellectual superiority and behaved accordingly. First proud of his pupil, whom he once described as a deep-fathomed sea, the master al-Juwayni felt jealous. When abu-Hamid showed him his first book, the shaykh remarked, "Do you want to bury me while still alive? Wait until I am dead before you cause my books to disappear."

It was time to change. From Naysabur al-Ghazzali moved to Baghdad to join the brilliant circle of scholars and poets gathered around and patronized by Nizam-al-Mulk, the enlightened Persian vizir of the Saljuq court. The reputation of the twenty-seven-year-old newcomer had preceded him and he was received with honor. Nizam was then at the height of his power in the court, a monarch in all but name. His rise began earlier under Alp Arslan (1063–1072), second of the Great Saljuqs, on whose death the vizir dominated the eighteen-year-old sun-successor Malikshah (1072–92). Nizam represented Persian culture at its best in a court interested in war more than in culture. He lavished his patronage on religious teachers and poets, built Sufi "monasteries," inspired the reformation of the calendar and more importantly established those theological colleges named after him. At least nine of them were started in the leading cities of Iraq and Persia. They served as models for later educational institutions with stipends for professors and scholarships for students. On his suggestion Malikshah called a conference of astronomers, among whom was the famous mathematician and poet 'Umar al-Khayyam, to bring the old Persian calendar into accord with the results of new observatories' calculations. In 1091, it will be recalled, the Assassins, whom Nizam bitterly opposed, gained possession of Alamut and the following year one of them, disguised as a Sufi, stabbed him to death. In a biography, ibn-Khallikan quotes a couplet elegizing him:

> A precious pearl was Nizam-al-Mulk,
>   formed by God of pure nobility.
> So rare was it that its contemporaries
>   did not appreciate it;
> So its Maker, zealous for its honor,
>   returned it to its shell.

Six years after his advent at the court, al-Ghazzali was appointed professor of theology at Baghdad's Nizamiyah, a position he occupied for four years. He soon dwarfed his colleagues. His popularity spread beyond the lecture hall filled with three hundred listeners. Established scholars from near and far came for consultation if not for learning. The Berber founder of the Murabit (Almoravid) dynasty in Morocco and Spain, Yusuf ibn-Tashfin, addressed a query soliciting his legal opinion. But all that failed to satisfy something in him. Earlier, when still in Naysabur, he had begun to show signs of intellectual and spiritual dissatisfaction. Like Descartes, father of modern European philosophy, mere authority lost its hold on him. His highly developed sense of curiosity carried him all over the units of the intellectual spectrum—as indicated by the quotation at the head of this chapter.[1] But all that—Scholastic theology, jurisprudence, philosophy, mysticism—was tried and found wanting. Skepticism dominated his thinking. Dogma and tradition had no more sway over him. Disparity between his colleagues' teachings and conduct must have confirmed him in his skepticism. Tortured mentally and physically, he broke down, resigned his post, turned his back on the greatest intellectual center in Islam and sought peace

---

[1] Al-Ghazzali, *Al-Munqidh min al-Dalal*, ed. 'Abd-al-Halim Mahmud (Damascus, 1385), pp. 70–71; cf. C. Field, *The Confessions of Al Ghazzali* (London, 1905), pp. 12–13.

in solitude and contemplation. His brother Ahmad occupied his chair.

Damascus, then under a Saljuq dynast, was his destination. He entered it as a dervish early in 1095, made the Umayyad Mosque his home and, as he tells us in his *Al-Munqidh,* "climbed every morning its minaret, closing the door behind him." He pursued the ascetic way of life, wearing coarse, shabby clothes, leaning on a staff and dangling from his shoulder a bag for his scanty provisions and possessions. By abstinence, self-discipline, contemplation and prayer he sought the peace of mind that fame, money and friends had failed to give him. Part of his sustenance, a historian tells us, he earned by copying. This may mean selling copies of the book he started writing, *Ihya' 'Ulum al-Din* (revivification of the sciences of religion), his masterpiece. The title suggests that al-Ghazzali began to think of himself as the "revivifier," promised Islam by God, in accordance with an accepted tradition, at the head of each century. The fifth Moslem century was drawing to a close. In 1961 the city where al-Ghazzali spent the first two years of his retreat held an international celebration in his honor.

At some time, perhaps 1099, nostalgia drove him to interrupt his solitude and return home for a visit with his family. Before leaving them he had entrusted their care to a friend and given away the rest of his money. Whether he had one or more wives is a subject about which his biographers—like all others—are silent. At his death he had daughters but no surviving sons. In his old home he had only one brother but several sisters.

From the Umayyad Mosque the bewildered wanderer moved to the Dome of the Rock in Jerusalem, soon to fall from Fatimid into Crusading hands. With it as a base he visited Hebron, shrines and other places sacred to Jews as well as Moslems. These pilgrimages were climaxed by the one to Mecca and Medina. He traveled incognito, of course, but was recognized by many pilgrims and scholars who later mentioned having met him. According to one anecdote, he once entered a mosque school in Damascus and, hearing his name quoted by the shaykh, turned his back and hurried out lest Satan fill his heart with pride. According to ibn-Khallikan and others he included Alexandria in his itinerary and perhaps contemplated moving on to Morocco to visit the sul-

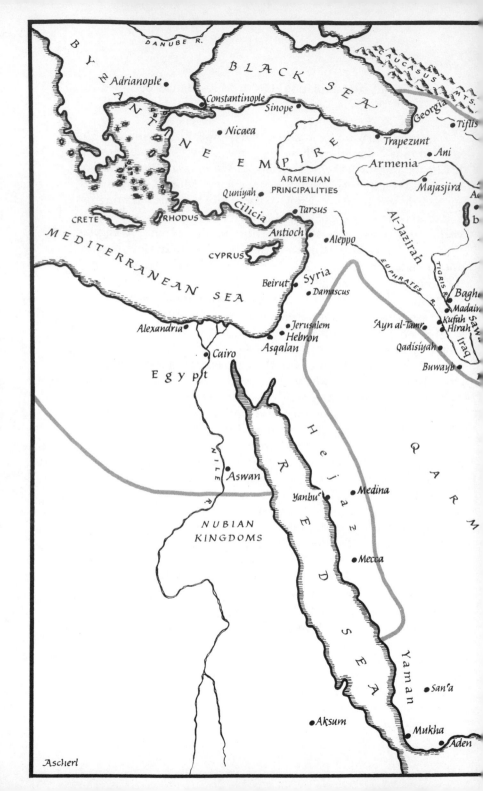

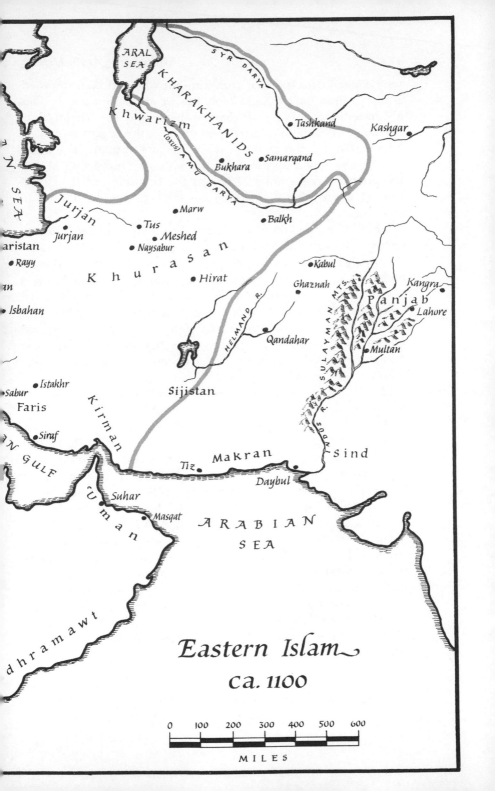

Eastern Islam
ca. 1100

tan who had corresponded with him but who had then just died. If so, this must have been in 1106. But we are certain that by then al-Ghazzali was holding the chair of theology at the Nizamiyah of Naysabur. This he did, after hesitation, at the urgent request of Nizam-al-Mulk's son who was then vizir at Khurasan. The vizir's plea was seconded by pious friends who, convinced that he was the promised renovator of Islam at the beginning of the (sixth) century, argued that such a high mission could not be fulfilled in seclusion.

Thus after a decade of alienation (1095–1105) a new Ghazzali, restored in health and reintegrated in personality, found himself occupying in the capital of his province a chair similar to that he had once held at the capital of the empire. This was brought about, in his own words in *Al-Munqidh min al-Dalal* (the deliverer from error), not "by proof or argument but by a light which God had put into my breast, the light that is the key to real knowledge." He insisted that to assume that profound truth rests upon marshalled arguments is to narrow unduly God's broad mercy.

He now had a textbook to use, the *Ihya'*, but it was not long before he discovered that his new philosophy of religion and outlook on life could neither be practiced nor communicated by lectures under the conditions in crowded halls and institutionalized agencies. Naysabur provided no more congenial an atmosphere than had Baghdad. Perhaps the assassination of his new patron by members of the same order who had killed his patron's father contributed to his discouragement. Again he yearned for personal tranquility and individual communication of knowledge.

His native town promised to offer the proper place. There he established a Sufi hostel (Ar. *zawiyah*, Pers. *khanqah*, corresponding to monastery) with a school, to commune with seekers after the mystic way and to indulge in his favorite manner of thinking. But time was not generous. On December 18, 1111, "God withdrew the gift which he had bestowed, calling it back to the glory of His presence." Under his head a paper was found bearing these stanzas:

> Do not believe that this corpse you see is myself. . . .
> I am a spirit and this is naught but flesh.   3

It was my abode and my garment for a time.
I am a treasure by a talisman kept hid,
Fashioned of dust which served me as a shrine,
I am a pearl which has left its shell deserted,
It was my prison, where I spent my time in grief.
I am a bird and this was my cage,
Whence I have not flown forth and it is left as a token.
Praise be to God, who hath now set me free.[1]

II

Al-Ghazzali was as prolific as a writer as he was profound as a thinker. An Egyptian scholar has listed (1961) 457 titles ascribed to him, of which 69 are of his undoubted authorship. Others are questionable, extinct, or spurious or bear duplicate titles. Several are brief essays. Hardly a branch of the humanistic studies escaped his treatment. Poetry was a hallmark of the cultured man and al-Ghazzali was responsible for a volume of verse, and he occasionally spiced his prose with stanzas of his own composition. Closely associated with poetry was music, frowned upon by theologians but allowed by him, together with song and dance, under strict conditions for intensifying religious feeling. All these aesthetic agencies have become fixtures in Sufi rituals.

The *Ihya' 'Ulum al-Din,* twenty-eighth in the chronological list, is the largest and weightiest. The first part treats of knowledge and the fundamental dogmas of Islam. This is followed by a part discussing acts of worship such as prayer and almsgiving. The third part takes up destructive vices, including lust, anger, greed and vanity. The last section studies the redeeming virtues, illustrated by patience, repentance, fear, asceticism, love, sincerity and meditation. The *Ihya'* took its place early among the classics of Islam. For Moslems it became as the *Summa Theologiae* of Thomas Aquinas for Christians. A thirteenth century jurist thought it came near being a koran. Another scholar of the same century declared, "Should all books on Islam be destroyed, the *Ihya'*—if spared—will make up for the loss." In Cairo about twenty editions of this book have been issued, and there are circles there which meet weekly for its study.

1 Margaret Smith, *Al-Ghazali the Mystic* (London, 1944), p. 36. (Reprinted courtesy of Luzac and Company, London.)

Open this or any work by al-Ghazzali and you immediately feel that its intellectual climate is different from the general run of theological works, in which verbosity seems to be considered a substitute for substantiality and much of the material appears impertinent, immaterial and irrelevant. It reads as if it had passed from the lips or pen of the transmitter to the ear or eye of the recipient without going through the brain of either. By contrast almost any page in al-Ghazzali feels vibrant with life. The style is as lucid as the thought is profound. The author uses anecdotes and parables reminiscent of Christ's. Farmers, animals and other homely objects are used. The self-deluded man, we learn, is like a gardener who is contented with pulling out the weeds without digging out the network of roots under the soil. Consider the bee—the author bids the sluggard—working diligently and intelligently picking its nectar from the choicest of flowers and building a hexagonal—not a square—wax house, because square corners waste space. Learn fidelity from the dog; he denies himself sleep for protecting his master and if necessary sacrifices his life for him. The chess game, evidently a favorite with al-Ghazzali, is used to drive home a point. Riders are admonished to dismount twice a day to spare their mounts.

Another work of al-Ghazzali cited above is *al-Munqidh min al-Dalal*. Small in size, *al-Munqidh* has an autobiographical sketch, including a confession, that makes it rare if not unique in Arabic literature. It reminds us of the *Confessions* of St. Augustine, who like him went astray before his conversion, yet became the most celebrated of the Latin fathers. Written at a late age, *Al-Munqidh* reports the stages of skepticism and self-examination through which the seeker after truth had passed and his recovery through the pursuit of the ascetic way of life.

In the passage from *al-Munqidh* quoted at the head of this chapter, we may note that the open-mindedness of our author made him study the current schools of thought with a view not only to criticizing but to discovering the secret of their success and perhaps to learning from them. His intellectual curiosity extended into the Jewish and Christian areas. In his *Ihya'* he refers to *Akhbar Da'wud* (news about David, Chronicles) and mentions the Torah and Psalms (*Zabur*). Of course several Old Testament characters were also koranic figures and known to him. So was

Jesus, the 'Isa of the Koran. Al-Ghazzali must have had access to an Arabic translation of at least the Gospels and the Pauline Epistles but, as in Judaism, several of his sources were apocryphal. "Said Jesus son of Mary, peace be upon him," is his favorite way of introducing the quoted material. Much of it can be found in the first quarter of *Ihya'*. In his treatise on morals and manners, *Ayyuha al-Walad* (O, child), he writes: "I read in the Gospel of Jesus, peace be upon him, that from the time the dead is laid on the bier until he is laid on the edge of the grave, God will ask him forty questions. . . ." His views on ethics and morality gave him a place among the highest ranking teachers in Islam.

At his time the tension between theology and philosophy had reached an acute stage. The two were natural enemies; one being anchored in revelation, the other in reason. An early work of al-Ghazzali, *Maqasid al-Falasifah* (the aims of philosophers), is an exposition of the views of philosophers as he understood them from original translations and from studies by two Arab exponents, al-Farabi (d. 950) and ibn-Sina (d. 1037). Both were Neo-Platonists and both were mentioned by him in his second book on philosophers. His introduction to Greek philosophy, begun while a student at Naysabur, was followed by independent study as a professor at Baghdad. Arab philosophers were often physicians, scientists and high court officials. In his *Maqasid* the author addressed himself to logic, metaphysics and natural science, ignoring mathematics. From these fields he chose for presentation only the material he promised to make the object of his critique *Tahafut al-Falasifah* (inconherence of philosophers), issued shortly before his nervous breakdown (1095). Towards Greek logic, particularly Aristotelian syllogism, he was more than kindly disposed. In *al-Munqidh* he not only acknowledged its usefulness but justified its use in theology and jurisprudence and employed it himself effectively against philosophers. Nor did he see any contradiction between mathematics and the teachings of Islam, but added a discouraging note that mathematicians tend to be unbelievers.

In *Tahafut* our theologian insists that philosophic theory cannot form a basis of religion; religion has an inner experience for basis. He worked out twenty points in which philosophic teachings conflicted with Islam, trying to show that reason, the mainstay of philosophers, does not in all cases lead to the ultimate truth. The *Maqasid* and *Tahafut,* among others by al-Ghazzali, were studied closely by two of his Spanish coreligionists, ibn-Rushd (d. 1198, whom we shall study later) and ibn-Tufayl (d. 1185). Ibn-Rushd bitterly and ibn-Tufayl mildly criticized him. Ibn-Tufayl owes his reputation to an original romance (*Hayy ibn-Yaqzan,* the living, son of the vigilant), a prototype of *Robinson Crusoe,* which supports al-Ghazzali's mystic thesis of man's inner light as a source of knowledge of the Divine. *Maqasid* and *Tahafut* were translated into Hebrew and Latin and introduced his name, Algazel, into the West.

The extent to which al-Ghazzali's strictures hastened the decline in philosophy after him cannot be ascertained, but the influence of philosophy on him is noticeable in his polemics, adoption of the Aristotelian syllogism and Neo-Platonic concepts. What he appropriated he incorporated into Islamic theology and there it became a permanent feature. Only the fundamentalist Hanbalis refused to extend hospitality to those influences. More than that his writings dissipated the mystery surrounding philosophy, making it look synonymous with rational thinking and within the reach of the intelligent man.

Of the numerous heterodoxies of Islam, the Isma'ilis (the Batinis of al-Ghazzali) were the ones against whom he leveled his heaviest batteries. A contemporary fellow Tusi, al-Hasan ibn-al-Sabbah, fortified himself in Alamut and was responsible for the assassination of his two friends Nizam-al-Mulk and his son. For almost two centuries the Fatimids had been challenging 'Abbasid supremacy in Islam. At the same time Qarmatis had controlled eastern Arabia, laid waste lower Iraq, threatened Syria and carried away (930) the Black Stone from Mecca. The secret of the success of the Isma'ili cause lay primarily in having found an heir to the charismatic quality of Muhammad in his son-in-law 'Ali, and after 'Ali in his imam descendants—a fact that did not escape al-Ghazzali's notice. The same kind of quality, passed on from Christ through Peter to the pope, has contributed to making the Roman Catholic Church one of the most enduring institutions in history. The imam taught with final authority. To this authoritative teaching was added the esoteric aspect enabling missionaries not only to brainwash their would-be followers but to fill the vacuum with whatever seemed necessary to meet their specific needs. In the case of the Sunnites the Prophetic charisma could not infiltrate the thick layers of Umayyad and 'Abbasid ungodliness and worldliness. The attempt to endow with that quality the entire community, in accordance with a generally accepted hadith: "My community shall not agree on an error," failed. The flow was too diffuse to be effective. Also ineffective was the attempt to confer the gift on the theologians in conformity with the hadith, "The ulema of my community are heirs of the prophets." The conduct of many theologians and jurists did not encourage acceptance. Thus Sunnis were unable to do what Shi'ites—particularly their Isma'ili branch—did: keeping the dynamic image of an inspired leader alive in the hearts of their followers.

The first of half a dozen critiques penned by al-Ghazzali was written (1095) at the request of the new young caliph al-Mustazhir and titled *Fada'ih al-Batiniyah wa-Fada'il al-Mustazhiriyah* (exposé of the vices of the Batinis and an exposition of the virtues of al-Mustazhir). Expectedly, the author devotes ample space to arguing the legitimacy of the 'Abbasid caliphal claims against those of his Fatimid rival. As an intellectual he could not countenance the idea of an infallible imam. His strictures brought out inconsistencies in Isma'ili teachings, including their esoteric aspect, and their irrational emphasis on authoritative instruction. His writings were probably responsible for accelerating the decay in the movement.

The two most conspicuous learned groups (ulema) of the day were the theologians and the jurists. The starting point of both was the same, the Koran, with the jurists making more use of the hadith and devising certain legal fictions to meet problems not faced before. By this time the Sunnite system of theology had taken shape, and so had the four orthodox schools of jurisprudence. Al-Ghazzali was trained in both theology and canon law, but had the moral courage to criticize openly both groups. In theology he followed the Mutakallim school inaugurated by al-Ash'ari (d. 935), once a Mu'tazilite and therefore inoculated with Greek thought and conscious of the value of logical reasoning. In his jurisprudence al-Ghazzali followed al-Shafi'i (see next chapter). In the introductory chapter of *Ihya'*, he points out the gap between what colleagues profess and what they practice. They are contented with the role of guardianship of dogma and tradition, while dogmatic theology and hadith as such cannot enable an individual to attain the ultimate goal of life: salvation and bliss. Theologians are concerned more with material than spiritual values. Since al-Ma'mun's inquisition (discussed earlier) they as well as jurists had become subservient to the rulers. Canon lawyers, mostly judges, were as self-seeking and worldly as the governors they served. Their preoccupation, like that of theologians, was more with trivialities rather than with essentials.

Al-Ghazzali's influence on both groups was effective and lasting. Through it theology became more rational, more relevant and at the same time more spiritual. Jurisprudence became more sensitive to changing conditions, expanded beyond the narrow bounds of religion and was lifted to a higher intellectual level.

Our theologian was introduced to mysticism early in life and never parted company with it. His first teacher at Tus was a Sufi (from Ar. *suf,* wool, the garb adopted in imitation of the Christian monastic costume). Mysticism sustained him in his crisis, its ascetic aspect was practiced by him in his wanderings and its ideology formed the subject of more than one of his books and overflowed into many others. The contrast he noted between Sufi conduct and theologian behavior must have confirmed him in the high esteem in which he held Sufism.

> At last I became convinced that Sufis are the true travelers on the path of Allah, that their behavior is the finest of all behaviors, that their path is the rightest of all paths and that their character is the noblest of all characters. Indeed, if all the intellects of intellectuals, the wisdom of wise men, the knowledge of jurists and theologians were to get together with a view to changing a thing in Sufi behavior or character for something better, they could not find it.[1]

Mysticism, according to this intellectual mystic, if the motivation is fear of Hell, is of a lower grade than the desire for reward in Paradise. The highest, however, is that of love of communion with the Divine and contemplation of God's beauty. This Beatific

[1] *Al-Munqidh,* p. 128.

vision became a favorite theme in numberless Sufi prayers, illustrated by the following:

> O God, if I adore Thee in fear of Hell, send me to Hell. If I adore Thee in hope of Paradise, exclude me from Paradise. But if I adore Thee for Thy sake only, withhold not Thine everylasting beauty from me.

The traveler along the mystic way goes through these stations: knowledge—gnosis acquired by intuition (*dhawq*) or inner light (*nur*); feeling—longing (*shawq*) and passion for the Divine; and action involving self-discipline. The inner light in man derived from the Light supernal by the process of emanation. This theory of light al-Ghazzali developed in his *Mishkat al-Anwar* (niche of lights), a commentary on Koran 24:35: "God is the light of the heavens and the earth. The similitude of His light is as a niche wherein is a lamp. The lamp is in a glass. The glass is as it were a shining star."

Man's soul also stems from the universal Divine. The Divine is then its ultimate goal, and its greatest quest is ascent to it. Al-Ghazzali's balanced judgment kept him away from extremists who identified themselves with the Divine and whom he did not spare. Action begins with control of the natural appetite and emotion, including hunger, lust and anger as a means to purifying the soul. Self-indulgence is clearly incompatible with the strife against the flesh, the world and the devil. The intent of solitude is contemplation, of contemplation prayer and of prayer communion with the Divine—rather than acquisition. Contemplation of the Divine beauty inspires love; contemplation of the Divine majesty inspires awe.

Jesus' denunciation of the scribes and the Pharisees and his views on worldliness lent themselves to the Moslem gospel of mysticism. So did Paul's dichotomy between soul and flesh—basically a Neo-Platonic thesis. The Sermon on the Mount was drawn upon generously. In quotations from it we read about the "blessed humble and blessed poor" (Matt. 5:5*seq.*), "the salt of the earth" (Matt. 5:13), "the great in the kingdom of heaven" (Matt. 5:19), "The man who spent his life preoccupied with things of the world" (Matt. 6:31,33; cf. 9:16,23), "pearls on the

necks of swine" (Matt. 7:6). The oneness of Christ with God
(John 10:30) is, of course, refuted; the error is likened to that of a
viewer who, looking at a glass full of wine, fails to distinguish
between the glass and the wine. Certain miracles ascribed to Jesus
are spurious, others garbled; few are substantially correct.

Al-Ghazzali's impact on Sufism is manifest in the fraternal orders that sprang up following the period in which he flourished.
The first and greatest was the Qadiri order, founded by 'Abd-al-
Qadir al-Jilani. 'Abd-al-Qadir, who studied at Baghdad, died in
1166. His was followed by the Rifa'i order, bearing the name of
Ahmad al-Rifa'i (d. 1183), who flourished in Basrah. Abu-al-
Hasan al-Shadhili (d. 1258) of Tunisia, founder of the fraternity
named after him which gave rise to some fifteen other brother-
hoods still flourishing in Africa, based his teaching admittedly on
Ihya'. Other fraternal orders in Asia and Africa follow Ghaz-
zalian mystic ideas and use "monasteries" of which the Tus
Khanqah may be considered a prototype.

Meanwhile al-Ghazzali's mystic ideas were making him a number of professional enemies, as were his philosophical views. Some
criticized him for entertaining emotional notions basic to Sufism
but incompatible with rationalism and philosophically difficult to
explain. Others condemned his religious teachings as detrimental
to orthodoxy. This hostility expressed itself in violent terms when
the Murabit sultan of Morocco and Spain, 'Ali (d. 1143), son of al-
Ghazzali's old friend Yusuf ibn-Tashfin, banned and burned all
books written by al-Ghazzali and threatened with death any Moslem found reading them.

III

The concentric ripples generated by al-Ghazzali's teachings
reached the farthest ends of the world of Islam. The teachings'
mystic aspects left noticeable traces in Christian and Jewish
thinking in the East as well as in the West. The roster of his
students includes some of the more celebrated divines. Numberless scholars took advantage of their visits to Mecca, Baghdad or
Damascus to learn from the most learned man of the age.

When on the holy pilgrimage young ibn-Tumart (d. *ca.* 1130), founder of the Muwahhid (unitarian, Almohad) dynasty of Morocco and Spain, came to know al-Ghazzali at Damascus. He later followed him and for three years studied under him. Back home he proclaimed himself al-Mahdi, emphasized God's unity against anthropomorphism (then prevalent), practiced the ascetic life and opposed drinking and other manifestations of laxity.

Several factors contributed to the making of the message of our teacher-author appealing and effective. He brought an original mind to bear on all problems he treated. He took pains to reason logically and systematically and to express his conclusions with clarity and precision. His treatment of philosophic and mystic doctrines made them palatable to theologians and set the pattern for the development of Islamic thought. The vital spark supplied by his personal experience as he sampled the prevailing schools of thought added to the value and acceptability of his teachings. In him orthodoxy, philosophy and mysticism found a happy combination. Posterity memorialized its respect by bestowing on him two honorific titles: the imam and *hujjah* (the supreme authority on al-Islam).

His impact on non-Moslems was largely in the mystic field. Jewish scholars in both Eastern and Western Islam cultivated Arabic studies. Less than half a century after al-Ghazzali's death, a Jewish convert to Christianity in Toledo had his philosophical works translated into Latin. In the mid-thirteenth century *Mizan al-'Amal*, a compendium of ethics, was done into Latin by a Jew in Barcelona. Ibn-Maymun (Maimonides, d. 1204) of Cordova, the most celebrated Jewish philosopher of the Middle Ages, used his *Maqasid*. The compendium on mysticism, *Mishkat al-Anwar*, was translated later and aroused much speculation among Jewish scholars. These scholars' views on the soul and its emanation and on the spiritual agencies in their relation to the Divine light reflect Ghazzalian doctrines.

Among Syrian authors influenced by this Moslem author mention may be made of ibn-al-'Ibri (Barhebraeus, d. 1286), Jacobite bishop of Aleppo. Ibn-al-'Ibri lived for a time in Baghdad and wrote two mystical works in which he followed al-Ghazzali closely and in which the *Ihya'* is repeatedly quoted. Ibn-al-'Ibri's views on the knowledge of God, the steps involved in seeking Him and the place of love in the scheme also follow those of al-Ghazzali. Through al-Ghazzali a part of the debt Sufism at its inception owed Christian monasticism may be said to have been repaid.

In Western Christianity the response was greater. Thomas Aquinas (1225–74) was exposed to Islamic influence while a student at the University of Naples, the first university founded by a royal charter. The founder was the Norman King Frederick II of Sicily, who patronized Arabic learning and had the works of ibn-Rushd and other Moslem philosophers translated into Latin and used as texts. There, Thomas studied Algazel. In places the analogy in thought and expression between his and his predecessor's writings is striking. The two leading theologians of Christendom and Islam agree on the kind of gnosis for perfect knowledge of God which St. Thomas calls grace. Both agree that the contemplation of God (Truth), a distinctive feature of man, is the highest goal man can have, and the Beatific vision an end in itself. Long before St. Thomas, al-Ghazzali wrote in his *Ihya'* that heavenly bliss is proportionate to the intensity of the love for God, and this love is commensurate with the knowledge of God gained by the elect on earth.

A contemporary of St. Thomas, the Catalan Dominican scholar Raymond Martin, quotes *Maqasid* and *Ihya'* and closely follows al-Ghazzali in making happiness in the next world purely spiritual involving the vision of God. The well-known French physicist Blaise Pascal (d. 1662) experienced a spiritual crisis similar to that of al-Ghazzali and likewise found relief in mysticism. His *Pensées* betray Moslem influence.

Another Christian mystic who was exposed to Islamic influence was the great poet Dante (d. 1321). In his minor prose works Dante frequently quotes ibn-Sina, ibn-Rushd and al-Ghazzali. Dante's views on the inner light, the Beatific vision and the ascent through the seven Heavens follow those of the Spanish mystic Muhyi-al-Din ibn-'Arabi and were largely anticipated by al-Ghazzali. Aware of his indebtedness to Moslem philosophers, the famed Italian poet did not consign them to the inferno, as he was bound to do by the teaching of his church, but to the border region termed limbo.

IV

The salient features of al-Ghazzali's personality and character may be inferred with greater certitude from his writings than from biographers' portrayals. We have already noted on the intellectual side his eager curiosity, passion for knowledge, openmindedness and devotion to truth. On the ethical side the reader is impressed by his otherworldliness, his moral courage in espousing unpopular causes—such as music—as an instrument of piety, his criticism of his colleague theologians and jurists, his tolerant attitude towards Christianity and his insistence on the superiority of spiritual over material values in this world and the next. Even in Paradise, to him and his like, the joys are spiritual rather than sensual as understood from koranic passages. In regard to the acceptability of Christian views, he had no objection except in case of conflict with orthodox Islam. He disapproved of cursing the second Umayyad caliph Yazid, generally held responsible for the death of the Prophet's grandson Husayn. Any Moslem, thought he, who curses another Moslem becomes accursed. His *Ayyuha al-Walad,* written at a mature age, reveals his religious ideal as that of an inner life and personal experience, not dependent upon stereotyped creed and formalized worship but manifesting itself in good deeds. His strife to attain that ideal, the measure of success he achieved and the nobility of his character entitle him to a niche in the hall of the world's saints.

In the absence of adequate information about his family life, his writings again serve as the main source. Only his brother Ahmad, according to all sources, was by his bedside at his death. We are sure of one wife, who survived him, but we do not know her name. Nor do we know his daughters' names. Like other young Moslems of his time, he married before he was twenty. His title abu-Hamid (father of Hamid) does not necessarily imply that he did have a son by that name. Such titles were often given arbitrarily. On the other hand, his keen and reasoned observations about children's behavior and their education would suggest that he did have ample opportunity to acquire firsthand knowledge of boys. His mother, who brought up her orphaned children alone, happily lived long enough to see two of them achieve distinction.

Of special interest in this connection are al-Ghazzali's views on marriage. He who marries a woman because of her faith, he tells us in the first part of the *Ihya'*, receives from God both wealth and faith, but he who marries for wealth and beauty makes wealth and beauty unlawful to him. His silence on the girls' education indicates that he did not rise in his views on women above the general level of his age. But he does enjoin the husband to teach his wife the requirements of prayer and other rituals, and makes the mother share with the father the responsibility for the children's upbringing. Parental education should aim first and foremost at character building. Stealth and lying are the earliest temptations. Parents should curb the child's appetite for food and render unattractive to him all forms of luxury and high living. He should be warned against bad company. Among his early lessons should be eating slowly, with the right hand, and avoiding soiling his clothes. White clothes are preferable to colored and gaudy clothes favored by effeminate boys. The teacher begins where the father ends. He takes his place.[1]

––––––––––––

Abu-Hamid Muhammad al-Ghazzali, theologian, jurist, philosopher, mystic, saint, reconciled reason and faith and fashioned a system of philosophical religious thought that has endured and satisfied the solid core of the Moslem community.

[1] In addition to Margaret Smith's book cited above the English reader has in W. Montgomery Watt, *Muslim Intellectual* (Edinburgh, 1963) a sober treatment. The Arabic reader is referred to al-Jumhuriyah al-'Arabiyah al-Muttahidah, *Abu-Hamid al-Ghazzali* (Cairo, 1962).

Al-Shafi'i: Founder of the Science of Islamic Law

Whenever I face an opponent in debate I silently pray, "O Lord, help him so that truth may flow from his heart and on his tongue; and so that if truth is on my side, he may follow me, and if it be on his side I may follow him."

—Al-Shafi'i

OF all the peoples of antiquity the Semites, judged by their contribution, were the most religiously-minded body. The three major monotheistic religions stand out as an enduring monument to their spiritual sensitiveness and religious activity. No other comparable group can match that. They were perhaps also the most legalistically minded. Their developed society was based on law. The Babylonian code compiled by Hammurabi (d. *ca.* 1686 B.C.) was more elaborate and far-reaching than the Sumerian or any other contemporary body of laws.

The stele recording the code represents the king standing in worship before the sun-god Shamash to receive the laws. This was the first step to establish a vital contact between religion and legislation. In primitive societies religious belief did not form a prominent source of law. The Babylonian monarch sought divine sanction for his laws, which comprised earlier Sumerian elements. The Hebrews carried on from there. Not only did the Hebrews make all legislation in Exodus, Leviticus, Numbers and Deuteronomy a direct revelation from Jehovah through Moses (Ex. 25:1, 35:1; Deut. 6:1) but in one place (Ex. 24:12, 31:18) they represented Jehovah as handing to Moses the Decalogue as written by His own hand. The Old Testament law thus distinguished itself from all other Near Eastern laws in being in its origin and entirety holy and revealed. God was the ultimate legislator and the judge.

I

Islam carried on from where Judaism left off, juridically speaking. It bypassed Christianity. The founder of Christianity was more spiritually than legalistically minded. Christ's follower Paul, founder of Gentile Christianity, was like minded. The Old Testament law forms a background for the narrative of the New but not an integral part of it. Islam, in common with Judaism, starts out with the assumption that God, the creator of man and the source of all power and authority, is entitled to thoroughgoing service on the part of man. This man cannot give without knowing God's will. That will is revealed through the prophets, greatest and last among whom was Muhammad. The Divine will is revealed not only to be believed but to be obeyed. Disobedience is sin—more than a civil crime—to be punished by God in the next world. Far from being a yoke, Divine law becomes to the believer a privilege with ample reward.

Islamic law (*shari'ah*, literally path to a watering place) is more than revealed or dictated. It is the Word of Allah incarnate. It coexisted with God. It was originally in a heavenly book of which the earthly one, the Koran, was a replica. It is perfect, eternal, universal, good for all men at all times in all places—at least in theory. It is authoritarian and totalitarian. The state does not create law; it enforces it. Law existed before the state and before the society. It sets forth man's relation and obligations to God and regulates his relations with his fellow men. It provides members of the society with guidance to achieve the good life prescribed by God. No such dogmatic stand was taken by any other people. The Greeks conceived of law as something man-made. So is its modern conception. The Romans, greatest legislators of early days, had a double foundation for their law: Divine revelation and human ordinance.

As long as he lived Muhammad, as God's spokesman, performed the treble function of legislator, judiciary and executive. No difficulty could have been insurmountable. With his death Divine legislation ceased, never to start again. His successors did not inherit the legislative aspect of his prophethood. As heads of state, they exercised the necessary judiciary and executive functions, of course. But the community of Islam (*ummah*) was now no more Medina-wide; it was world-wide, and need was felt for sources supplementary to the Koran. Besides, the koranic legislation does not always specify the procedure or method of observance. Ritual prayer, for instance, is enjoined with no instructions as to what formulas to repeat and how many genuflections and prostrations to perform. The usage (*sunnah*) of the Prophet lay at hand to establish a precedent. His behavior became an established model. His usage of a local procedure gave it sanction. All this became a living tradition followed by his Companions (*sahabah*) and by the first generation of their successors (*tabi'un*). In due course both generations passed away, necessitating the recording of their versions of the sayings, deeds and tacit approval (*taqrir*) of the Prophet in what became known as *hadith* (literally, narrative). Hadith worked its way into second place after the Koran as a source of law.

But after all, the laws of the Koran were limited, those of the hadith were limited, while the new crop of cases was unlimited. Resort must be had to new devices. One was to widen the base of hadith to include sayings and deeds of the Companions, even of their immediate followers. But even here the supply was exhaustible. A richer source was personal judgment (*ra'i*, opinion) involving speculation. By this time the output of hadith, competing for recognition, had reached the bewildering stage. No criteria were as yet set for verification and no written collections had yet been standardized. Each populous city from Marw and Naysabur to al-Qayrawan and Cordova had its leading jurist with a local following. The jurists had access to legal opinions of earlier generations for use as guide, but no collection and no jurist had achieved recognition on a national scale, with the possible exception of the Syrian al-Awza'i (d. 774 in Beirut). A variety of judicial opinions, reflecting local economic and social conditions, were competing for wide acceptance.

Amidst this confusion two towering figures emerge and gradually dominate the scene, one in the intellectual and the other in the religious center of Islam. They are those of abu-Hanifah (al-Nu'man ibn-Thabit) and Malik ibn-Anas.

II

Abu-Hanifah (699–767), a Kufan grandson of a Persian slave, was neither a professional lawyer nor a judge but a silk merchant. Malik (718–796) was a Medinese theologian and jurist. One was a theoretic scholar, the other was a practicioner. Each was the center of a circle of disciples—that of abu-Hanifah more private— but neither aimed at founding a school. The eponym of the Iraqi school composed no books. His teachings reached us through his pupils headed by abu-Yusuf, judge of Harun al-Rashid. The Hanafi turned out to be the first of the four orthodox schools of Islamic law and held the leading position among them. Malik's masterpiece *al-Muwatta'* took its place as the first conscious attempt at a law manual of Islam, law as viewed in Medina, home of the Companions and nursery of tradition. The Maliki school not only widened the base of hadith but made more extensive use of it as against its Iraqi rival, which leaned more on personal judgment. By biography and ancestry abu-Hanifah was not closely attached to Medina. As the Hanafi school leaned less on hadith and more on juridical opinion, it developed a new method of legal reasoning, approval (*istihsan*), and instituted a new form of speculation, analogy (*qiyas*). Malik made a limited use of a new form *istislah,* what was considered by the scholarly consensus to be for the good of the community.

Rivalry between the Iraqi and the Hijazi schools involved charges and countercharges hard to justify. The Hanafi use of opinion was controlled by several considerations as was the Hijazi use of hadith. Although in general one might seem more liberal and the other more conservative, in many cases the distinction between the two is as difficult to make as one between Democrats and Republicans in American politics.

The early 'Abbasids favored the Hanafi system and thereby gave it prestige and an opportunity to spread eastward, while the Maliki system spread westward into North Africa and Spain. The Saljuqs followed the 'Abbasids in their adoption of the Hanafi school and were in turn followed by their Ottoman cousins. The modern Arab states of Iraq, Syria, Lebanon and Egypt inherited this school for official use, while most of their citizens owe allegiance to other schools. The Azhar shaykhs are predominantly Shafi'is.

Between the "people of opinion" school, as the Iraqi was styled, and that of the "people of hadith" of Medina there was room for a third one, the Shafi'i. The founder of this third classical school was conveniently born in Palestine, between Hijaz and Iraq, took his education in Medina and Baghdad, and labored in Mecca, Baghdad and Cairo. He was more cosmopolitan than his two predecessors.

III

When in 768 Muhammad ibn-Idris al-Shafi'i was born at Ghazzah (Gaza) and shortly after lost his father, his impoverished mother saw no future for her son—the statement in ibn-Khallikan and other biographers connecting his birth with Jupiter shooting from Palestine to Egypt and spraying fragments all over the area notwithstanding. Ghazzah was often visited by merchants from Mecca, one of whom, Hashim, a great-grandfather of the Prophet, had died there. The city thereby acquired particular dignity. After the conquest it provided hospitality to Arabian emigrants, one of whom was Idris al-Shafi'i. The widow carried her two-year infant to Mecca "just to preserve the noble pedigree" of the father, a descendant of Muttalib of the Quraysh.

From their modest apartment to the Haram Mosque the lad daily commuted on foot and went through the standard curriculum. From the mosque school, following a recognized procedure, he was graduated to the desert school, there to live with a Bedouin tribe, learn such characteristic skills as horsemanship and archery and above all acquire the correct form of Arabic, unadulterated by urban life. The tribe our young man chose roamed between Mecca and Medina and was noted for the "purity of its tongue." The apprenticeship lasted ten years. His interest was equally divided between learning and archery. In ten arrow shots he rarely missed one. In the course of his learning he memorized "ten thousand verses" of the tribal poetical lore. The desert school left a distinctive imprint apparent in his elegant prose, eloquent speech and poetical composition. Clearly he was headed for a literary career.

But the chance fall of one book into his hands changed the course of his life. It was Malik's *Al-Muwatta'* (trodden path), a collection of his lectures incorporating the prevailing opinion in Medina's juridical circles. Al-Shafi'i's biographers tell us—predictably—that he memorized the book from cover to cover (1,004 printed pages in the two-volume Cairo edition of 1951). Not satisfied, the eager student sought the source. For eight months he sat at the feet of the aged master in Medina, from whom only death separated him.

By now the subject of our study was twenty-eight years old. It was time he married and earned his living. For wife his choice fell on Humaydah, a descendant of 'Uthman ibn-'Affan, by whom he had a son named abu-'Uthman and two daughters. This is the only spouse known to us. But he did have a concubine whose only son died in infancy. Abu-'Uthman followed in his father's steps and became judge in Aleppo. Shortly after his marriage al-Shafi'i met the governor of Yaman while on a pilgrimage, and accepted an appointment at his court. This province was then seething with 'Alid dissension. Several years later, he and nine Yamanis were led in chains to Harun al-Rashid's court charged with treason. One after the other of the prisoners was beheaded. The turn of al-Shafi'i came. In the august presence of the supreme ruler of the realm, he unhesitatingly and with unfaltering voice recited the proper greeting of peace. The caliph repeated the convential formula invoking God's peace and mercy, following it by a rebuke for venturing to speak without permission. The captive reminded his captor that God's mercy, graciously bestowed on him, entitled him to a measure of impunity. Taken aback, the caliph asked him to go ahead and explain his behavior in espousing an

'Alid pretender's cause. "But how can a man talk," shot back the bold prisoner, "with chains on his feet?" The caliph ordered him freed.

This enforced visit to Iraq gave the seeker of learning a golden opportunity to imbibe from a new source, the Hanafi. In Baghdad he established firsthand contact with the disciples of the departed master. Throughout the association the Hijazi scholar reserved to himself—as a Maliki—the right to dissent, discuss and debate. But he must have been in the meantime absorbing more Iraqi views than he realized.

After two or three years' sojourn he returned home with a "camel-load of books" to occupy a chair in the Haram, where he had received his elementary education. His audience at times included pilgrims from all over the world of Islam. For nine years he preached, taught and wrote, but evidently missed the intellectual stimulation that only Baghdad could provide. After Malik Hijaz was short on productivity in scholarship. Malik's disciples contented themselves with rehashing what the master had taught, and his followers started surrounding his head with a halo of veneration. Particularly dismayed was al-Shafi'i by the report that in distant al-Andalus his teacher's cap was being used in the ritual prayer for rain. This he denounced vehemently by voice and pen, not realizing that some day he would be given the same kind of treatment. Again he turned his face to the "learned's nest" in the northeast, this time not as a Maliki, nor as a Hanafi, but as al-Shafi'i, an exponent of a new school, a school destined to influence its two predecessors and supersede them in many parts of the world.

It was not long before the newcomer was a recognized imam, a religious leader in his own right. Of the fifty circles then flourishing in the capital, his began with six pupils but soon outstripped them all. The circle (*halqah*) was so called because it consisted of a group of students seated around a professor usually on the floor of a mosque. The professor sat on a cushion leaning on a pillar; the students squatted on a mat. The practice is not entirely obsolete.

By his reasonableness and reasoning al-Shafi'i gained followers from upholders of private judgment and from upholders of tradition as well as from the non-committed. To them he looked more an eclectic reconciler of the two schools than an originator. One of his ardent admirers was ibn-Hanbal, the future victim of al-Ma'mun's inquisition, mentioned above. When on a pilgrimage to Mecca, this Iraqi scholar had met al-Shafi'i. He is credited with the saying "jurisprudence (*fiqh*) was a closed science until al-Shafi'i provided the key," and with expressing the hope that his master would be recognized as the restorer of the faith at the head of the third Moslem century, after the pious Umayyad caliph 'Umar ibn-'Abd-al-'Aziz, the initiator of the series at the second century. Ibn-Hanbal later broke off from the Shafi'i school to become the founder of the fourth and most conservative of the orthodox schools.

While in Baghdad the new imam issued the first edition of what became known as *Al-Risalah* (epistle), generally considered the earliest scientific treatment of Islamic law. It spread the author's reputation far and wide and has since been used as a textbook in school of law.[1] He added to his reputation and to his store of knowledge by visiting the neighboring lands of Syria and Palestine in which he must have had friends since his Meccan days.

In 815 (199 A.H.) we see him leaving for Egypt in the company of a newly appointed governor. This is surprising in view of the fact that no city there was then in the limelight of intellectual activity. Neither he nor any of his biographers offers an explanation. Whenever asked he would jokingly say, "because of my fondness of sugar cane." But evidently the new climate generated by al-Ma'mun was not considered congenial by this intellectual. The hero's reception given him in his new home left no doubt that his reputation had preceded him despite the difficulties of long distance communication. Those were times in which neither actors nor athletes but religious leaders were the occupants of the limelight. The imam was accepted as the restorer of the faith promised by God at the "head" of each new century—according to a Prophetic tradition. Al-Ghazzali, a follower of the Shafi'i school, was another such restorer, as we have noted before.

From his residence at Fustat the imam walked daily after the early morning prayer to lecture at the Mosque of 'Amr ibn-al-'As.

[1] For a translation see Majid Khadduri, *Islamic Jurisprudence: Shafi'i's Risāla* (Baltimore, 1961).

The first lecture dealt with the Koran and lasted till sunrise, when hadith was treated. The remaining part of the forenoon was divided between one lecture dealing with polemics and debate, and a last one devoted to grammar and poetry. At the close of each lecture opportunity was given for questions and discussions.

After five years of teaching and writing the health of the fifty-two-year-old man gave way (820) because, we are told, of hemorrhoid bleeding. The astrologers' prophecy was fulfilled. The Jupiter that rose from Palestine and shot to Egypt did illuminate the area. The pilgrims that visit his tomb at the foot of the Muqattam, bearing the dome built (1211) by al-Malik al-Kamil (Salah-al-Din's nephew), bear witness to the fact. Salah himself was a follower. The deceased's preference for burial in Old Cairo was unmistakably expressed by strong odor emanating from the body when an attempt was made to carry it to Baghdad. Throughout his lifetime, we are also assured, no plague ever afflicted a land of which he was a resident.

His mail did not cease with his death. In fact it continued to the present day. A 1965 scholarly study (in 387 pages) divides the correspondents exactly equally between males and females and the contents almost equally between complaints and requests. The complaints relate mostly to injustice or other forms of wrong perpetrated against the writer by private or public persons. The requests are largely for vengeance in return for an injury or offense, or for cure from some incurable disease, such as blindness or paralysis. In many letters the holy man is addressed "ya-Shafi'i" (O my intercessor), which suggests that the name he bore (from a great-grandfather, Shafi') lent itself to the posthumous role he played. The study could not include mail delivered by hand and burned weekly by the custodian of the shrine.

IV

The science of Islamic jurisprudence, of which the foundation was laid by al-Shafi'i, was termed *fiqh* (literally, intelligence) as against *'ilm* (literally, knowledge), applied to other sciences. The implication was that its acquisition required a high degree of native talent. A *faqih* more than an *'alim* should be capable of independent judgment. This new science may be considered unique in the sense that, unlike mathematical or medical sciences, it had an entirely indigenous origin. It received no stimuli from Indo-Iranian or Indo-European sources and followed no pattern. Its founder showed no interest in Greek philosophy including Aristotelian logic. Nor did he favor the dialectic (*kalam*) form of theology. Yet he lived in an environment where Mu'tazilites, Shi'ites, philosophers and theologians were engaged in hot debates, employing logical reasoning and sharpening didactic and polemic tools which he could not but have partly acquired.

To al-Shafi'i and to his fellow jurists *fiqh* was meant to regulate all man's relations to God (*'ibadat*), to himself and to other men (*mu'amalat*). This made it inclusive of theology and made jurists antedate theologians. This comprehensive science provided regulations (*ahkam*) for religious obligations and for the performance of such basic dogmas as prayer, fasting, almsgiving and pilgrimage. It supplied laws regarding criminal and civil cases and went beyond that to what constituted courtesy and good behavior in social relations. All acts of man were thus divided into what is legally permitted (*halal*) and what is legally forbidden (*haram*), with several gradations in between. What is legally permitted may be an obligation (*fard*), expressly commanded in the Koran or sunnah, or a desirable thing to do (*mustahabb*), recommended by the sunnah. Otherwise the act is reprobated (*makruh*) or absolutely forbidden (*haram*). Then there is the category of indifferent acts (*mubah*).

The Koran as the uncreated word of God was, of course, the ultimate source of all legislation. All other sources were subsidiary to it and largely derived from it. Any law was explicitly or implicitly in the Koran. This was the orthodox view and the new imam concurred. The Koran tells us it was revealed in Arabic (12:2; 13:37; 20:112; 39:29), making it incumbent on the scholar to master all the intricacies and niceties of this sacred language, and on the believer to study it and recite his ritual prayers in it. A marriage contract in a language other than Arabic, al-Shafi'i taught, could not be considered valid in the case of a Moslem. On the other hand the Hanafi school authorized the recital of the opening surah of the Koran in Persian.

After the Word of Allah, the practice (*sunnah*) of His Messenger established itself as a source of canon law. It was al-Shafi'i who defined it as the Prophet's model behavior. Even in the Prophet's lifetime his behavior became a model sanctioned by revelation. More than once the believer is ordered to believe in "Allah and His Messenger" (7:158; 64:8; cf. 4:169, 59:7). Al-Shafi'i went further and arbitrarily identified koranic "wisdom" (*hikmah*, 3:43; 5:110; cf. 2:123, 146; 4:113; 62:2) with hadith. A reading of the Arabic text where God promises to send one who teaches the "Book, the Wisdom, the Torah and the Evangel," suggests that the reference echoes Hebrew *hokhmah*, the wisdom literature of the Old Testament.

Here al-Shafi'i parted company with the Maliki school. That school utilized the prevalent usage or living tradition, including the practices of the Companions and their successors. To the new legislator, the practices of the Prophet's associates, whether confirmatory or contradictory, were of little value. Having limited the sunnah to the Prophet's practice and raised it to a level close to the Koran, he set out to establish criteria for the interrelationship between the two. The sunnah should be well-authenticated. The chain of authorities transmitting its record (hadith) should be uninterrupted; it should also reach back to the Prophet. Well-established hadiths should not disagree. If they do the one more in keeping with the Koran is the one to be accepted. A number of hadiths in Malik's *al-Muwatta'* with incomplete chains are thus rejected. The Prophetic hadith should not contradict the Koran. Nor can it abrogate it. A koranic text can be repealed only by a koranic text. God is free to change His decision, necessitating a corresponding change in Muhammad's sunnah. The sunnah then explains or clarifies the sacred text. Once fully authenticated, a Prophetic hadith should be accepted without questioning. The "why" and "how" are no more applicable to it than to a koranic prescription. It then partakes of the authority of revelation. This raises the hadith's authority to the level of the Koran's, leaving one important difference: In the Koran God speaks; in the sunnah the Prophet speaks. The one is inspired in meaning and letter, the other in meaning only.

In his *al-Risalah* al-Shafi'i states that a hadith may be in full agreement with the sacred text, it may be explanatory to it or may not be directly connected with it, but under no condition can it alter or repeal it. This firm stand confronted him with difficulties, necessitating stretching the meaning of the hadith's function in the explanation or clarification of the text. The Koran (5:42) punishes the thief with the cutting off of his hand, but a hadith of the Prophet indicates that this punishment could be waived in case the theft was of an insignificant amount. The Koran (24:2) prescribes a hundred lashes for an adulterer. But in case the act was committed under certain aggravating circumstances a Prophetic hadith authorized stoning the adulterer.

In the domain of hadith al-Shafi'i made a major contribution. Not only did he establish it alongside the Koran as a leading source of legislation but he set it on the path of becoming a science in its own right. We know of no other people who reduced their religious tradition to a science. The influence of al-Shafi'i is reflected in the collections of hadiths which began to appear shortly after his time and acquired canonical status.

By the mid-third century after Muhammad an overwhelming avalanche of hadiths—valid, dubious, contradictory, spurious— had accumulated. Whenever a religious, political or social issue arose, it yielded a new crop of sayings and deeds attributed to the Prophet. Tradition collectors scoured the four quarters of the world of Islam. Each party sought sanction for its views in a hadith, if not readymade, made to order. The Shi'ite schism offered an almost irresistible temptation to fabricate the stuff. For a time committing hadiths to writing was not favored, because of possible confusion with the sacred text. The failure of the retentive faculty was therefore responsible for many faulty sayings. In certain cases the fabrication was made by well-intentioned traditionists in their zeal to guide the hesitant along the righteous way. More often the motivation was mercenary. Storytellers, under the guise of traditionists, thrived on the assumption that the more extraordinary the hadith the better for the trade. One such manufacturer, executed at Kufah in 772, confessed to having circulated 4,000 hadiths of his own invention. A Companion, abu-Hurayrah, reportedly transmitted 5,374 hadiths, many of which were evidently foisted on him after his death. As Christians and Jews embraced the new faith, words were put into the Prophet's mouth and deeds were ascribed to him analogous to those in the Bible. In a reply to a question as to how many times a man should forgive his slave, the Prophet is made to say "seventy times a day." After a battle outside of Medina (627), Muhammad fed from one chicken and some loaves of barley bread a thousand tired, hungry troops.

Thus did hadith serve as a vehicle for introducing alien practices and concepts into Islam, and a means of softening the rigidity of its Divine law. It promoted a folk religion alongside the learned religion.

It was time for a critical study of the amassed corpus, with a view to systematization and standardization. The way had been paved by al-Shafi'i. A member of his school, born in Bukhara, was the first to undertake the project. Al-Bukhari (d. 870) reportedly selected his 7,397 hadiths from 600,000 gathered from a thousand shaykhs, in the course of sixteen years of travel and labor in Persia, Iraq, Syria, Hijaz and Egypt. Of the abu-Hurayrah collection he accepted only 446. Before committing a hadith to writing, the conscientious author would perform the ceremonial ablution and recite his prayer. The collection, titled *Sahih* (genuine), took its place as the earliest and most authoritative work of its kind.

The pattern was set. To be valid a hadith had to consist of two parts: a chain of authorities (*isnad*) and a text (*matn*). The hadith should be in direct address involving a direct quotation. A related to me that B related to him that C said. This formula was introduced into theology, historiography and other sciences. The validity of a hadith depended, moreover, on the piety and character of every transmitter and the possibility of having had firsthand contact with the nearest man to him in the chain. Four categories were recognized: genuine or sound (*sahih*), good or fair (*hasan*), weak (*da'if*) and invalid (*saqim*), mostly on an external critical appraisal, directed largely to the sayers rather than to the sayings.

The second major contribution of our jurist was in what became recognized as the third source of law in the descending scale: consensus (*ijma'*, literally agreement). Before him this principle was extensively used, but among the legists themselves there was no consensus as to what constituted consensus. Was it the agreement of a local community or the entire community of Islam? Was it a unanimous agreement of all jurists or a majority of them?

At different times in different places al-Shafi'i held varying views on this subject as indicated by a study of the book under his name entitled *Al-Umm* (the mother). This comprehensive law book has come down to us in an edition by his favorite Egyptian disciple (the Cairo 1961 edition in eight volumes). But it is clear that the master was critical of the provincial use of this doctrine by the Medinese, as he was of its Iraqi concept as the consensus of scholars in each generation. On the positive side he broadened its base to include the community at large as expressed unanimously by its most learned jurists. In all cases ijma' was not arrived at formally in a council, but accepted as a *de facto* agreement. Throughout al-Shafi'i insisted that a clear saying of the Prophet overrules any prevailing practice of the Moslem community.

Apparently the brilliant canonist failed to appreciate the full potential of this unpretentious instrument of legislation. Its advocates had difficulty finding sanction for it in the Koran. The references to the believers as a "middle community" (2:137) and to disagreement among them were far-fetched. Tradition was more accommodating. It first prepared the way for ijma' and later, after al-Shafi'i's time, signed a lifelong alliance with it. This was expressed in the above-quoted hadith: "My community shall not agree on an error," four words in Arabic but long enough to insure the new doctrine unlimited success.

Ijma' found more functions to perform than filling vacancies left by the Koran and the hadith. It furnished assurance, where assurance was necessary, for institutions or decisions. By ijma' the text of the Koran, as compiled by Caliph 'Uthman, became the canonical text. By ijma' circumcision, an early Semitic practice uncited in the Koran, became a hallmark of Islam corresponding to baptism in Christianity. Under its umbrella other pre-Islamic practices and institutions were smuggled in. Even what the learned religion would first consider innovation, if not heresy, was—thanks to ijma'—universally, or almost so, accepted in folk religion. The sinlessness of the Prophet and the cult of saints—referred to earlier—come to mind by way of illustration. Moreover, this third source has an advantage in possessing a quality of self-renewal denied the other two. Revelation ceased with the Prophet, and hadith ended some three centuries later. But the operation of

ijma' can make a present or future Moslem community introduce
a change into its corpus of belief and practice.

The Shi'ah, for obvious reasons, had as little to do with ijma' as
with Summite hadith. They had their own equivalent of both.
For ijma' they substituted an infallible mahdi.

Reasoning by analogy (*qiyas*, literally measurement) became
the last root (*asl*) of Islamic jurisprudence. This fourth legal doctrine was no more initiated by al-Shafi'i than the third. Nor did
abu-Hanifah, who used it extensively, invent it. At times al-Shafi'i
refers to the Iraqis as "people of qiyas." But Malik's school placed
little reliance on it, and fundamentalists had no use for it.

Qiyas is a form of personal opinion. It involves deduction subsequent to establishing parallelism between a case treated in the
Koran or sunnah and a newly risen case. Its advocates had even
more difficulty in finding support for it in the sacred text than in
the case of ijma'. It met vehement opposition from the conservative and literalist wing. The Hanbalis clung narrowly to the letter and vetoed innovation. Al-Shafi'i showed no enthusiasm for it.
In *Al-Risalah* he justifies its use only in cases not dealt with in the
Koran or the sunnah and not covered in the ijma'. It was the only
form of opinion admitted by him and hardly accepted as a fourth
root. A new restriction beyond the points of resemblance was imposed: consideration of the reason (*'illah*) behind the rule in the
Koran or the sunnah. The restriction gave qiyas respectability.

With qiyas the work of the great imam was completed. He
found all the fundamental legal terms already in existence but in
loose use. He exerted himself to define them, evaluated them, established their mutual relationship and thus constructed a coher-
ent system. The theory of sources he laid out became the classical
one. The constitution of Islamic law he formulated has been generally accepted. All that remained was to find a supporting
hadith, and that was not difficult to do. When Muhammad sent
to Yaman a Companion, Mu'adh ibn-Jabal, as governor and dis-
penser of justice, he subjected him to this test:

  —How will you decide when a case arises?
  —In accordance with the Book of Allah

—And if you find naught therein?
—In accordance with the sunnah of the Messenger of Allah
—And if you find naught therein?
—Then shall I apply my reasoning.[1]

Thereupon the Prophet praised Allah for enabling His Messenger to choose a messenger qualified to do what is pleasing to Him.

With that the door of personal reasoning (*ijtihad*) was forever closed. Every orthodox Moslem has since belonged to one of the four classical schools: Hanafi, Maliki, Shafi'i or Hanbali. He is free to change, but so long as he owes allegiance to a school its decisions are binding on him.

V

The biographers of al-Shafi'i found nothing weak in his character to record. Nor can a sensitive nose smell anything wrong in the record. Besides, we have his published poems (*diwan*) and his essays and conversations (*adab*), which give us firsthand information and mirror his inner self. Incidentally, his literally output, bearing the influence of his early desert schooling, is considered of the highest order. Lucid in style and rich in wisdom, his verses are still memorized and quoted. Asceticism, generosity and modesty shine among the qualities of this gentleman scholar. Numberless anecdotes are given in evidence of his generosity; the one most often repeated tells about the distribution of the 10,000 dirhams in his pocket among those who met him on his visit to Mecca when on an appointment in Yaman. His mother had instructed him to empty his pocket whenever he entered the Holy City. In Cairo he often gave the last coin in his possession for a service or in response to a request. When his books were discussed in his presence his usual comment was, "I'd rather see people utilize my work than ascribe a letter of it to me."

Of special interest to us is his intellectual honesty, his dedica-

---

[1] The authoritative study of al-Shafi'i's work is Joseph Schacht, *The Origins of Muhammadan Jurisprudence* (Oxford, 1950). The most comprehensive in Arabic is Muhammad abu-Zuhrah, *Al-Shafi'i: Hayatuhu wa-'Asruhu,* 2nd ed. (Cairo, 1948).

tion to truth. An effective speaker and debater widely considered unbeatable, he tells us:

> Never do I argue with a man with a desire to hear him say what is wrong, or to expose him and win a victory over him. Nor do I enter into a discussion with anyone except with the desire that he be helped and get better. Whenever I face an opponent in debate I silently pray, "O Lord, help him so that truth may flow from his heart and on his tongue; and so that if truth is on my side he may follow me, and if it be on his side I may follow him." [1]

Theologian, poet, essayist, teacher, jurist, saint, al-Imam al-Shafi'i laid the scientific foundation of a system of jurisprudence hardly paralleled in its reach and scope, a system that has regulated the relations of millions of moslem believers to their God, to themselves and to one another.

[1] Cf. ibn-abi-Hatim, *Adab al-Shafi'i wa-Manaqibuhu*, ed. 'Abd-al-Ghani 'Abd-al-Khaliq (Cairo, 1953), pp. 91, 92–93; Muhammad ibn-'Umar [Fakhr-al-Din] al-Razi, *Manaqib al-Imam al-Shafi'i* (Cairo, 1237), p. 130; abu-al-Faraj ibn-al-Jawzi, *Talbis Iblis*, ed. Muhammad Munir al-Dimashqi, 2nd ed. (Cairo, 1950), p. 120.

Al-Kindi:
Philosopher of the Arabs

*The noblest in quality and highest in rank
of all human activities is philosophy. Philosophy is defined as knowledge of things
as they are in their reality, insofar as man's
ability determines. The philosopher's aim
in his theoretical studies is to ascertain the
truth, in his practical knowledge to conduct himself in accordance with that truth.*
—Al-Kindi

STRICTLY there was no such thing as Arab philosophy. Unlike
Arabic literature, Arab philosophy was an importation. Hence its
foreign name *falsafah* and the designation of its practitioner as a
faylasuf.

The Arabians did have *philosophia* in its etymological—not
technical—meaning. Their literature from its earliest days is
studded with proverbs, wise sayings, anecdotes and fables intended to inculcate courage, generosity, tribal solidarity and
other virtues high in their scale of values. Their fabulist and
proverb-maker Luqman (al-Hakim, the sage) was adopted by the
Koran and passed on to legendary history. As Luqman became
the Aesop of the Arabs, so did 'Ali ibn-abi-Talib become their
Solomon. Countless nuggets of wisdom (*hikmah*) have been fathered on him. But falsafah is in no way related to hikmah.

With Islam a new type of philosophical thought makes its appearance, theology. Islamic theology, anchored in the Koran and

hadith (tradition), sets up a well-balanced, comprehensive system encompassing all aspects of human life. It defines the identity of God and designates His attributes. It explains the origin and nature of man and specifies his relations to God, his fellow man and nature. Theologians and jurists enshrined the system in the *shari'ah* (canon law). But falsafah in its origin had nothing to do with shari'ah. In its essence the so-called Arab philosophy was Greek philosophy, rendered into Arabic by Christian translators and reworked by Moslem commentators to meet the proclivity of the Arab mind and to harmonize with koranic dogmas and Islamic tenets of faith. Its general framework, scope and basic assumptions remained largely Greek.

Until the mid-ninth century, when al-Kindi flourished in the 'Abbasid court, orthodox theologians, scholar-jurists, radical Mu'tazilites and mystic Sufis were the only competitors for the mass mind. All were of indigenous origin. Of the two exotic cultural influences that had by that time intruded, the Indo-Persian presented no challenge, but the Greek did. The Greek element, we recall, was introduced by Christian Syrians, mostly physicians, under Harun and al-Ma'mun. For a thousand years prior to that, under Seleucids, Romans and Byzantines, Greek thought had been domesticated in Syria and Egypt. For five hundred years Christian scholars of the Fertile Crescent had been studying the classical legacy and integrating aspects of it in their Semitic culture. The Apostle Paul knew Greek and was familiar with Greek philosophy. Several theses in his Epistles, such as those relating to human nature and to the analysis of the body into earthy or natural, and heavenly or spiritual, go back to Greek origins. Stoicism first and then Neo-Platonism were the two influential pagan systems with which the Christian system had to establish a give-and-take relationship. Stoicism was founded by a Cyprus-born Phoenician, Zeno (333–261 B.C.), whose *stoa poikile* (painted porch), in which he lectured at Athens, gave the name to the school.

Paul and the early Christian Fathers of Alexandria Hellenized Christianity, rendered it palatable to the Greco-Romans and facilitated its world-wide expansion. In Alexandria, where waves of pagan, Jewish and Christian thought met, clashed and had to be reconciled, flourished in the last decade of the second century a

Christian catechetical school headed by Clement. Originally a pagan deeply read in Greek philosophy, Clement became founder of the Alexandrian school of Christian theology. His more celebrated pupil, Origen, born in Egypt to a pagan family, carried on the work of harmonizing the best in the antique culture with Christian thought. To that end he made extensive use of allegorical interpretation. A Jewish contemporary of St. Paul, Philo, also of Alexandria, led the way in his endeavor to reconcile the Platonic-Aristotelian philosophy with the doctrines of the Pentateuch. He explained those doctrines in terms of contemporary Greek thought. By the same token it can be said that these early Christian and Jewish scholars were Semiticizing Greek learning, preparatory to Christianizing and Judaizing it.

I

Moslem religious thought in this field followed the Judaeo-Christian antecedent. It gave prophethood and the intuitive acquisition of truth supreme place. As in the case of Christianity and Judaism, Islam depended on revelation and employed faith for its acceptance. To the Semitic mind the supernatural was not necessarily irrational. On the other hand the Greeks enthroned reason and made it the arbiter in determining what is true. Their philosophy depended upon the human mind and employed logic —the principles of valid inferences—as its instrument. No other people of antiquity trusted man's intellect and its working to such an extent.

It was against this background of European philosophy in itself and in its Judaeo-Christian variety that Arab philosophy arose. Its rise was an interesting illustration of the ability of thought to transcend time and space and to overcome religious and national barriers. The rise, however, was not due to the impact of that pre-Christian fourth-century system of Plato and his pupil Aristotle, but to its latest development of the fourth Christian century known as Neo-Platonism. Neo-Platonism evolved in the city bearing Alexander's name as a synthetic system of Neo-Pythagorean elements with their undue reverence for numbers, Platonic elements mainly metaphysical, Aristotelian doctrines derived from his logic and Stoic ethical teachings. The movement picked up

Oriental mystical and later Jewish rabbinical and Christian pa-
tristic elements.

Three early exponents of Neo-Platonism were Near Easterners.
Its founder Plotinus (d. A.D. 270) was born in Egypt and educated
in Alexandria, and taught in Rome. His pupil Porphyry (clad in
purple, d. *ca.* 305) was a Tyrian by birth whose real name, Melik
(king) betrays his Semitic origin. It was he who expounded Plotinus and inaugurated a system that for centuries was dominant.
His Syrian-born pupil Iamblichus (d. *ca.* 333), following the Neo-
Pythagorean pattern, ascribed to numbers higher significance
than they mathematically possessed.

The confrontation of Greek and Islamic thought in ninth-
century Baghdad made the era one of the two most intellectually
exciting ones in the history of the Arabs. A thousand years had to
pass before anything similar was experienced. At the early confrontation the two parties looked at each other with enemys' eyes.
Moslem intellectuals, largely theologians, saw no possibility of coexistence. It was the recurring problem faced earlier by Jewish
and Christian theologians. The encounter seemingly involved
either the subordination of theology to philosophy, which would
mean no more Islam, or the subordination of philosophy to theology, which would mean no more philosophy. Neither could accommodate or tolerate the other.

It was a time of impasse, and with the time came the man. He
was a man with a first-class mind which addressed itself to the
study of the new philosophy. It was an encyclopedic mind to
which no aspect of human knowledge seemed alien. It made the
author feel at home in alchemy and medicine, astrology and astronomy, mathematics and geometry, physics and metaphysics, as
it did in philosophy—Hindu or Greek, theology and logic. This
generalist was not original or creative in his thinking, but had
enough originality to realize that a modus vivendi could be established between the alien and the indigenous thought. His studies
in Greek science gave it a home in the Arabic language and Moslem culture; those in philosophy singled out congenial strands
and integrated them with theology. He thus pointed the way toward further accord. Al-Kindi's place in history is that of a pioneer, a guide, blazing a new trail. The series of Moslem thinkers

he initiated spread over the area to Spain and extended in time
to the twelfth century. They did not cease until philosophy was
made an integral part of the intellectual heritage of Islam.

The homage almost all of them paid Islam does not hide the
fact that their intellectual home was more in Alexandria and
Athens than in Mecca and Medina. Of this school al-Razi
(Rhazes, d. 925) of Persian origin was the most original and the
most radical. In fact he was exceptional. A pure rationalist, he
subordinated theology to philosophy. To him the prophets—including Moses, Jesus and Muhammad—were impostors. Al-Razi
was followed by al-Farabi (Alpharabius, d. 950) of Turkish ancestry. Al-Farabi was honored by his people with the title "the
second teacher" (after Aristotle). He belonged to the second generation of Moslem philosophers and is credited with writing the
first systematic exposition in Arabic of Aristotle's and Plato's philosophies. Generally recognized as the real founder of Moslem
Neo-Platonism, al-Farabi constructed a clearer and more consist-
ent system than al-Kindi's. Two other of these thinkers, ibn-Sina
and ibn-Rushd, will be fully studied in later chapters.

II

Abu-Yusuf Ya'qub ibn-Ishaq al-Kindi was born about 801 at
Kufah during the governorship of his father, who died shortly
after that date. His grandfather had held the post earlier. The
surname indicates ancestry in the royal tribe of Kindah of Yamanite origin. The tribe took justifiable pride in its royal ancestry
and particularly in Imru'-al-Qays (d. *ca.* 545), the greatest of the
seven authors of the "suspended odes." The celebrated al-Nadim
of Baghdad (d. 995), author of *al-Fihrist* and earliest of al-Kindi's
biographers, devotes four lines to his pedigree, one long sentence
to his life and six pages to an enumeration of his writings. As a
matter of fact the honor Ya'qub bestowed upon the tribe by his
learning eclipsed that bestowed by his noble ancestors. It made
the name Alkindus (Elkindus) known in the West and immortalized in its Arabic form. To his people he became known
as Faylasuf al-'Arab; this he was in more than one sense. He was
the only notable philosopher of pure Arabian blood and the first
one in Islam. In 1962 Baghdad held a millenary anniversary of its

philosopher to which it invited participants from four continents.

In al-Nadim's judgment, al-Kindi "was the most learned of his age, unique among his contemporaries in the knowledge of the totality of ancient sciences, embracing logic, philosophy, geometry, mathematics, music and astrology." Subsequent Arab biographers, including those who specialized in physicians and philosophers, from the Spanish Sa'id (d. 1070) to the Egyptian Qifti (d. 1248) and the Syrian ibn-abi-Usaybi'ah (d. 1270), had but little to add about his domestic life. None mentions his dates of birth or death, the names of his shaykhs, his mother, wife or wives and of his children, one son excepted. His aristocratic ancestry and voluminous output occupied their attention.

Ya'qub received his early education in Kufah and Basrah. Founded under the second caliph as military camps and depots for the army, these sister cities developed into brilliant depots of learning, vying with each other for supremacy. Basrah was the birthplace of Hasan al-Basri and al-Ash'ari, founders of orthodox theology; it also cradled those early champions of reasonable creed styled Mu'tazilites. Al-Kindi's early introduction to Mu'tazilite doctrine made him receptive to what was in store for him. Kufah was the home of celebrated traditionists. The two cities contributed to the rise of the science of philology that still holds sway wherever Arabic is taught.

From there the young man was graduated to the greatest intellectual center of Islam and one of the greatest in the world, Baghdad. He was attracted to al-Ma'mun's court, serving in varied capacities and enjoying—in common with a galaxy of intellectuals—caliphal patronage. This was indeed a golden opportunity, and we can be sure he took full advantage of it, pursuing his studies independently and specializing in Greek philosophy and science. Accessible to him were Hunayn ibn-Ishaq's fresh translations headed by Aristotle's *Metaphysics* (*Ma wara' al-Tabi'ah*) and the so-called Aristotle's theology (*rububiyah*), the work of an unknown Neo-Platonist commented upon by Porphyry and translated for al-Kindi's special use by a Christian from Hims, 'Abd-al-Masih ibn-Na'imah. The budding Arab philosopher adapted the pseudo-Aristotelian work for the needs of his pupil Ahmad, son of Caliph al-Mu'tasim (al-Ma'mun's brother-successor in 833). These were the two books which more than any other ones left their deep imprint on Arab philosophy. By this time evidently al-Kindi had become an influential figure in the 'Abbasid court, a consultant as well as a tutor.

The list of works written by or ascribed to this author is one of the most impressive in Arabic—perhaps all—literature. Al-Nadim cites 231 titles. A modern researcher lists 361, of which 27 are philosophical, 22 psychological, 22 medical and the rest are grouped into mathematics, optics, music, astronomy, astrology, geography, logic, physical science, politics, polemics and miscellaneous (perfume, swords, minerals, mirrors, watches). A number of these are essays of one or two pages each; several are duplicates with varying titles; many are spurious; most are lost. Ironically, Latin has preserved more than the original Arabic.

An early biographer, al-Qifti, credits al-Kindi with a translation of Ptolemy's geography from Syriac. Ibn-abi-Usaybi'ah and others include him among the expert translators. That he knew enough Greek or Syriac to undertake a translation is doubtful. The Christian translators studied Greek mostly in Asia Minor and Syriac in monasteries, both sources not readily accessible to a Moslem. What al-Kindi did was probably to edit and revise, re-Arabicizing translations by Syrian Christians.

III

In introducing his treatise *Risalah fi al-Falsafah al-Ula* (epistle on the first philosophy) to his caliphal patron al-Mu'tasim, our philosopher writes:

> The noblest in quality and highest in rank of all human activities is philosophy. Philosophy is defined as knowledge of things as they are in reality, insofar as man's ability determines. The philosopher's aim in his theoretical studies is to ascertain the truth, in his practical knowledge to conduct himself in accordance with that truth.[1]

[1] Muhammad 'Abd-al-Hadi abu-Ridah, *Rasa'il al-Kindi al-Falsafiyah*, vol. I (Cairo, 1950), p. 97. This work in two volumes is the most complete study of the life and philosophy of al-Kindi. For a general study of Arab philosophy M. M. Sharif, ed., *A History of Muslim Philosophy*, vol. I (Wiesbaden, 1963) (with articles on al-Kindi, ibn-Sina and ibn-Rushd) is recommended.

The Platonic overtone of the above definition is evident. So is the following assertion that truth as ascertained by philosophy is universal and supreme, transcending nationality and denomination. In anticipation of his readers' reaction to advocacy of foreign ideas, he continues:

> We should never be ashamed to approve truth and acquire it no matter what its source might be, even if it might have come from foreign peoples and alien nations far removed from us. To him who seeks truth no other object is higher in value. Neither should truth be underrated, nor its exponent belittled. For indeed truth abases none and ennobles all.[1]

In another place al-Kindi warns the would-be philosopher:

> For a seeker of learning aspiring to be a philosopher six prerequisites are essential: a superior mind, uninterrupted passion, gracious patience, a free-from-worry heart, a competent introducer and a long, long time. Should one of these prerequisites be lacking, the student is bound to fail.

By his characterization and definition of philosophy al-Kindi committed himself to the perilous theory that philosophy was superior to theology with its cognate sciences of jurisprudence and ethics, a theory unacceptable to spokesman of orthodox Islam. He argued that theology was a branch of philosophy; one depends on revelation, the other on reason; one employs logic, the other faith, but the truth attained by theology is not in conflict with that attained by philosophy. He further argued that the truth revealed through the prophet is in accord with the truth as attained by the philosopher. He insisted that theologians should use logic, philosophy's tool, in their argumentation. But all that was an exercise in futility. To the exponents of Islam, Mu'tazilite views plus philosophic views made Kindite doctrine doubly atheistic (*kufr*).

But, eager to keep both feet within the fold of Islam, the young philosopher modified his position. In his contribution on Aristotle's works (*Kammiyat Kutub Aristutalis*), he admits that di-

[1] Abu-Ridah, vol. I, p. 103.

vine science (*al-'ilm al-ilahi*) is superior to human science, but insists there is no contradiction between the conclusions of the two. Clearly prophetic knowledge is spontaneous and stems from inspiration, requiring no effort and no research. It is in a class by itself. In contrast, philosophic knowledge is acquired the hard way, open to demonstration and expressed through logic. Prophethood is the prerogative of the rare; it is the perfect faculty. Philosophy is open to all. Nevertheless, al-Kindi insisted, knowledge produced by the true prophet is identical with that produced by the competent philosopher. This makes koranic arguments in such cases as the creation of the world from nothing and the resurrection of the dead more certain than the philosophic. Here the koranic conclusions are acceptable—by faith.

Islamic revelation is specific on this double creation-resurrection problem. In surah 36:78–79 God instructs Muhammad to answer skeptics who rhetorically ask, "Who will give life to bones that have been reduced to dust?" by, "He who originally produced them will give life to them." The Koran goes on to explain: "All that He needs to do, when He wishes a thing, is to say to it 'Be' and it is" (36:82). On this al-Kindi comments that God as creator is an originator (*mubdi'*). He needs no matter and no time. Man needs both. God does it by His creative will and absolute power, of both of which man is deprived. As for the objection as to how God could address something nonexistent, al-Kindi meets it with a novel explanation, the allegorical use of "Be," a device he developed in another context.

In the epistle addressed to his pupil Ahmad ibn-al-Mu'tasim the teacher answers a question raised by a puzzled student. It relates to surah 55 verse 6: "The stars and the trees offer worship (cf. 22:18, where we are told the sun, the moon, the stars, the mountains, the trees and the beasts offer worship). Our exegete takes pains to offer an intellectually satisfying interpretation. The verb *yasjud* in this case simply means that all these objects, inanimate and animate, follow in their growth, development and movements laws established by God. They obey, rather than prostrate themselves or worship. Herein the Moslem philosopher took a radical step, the full significance of which he may not have appreciated. He opened the way for allegorical interpretation of scriptural material. This was pursued by later philosophers, becoming a major contribution to Islamic thought. The device has become a main resort of modern reformers. From figurative to esoteric interpretation the step was not hard to take and was taken by ultra-Shi'ites.

In committing himself to the koranic doctrine of creation from nothing (*ex nihilo*), al-Kindi deviated from the Aristotelian view but was not followed by his successors. Both ibn-Sina and ibn-Rushd adopted a modified Aristotelian doctrine and won the condemnation of their coreligionists.

From the premise that matter is finite al-Kindi proceeds to argue philosophically to establish the existence of God. Being finite, matter is neither self-creating nor self-perpetuating. It requires an infinite to bring it into existence. That infinite is God. Not only is God the creator, the originator, but He is the sustainer. Anything not sustained by Him is no more. Natural laws are the courses set by God for the operation of the material world. The series of causes in operation are finite in time and place. He is eternal (*qadim*). He is the prime cause, the true cause, the cause of causes. He acts but is not acted upon, sees but is not seen, causes movement but does not move.

The regularity, this author further argues, with which celestial bodies, human beings, other animate and inanimate objects conduct themselves, the hierarchical arrangement of their parts, the consistency with which all perform their functions, provide another proof of God's existence. The systematic behavior of heavenly and earthly bodies did not, of course, escape the attention of Greek philosophers beginning with Socrates, as indicated by their use of the term *kosmos* (order, harmony), but its attribution to an outside, unified, ethical, all-embracing force was nowhere developed.

The Kindite view of the soul is more Platonic than Aristotelian. Strictly it is Neo-Platonic as worked out by Plotinus in the *Enneads* and wrongly ascribed to Aristotle. The soul is not a body, it is a simple entity emanating from God in the same way as rays emanate from the sun. In substance, therefore, it is spiritual, in origin divine. Insofar as it is limited to the human it is in transit on earth but governed by celestial spheres. Its nobility of character sets it apart from the body with its passions. As it separates from the body it returns whence it came, the Divine light, and gains vision of the supernatural. This Kindite doctrine of duality is reminiscent of the Pauline. Clearly the Arab philosopher has nothing to contribute on this subject. His treatise *Fi al-Nafs* (on the soul) closes thus:

> O you, foolish man, don't you realize that your sojourn here on earth is but for a glance, after which you return to the real world, the world in which you stay for ever and ever? Verily you are nothing but a passer-by, following the will of your Creator—the mighty, the majestic.[1]

On the subject of intellect, usually discussed together with the soul, al-Kindi the scientist does not seem clear. He is confused among Aristotle, Plato and Plotinus. Aristotle distinguishes between two intellects, one potential which receives and is perishable, and the other active which produces and is eternal. The active agent has a distinct metaphysical entity, is and remains incorruptible. It serves as the intermediary between the spiritual world and the human mind. Some Moslem writers recognized in this intellect the spirit of holiness, in other words, Gabriel, the carrier of the revelation.

Al-Kindi holds a four-fold concept of intellect (*al-'aql*). In his opuscule on this subject he stresses the distinction between one intellect which simply acquires knowledge and another which practices it. The one, he explains, is similar to him who learns handwriting and possesses it as an art, and the other to him who actually practices the art. In another connection he teaches that freedom and immortality exist only where intelligence exists. By intelligence, knowledge of God and good works, man attains the highest possible good for himself.

To al-Kindi, as to others of his kind and age, philosophy was the mother of science. In his amplified definition of philosophy he makes it the ascertaining of the reality of things in their being and their becoming. Traces of this medieval concept are noticeable in the wording of doctorates of philosophy bestowed by our universities in the physical and social sciences as well as in the humanities.

---

[1] Abu-Ridah, vol. I, pp. 279–80.

Professionally this philosopher was a physician. Philosophy and medicine, we learned, went together; the same title (*hakim*) was used for both practitioners. Al-Kindi served as court physician to the caliphs under whom he flourished but, judging by an anecdote in al-Qifti, his private practice was limited. He must have felt more at home with books than with patients. A wealthy merchant neighbor had a paralyzed son, whom no physician in Baghdad could cure. Finally he learned to his surprise that his distinguished neighbor was as brilliant a physician as he was a philosopher. Al-Kindi responded to the request and cured the boy by the use of music.

In what has survived of the thirty-six medical essays authored by him, not much could be called original, unless it be a curious attempt to establish dosology on a mathematical basis. A modern researcher has discovered in his opuscule dealing with compound drugs an embryonic concept of psychophysics. In chemistry we know of two treatises on the production and use of perfume, in particular rose water (*'itr*, attar), and two other treatises criticizing alchemists for deceptive claims and for vain attempts to convert base into precious metal. It should be acknowledged here that al-Kindi the scientist, like al-Kindi the philosopher, conceived of his mission as that of a transmitter, transmitter of the "learning of the ancients." In addition to preservation his contribution lay in the field of presentation. This involved paraphrasing the original and making it comprehensible and adaptable to specifically student needs. He devotes an opuscule to definitions of a hundred technical terms in philosophy and science; it is a work that may be considered the earliest technical dictionary in Arabic. His advice to the would-be-physician is concise as well as meaningful:

> Let him who plans to practice the art of healing fear God the most high, and take no risks, bearing in mind that for health there is no substitute. To the extent to which he likes to be mentioned as the restorer of a patient's health, he should guard against being cited as its destroyer and the cause of his death. The physician who is not wise (*hakim*) is himself ill.

It is to the credit of this scientist that he was the first writer in Arabic to give a comprehensive and systematic classification of the sciences, a subject that had not escaped earlier Alexandrian scholars. He recognized two categories; philosophical and theological. Under philosophical he listed mathematics, physics, metaphysics, politics and logic.

Next to medicine, mathematics had perhaps the greatest claim on the philosopher-physician's interest. He penned fourteen works on this subject, most of which did not survive. Four treat the Hindi numerals and their use. One book he divides into five chapters "corresponding to the five material elements in nature, five fingers of the hand, five planets, five circles of latitude and five types of voice pitch." Obviously he shared the Neo-Pythagorean view that numbers existed before the objects numbered and possessed some exotic, mysterious value beyond their mathematical one. His undue regard for mathematics made him give it priority in learning over not only physical but philosophical sciences.

Closely allied to mathematical was astronomical science, in which forty-four titles are ascribed to him. In those extant the Ptolemaic system, as expounded in *Almagest,* is apparent. In the astronomy-astrology field al-Kindi was not as critical as in the chemistry-alchemy field. He acknowledged astral influences over human affairs without, however, compromising God's almightiness. Several of these works were early translated into Latin, establishing his reputation in the West. Many Western Europeans came to know him as an astrologer.

Another science which spread Alkindus' name in Europe was that dealing with light and vision, optics (*al-manazir*). Here the author based his work on Ptolemy's *Harmonics* and two books attributed to Euclid, all three available in Arabic. According to him light takes no time to travel, and vision is achieved through rays sent from the eyes to the object. In the other four senses the organs receive the impressions. The blue color of the sky is explained in a special essay as a result of the admixture of the light of dust and vapor in the air—illuminated by the sun—with the darkness of the sky. His works translated into Latin introduced the science of optics into Europe. The celebrated English philosopher-scientist Roger Bacon (d. 1294) and the Polish physicist-mathematician Witelo (Erasmo Ciolek, d. 1285), among others, benefited by them. His works in this field were superseded by those of another scholar, al-Hasan (L. Alhazen) ibn-al-Haytham (d. *ca.* 1039 in Cairo), the greatest physicist in Islam and one of the greatest optic students of all times. Ibn-al-Haytham excelled his predecessor in originality and critical approach. In an unedited critique of Ptolemy, ibn-al-Haytham insists that "truth should be sought for its own sake, and he who pursues something for its own sake has only one concern: finding it." He goes on to say that God did not make scientists immune against error and that knowledge of the truth can be gained only by severe criticism of others' views, by guarding against one's prejudices and by remembering that there is no such thing as truth in a pure and manifest form that can be readily recognized.

In all the sciences treated above—optics excepted—al-Kindi had no predecessor. In one major field, music, he was his own predecessor. Arab bibliographers cite early titles on song (*ghina'*) originating in Arabia and influenced by Persian models, but hardly any survived and presumably none could be compared in scientific treatment and comprehensive presentation with al-Kindi's. He had, of course, Greek-writing predecessors, Neo-Pythagorean as well as Neo-Platonic, from whom he benefited. His contribution consisted primarily in transmitting. Transmission entails preservation and involves presentation. In presentation al-Kindi had the specific needs of the learner in mind. On the originality side he was not entirely lacking. He added a theoretical fifth string to the lute (from Ar. *al-'ud*) and thereby reached the double octave without resorting to the shift. The scale he used is still in vogue. By using alphabetic notation for one octave he made advance on the Greek method. Fifteen treatises on this newly found treasure of the ancients appeared under his name. Only five survive. In one, the word *musiqi* (now *musiqa*) is used for perhaps for the first time in a title. The treatment comprises composition (*ta'lif*), melody (*lahn*), rhythm (*iqa'*) and related subjects.

Al-Kindi the musician, like al-Kindi the philosopher, opened the way for the two scholars who excelled him: al-Farabi and ibn-Sina. Al-Farabi devoted three major works to this subject, which placed him highest among Moslem music theorists.[1]

[1] On al-Kindi as a scientist consult Ahmad F. al-Ahwani, *Al-Kindi: Faylasuf al-'Arab* (Cairo, 1962?).

Our author was fortunate in having had early and competent translators. His multi-faceted reservoir of learning gave him an unusually wide reading audience. Mid-twelfth century Spain was the scene of the height of the translators' activity, but the personnel was cosmopolitan. Toledo after the Christian reconquest (1085) remained a center of Islamic learning and became a main channel for transmitting the treasures of Arab erudition. Through the initiative of Archbishop Raymond of the city (1126–1152), a school of translators flourished and attracted interested scholars from the continent as well as the British Isles. Toledo continued its work in this field for more than a century. In 1250 it was chosen as the site of a school of Oriental studies— the first of its kind in Europe—founded by the Order of Preachers for training missionaries to Islam and Judaism.

A pioneer translator in Toledo was the English mathematician and astronomer Robert of Chester, who labored from 1141 to 1147 and became known for the first rendition into Latin of the Koran. From al-Kindi he chose parts of *Ahkam al-Nujum* (principles of astrology, *De judiciis astrologicis*). Four treatises on this subject were done by John of Seville (d. 1157, Hispalensis), a Mozarab Christian whose works are confused with those of a baptized Jew bearing the same name. Another Spanish translator, Arnold of Villanova (d. 1260), was a physician who studied the Arabic language under Moslem colleagues in Valencia, his birthplace. He was responsible for doing *Fi Ma'rifat Quwa al-Adwiyah al-Murakkabah* (on the knowledge of the efficacy of compound drugs).

But the greatest translator in this series was an Italian, Gerard of Cremona. Gerard spent most of his working days in Toledo but finally returned to his native city, where he died in 1187. Of al-Kindi's works he chose three: *Fi Mahiyat al-Nawm w-al-Ru'ya*, (on the nature of sleep and dreams, *De somo et visione*), *Fi al-'Aql* (*De intellectu*), and *Fi al-'Anasir al-Khamsah* (the five essences of substances, *De quinque essentiis*).

Other than Latin, Hebrew was a recipient of Kindite works. By way of illustration, mention may be made of the opuscules on *al-Mawalid (nativities)* and on *al-Matar* (rain) by a Frenchman, Kalonymus Ben Kalonymus.

Not long after the invention of printing from movable type (*ca.* 1440) al-Kindi's Latin works found publishers, thus spreading and continuing their effectiveness. One of the first was published in Venice in 1507, to be followed by others in Strassburg (1531), Nuremberg (1548) and other cities. The intellectual avenue leading from the portals of Toledo crossed the mountains into France and central Europe as well as into the British Isles. The first book printed in England, *The Dictes and Sayengis of the Philosophres* (by William Caxton, Westminster, 1477), was based on *Mukhtasar al-Hikam wa-Mahsin al-Kalim* by Mubashshir ibn-Fatik (d. 1053), a collection of aphorisms and wise sayings including several from the writings of al-Kindi. The wisdom al-Kindi advocated accented quest of virtue, guidance by intellect, satisfaction with abstinence, patience, and acceptance of suffering and death as unescapable concomitants of our humanity. The sixteenth-century Italian physician and mathematician Geronimo Cardono counted Alkindus among the twelve great minds of history. More recently Western scholars have revised old editions and made new ones of his works.

IV

As might be expected what we know about this Moslem's family life does not satisfy our curiosity. In vain we search available sources for information. A passing reference to a son in connection with the will he left gives him the name borne by almost every Moslem, Muhammad.

Anecdotes sprinkled over Arabic literary works give us an insight into the behavior and personality of the man. With the accession of al-Mutawakkil and the reaction against the unorthodoxy initiated by al-Ma'mun—with which al-Kindi was identified —the courtier lost caliphal patronage. A report was spread that the discipleship of Ahmad, son of al-Mu'tasim, imbued the young prince with Mu'tazilite doctrine and militated against his succession to the caliphate. To make matters worse al-Kindi found himself the victim of a plot concocted by two jealous competitors, Ahmad and Muhammad, sons of Musa ibn-Shakir. By the caliph's order, the sixty-year-old man was given fifty lashes, and the two brothers confiscated his most precious possession, his library, known all over Baghdad by the name al-Kindiyah. This must have crushed the spirit of the scholar, but not for long. A friend came to his rescue; appointed by al-Mutawakkil to investigate the functional failure of a canal dug from the Tigris by the Shakirs at a great expense to the caliph, the inspector threatened to expose the two brothers unless they returned his friend's books to their rightful owner. The men knew that in case of an adverse report by the inspector, crucifixion on the river's banks awaited them. But from al-Kindi's humiliation as a man subjected to corporal punishment there could be no rescue.

With the courtier's loss of caliphal favor went loss of popular prestige, leading to a life of seclusion in a state of morose sulkiness. Certain features of his character must have contributed to his alienation from society. One of them was intellectual arrogance. Once, we are told, he entered al-Ma'mun's salon and took his seat above a theologian. "How dare you," protested the man, "occupy a seat above me, I an imam?" "Because," shot back the philosopher, "I know what you know, and you don't know what I know." In his writings he did not spare religious leaders who did not accept his philosophical views, calling them ignorant, bigoted, narrow-minded and merchants of religious commodities.

More serious perhaps was the charge of niggardliness repeatedly leveled against him by friend and foe. In characterizing him al-Nadim singles out this one trait. But his worst enemy was a contemporary, al-Jahiz. In his book *al-Bukhala'* (the misers), this renowned belletrist gave him a place of honor. In the scale of Arab values niggardliness and avarice occupy as low a place as generosity and hospitality occupy a high one. Al-Jahiz related that as a friend of the philosopher was dining with him, a neighbor dropped in and the host would not invite him to participate in the meal. "I felt," concluded the narrator "so ashamed of this man, the stingiest God ever made." Other reports cite al-Kindi's will, addressed to his son:

> Remember, O my son, the father is a master, the brother is a trapper, the uncle a carbuncle and the relatives venomous scorpions. "No" to a seeker entails no harm to you; "yes" reduces the enjoyment that is due. . . . The dinar is in a feverish state;

once you change it, you lose it in haste. The dirham is a prisoner; once out of the cell, never back again, never.[1]

The Arabic reads like a play on words (*al-ab rabb; al-akh fakhkh, al-'amm ghamm* and so forth) for pun and fun, not for edification. If a man of al-Kindi's caliber did write it, he must have been in his second childhood.

The date and cause of the unhappy man's death are not certain. The probable date is 873, at age 72. According to an unconfirmed report he met death by fire of undetermined origin. But a contemporaneous fellow astrologer, abu-Ma'shar (Lat. Abulmasar), who benefited by al-Kindi's works, plagiarized two of them and became the most frequently cited authority in medieval Europe, offers a more detailed explanation. The cause was a knee ailment which he treated by drinking old wine, but when he substituted honey the condition worsened, the pain became intolerable, spread to the brain and killed him.

Ya'qub ibn-Ishaq al-Kindi, pioneer in Arab philosophy, encyclopedic in knowledge, prolific in authorship, made Greek learning an integral part of Islamic tradition, blazed the way for harmonizing philosophy and theology and provided Greek thought with a permanent home in Arab culture.

[1] Ibn-abi-Usaybi'ah, *'Uyun al-Anba' fi Tabaqat al-Atibba'*, ed. August Müller (Cairo, 1882), vol. I, p. 209.

Ibn-Sina: Prince of Physicians and Philosophers

> *Thus I continued until I had mastered the totality of sciences. My comprehension of them then [at age eighteen] attained the limits of human possibility. All that I learned during that period is precisely what I know now.*
>
> —Ibn-Sina

By the early eleventh century, where we are in this study, Arab sciences had been initiated, classified and developed. The line of demarcation was sharply drawn between the "sciences of religion" and the "sciences of the ancients *(awa'il),*" the ancients being mostly Greeks. In the first category hadith, theology and jurisprudence, together with their linguistic and philological auxiliaries, were included. The second featured philosophy, comprising logic, physics and metaphysics, mathematics and astronomy.

Being of alien origin the sciences of the ancients, as we learned, started with a negative. Any Moslems engaged in them became suspect. Moslem philosophers, therefore, beginning with al-Kindi, strained their efforts to domesticate philosophic thought in Arab culture and to build bridges between philosophy and theology. Mathematics, represented by Euclid's and Ptolemy's geometry, served as a pillar. Logic was another. Early Moslem theologians engaged in polemics with their Christian counterparts—already imbued with Greek philosophic thought and dialetics—gradually adopted the methods of Aristotelian logic. Thus arose the Mutakallims, cited before, whose distinguished exponent was al-Ash'ari of Basrah and Baghdad (d. 935). Even al-Ghazzali, author of the influential critique of philosophers, defended the use of logic in theology.

Medicine stood in a class by itself. It had its start in pre-Islamic Arabian folklore and was transmitted by word of mouth. In the conquered Fertile Crescent it entered a more sophisticated stage, that of the Syro-Persian, already affected by Greek medicine. The physicians of the Umayyads and of the first 'Abbasid caliphs were Christian Syrians. The translation of Galen under al-Ma'mun gave Moslems their first chance. This turned out to be a field in which they achieved excellence. It offered them an opportunity for original contributions of lasting value and for international fame.

At its inception as a science, medicine established and for centuries maintained close association with philosophy. Moslem philosophers from al-Kindi in Baghdad to ibn-Rushd in Cordova were almost all physicians. Caliphs and other chiefs of state appointed them as court physicians, tutors and political advisers. If any of them, however, ever made a significant contribution in this third field of activity, his biographer must have forgotten to mention it.

Ibn-Sina was in that tradition. Al-Kindi awakened his people's mind to Greek thought but cannot be said to have left a system of his own. Al-Razi (d. 925) was too radical to be effective. His belief centered in man, reason and God; religion, prophecy and theology were of no import. In the history of medicine al-Razi is undeniably the most original of Moslem physicians. His treatise on smallpox and measles gives the earliest clinical distinction between the two diseases and is considered a treasure of medical literature. Al-Farabi (d. 950) in his system attempted a syncretism of Aristotelianism and Platonism. But he was more politically minded. His distinctive contribution was *al-Madinah al-Fadilah* (the superior city), modeled after Plato's *Republic*. He also achieved a distinction in musical theory unattained by any other Moslem.

It was then left to the man under study to construct a compre-

hensive, well-integrated system of Arab philosophy. The intellectual activity initiated by al-Kindi and advanced by al-Razi and
al-Farabi culminated in him. Climbing on the shoulders of his
predesessors, he overtowered them. His works in both philosophy
and medicine outlived theirs. The success and effectiveness this
physician-philosopher achieved in both fields were unmatched by
any competitor. In him Arab philosophy and medicine reach their
apex.

I

Abu-'Ali al-Husayn ibn-Sina was born in a small village,
Afshanah, near Bukhara, capital of Transoxiana. His father was
commandant of a nearby citadel under the Samanid amir Nuh
ibn-Mansur. The dynasty owes its name to a convert from Zoroastrianism whose sons distinguished themselves in al-Ma'mun's service and were rewarded by provincial governorships. Under this
enlightened dynasty, of which one member patronized al-Razi,
Bukhara developed into an intellectual center. The ibn-Sina family with three sons moved to it, and there our young boy got his
education.

By the time al-Husayn was ten years old, he had read the
Koran and studied Arabic literature. He had also been initiated
into the Isma'ili cult by his father, a new convert of an Egyptian
propagandist. At the age of sixteen—if we can believe him—he
had mastered a number of sciences, studied medicine (which he
"found easy") by himself and began teaching and practicing it. A
grocer had introduced him to "Indian" mathematics. Meantime
he was delving into jurisprudence. An itinerant philosopher was
offered the hospitality of the house in return for teaching the lad
Porphyry's *Isagoge* (introduction [to logic]), Euclid's *Elements*
and Ptolemy's *Almagest*. The contract was of brief duration, the
student having discovered that he could independently solve geo-
metrical problems which the teacher could not. Clearly the boy
was precocious, and he knew it. Possessed of what amounted to a
passion for learning, he persisted in gratifying it by himself.

The fame of this scholar-physician, still in his teens, reached
the Amir Nuh who was suffering from a malady. Al-Husayn cured
him and was granted the privilege of using the royal library.

"There," in his own words, "I saw books whose very names were unknown to many and which I had never seen before and have not seen since." With voracious appetite he fell on its contents and in some eighteen months he devoured them. A photographic memory and unusual power of assimilation served him well. Later this repository of learning was reduced to ashes by fire. Wagging tongues suspected its long-time user of wanting to be unique in his knowledge of its contents—a common motif in such tales. But such a device was hardly necessary in this case. Ibn-Sina would have been unique under all conditions. Before the conflagration, the only copies of the first two books he, aged twenty-one, had authored were deposited in it.

In his autobiography—a rare genre in Arabic literature—communicated at the age of thirty-two to his faithful disciple and life-long companion abu-'Ubayd al-Juzjani and preserved in full or in part in the three major "who's who's" in learned Islam, ibn-Sina provides us with interesting details about his method of study:

> Whenever a perplexing problem confronted me or a middle term in a syllogism escaped me, I would repair to the mosque, there to pray and implore the All-Creator until the hidden was revealed and the difficult eased. Returning home I would at night set a lamp before me and engage in reading and writing. Whenever sleep or fatigue came near overcoming me, I would resort to wine and drink until my strength was fully recovered. Thereupon back to reading I would go. In case slumber did overtake me, I would go on in my sleep considering what I was considering before. In fact many a problem was thus solved.
>
> Thus I continued until I had mastered the totality of sciences. My comprehension of them then [at age eighteen] attained the limits of human possibility.
>
> All that I learned during that period is precisely what I know now.[1]

With at least one science the self-assured intellectual did not reckon. A copy of the *Metaphysics* ascribed to Aristotle fell into

[1] Al-Qifti, *Ta'rikh al-Hukama'*, ed. Julius Lippert (Leipzig, 1903), p. 415; cf. ibn-abi-Usaybi'ah, vol. II, p. 3; ibn-Khallikan, *Wafayat al-A'yan wa-Anba' Abna' al-Zaman* (Cairo, 1299), vol. I, p. 272.

his hands and floored him. Forty times he read the manuscript without making much of it. Fortunately, however, for him and for the world, he later yielded to the entreaties of a bookdealer and almost reluctantly purchased a copy of al-Farabi's work on metaphysics. This turned out to be a landmark in his career. It signaled the beginning of a new direction to his mental activity. Philosophy, particularly Neo-Platonism, now began to claim the greatest share of his interest. Soon a third factor intruded into his already crowded life: the political.

For years the area where he lived had been the battle ground for mastery between Iranians and Turanians. The Iranians, represented by the Samanids, were cultured with a proud tradition of autonomy, if not sovereignty, but their representatives' star was now on the wane. The Turanians, led by the Turkish Ghaznawids, were upstarts in culture and rule. In 999 their great sultan Mahmud completed the conquest of Transoxiana, including Bukhara. Strict in his orthodoxy, ruthless in his treatment of heterodoxy, and lacking in respect for learning and the learned, the new sultan was not exactly the kind of patron under whom ibn-Sina could flourish. Shortly after the loss of his patron, the young scholar lost his father.

This set him on a path, long and tortuous, punctuated with ups and downs—mostly downs—and landing him at last in a Buwayhid amir's court at distant Isabahan. The Buwayhids were Shi'ite Persians who claimed descent from the pre-Islamic kings of Persia and for years had ruled in Baghdad while the caliph reigned. From one princely court to another—a dozen in all—the wandering scholar shuttled almost restlessly and as if aimlessly. In Jurjan, he found his would-be patron already dead. He crossed the desert to Khurasan, losing on the way several of his companions. He was now (about 1015) in Persian Buwayhid territory. For a time he seemed happily established at al-Rayy (five miles from modern Teheran) in the court of a princess. This astute widow kept the reins of government in her hands even after her son came of age, and kept Sultan Mahmud at bay by reminding the mighty conqueror of the scorn he would earn by attacking a woman's principality. What function the scholarly guest performed, we are not told. Two or three years later "circumstances forced him to leave."

Other equally obscure circumstances took him to Hamadhan, where he entered the service of Shams-al-Dawlah (the sun of the state). Successful treatment of an attack of princely colic served as an introduction. The physician was soon made vizir, the highest office he had thus far held. When he left Bukhara he was dressed in the green robe and neck scarf of the canon lawyers, but now he wore the long vizirial robe with a short jacket and a turban of coarse cloth. No sooner did he assume the high duties than the army for some undisclosed reason rose against him and demanded his death. For forty days the physician-vizir hid in a friend's home. Another attack of colic on the amir served this time to release him from his voluntary prison. Again he was appointed vizir in a special ceremony.

On the death of Shams-al-Dawlah, it was discovered that ibn-Sina had entered into secret correspondence with 'Ala'-al-Dawlah, amir of Isbahan. After four months' imprisonment in a fortress he was released. Disguised as a Sufi, he slipped out of the town with two slaves, his brother (who must have been in his company all along) and al-Juzjani. At the court of 'Ala'-al-Dawlah he was received (about 1023) with due ceremonial and lodged in a sumptuously furnished house. Here he apparently held no official position but dedicated himself to study and writing. Friday evenings were devoted to "seminars" under the princely patronage for discussing any scientific and philosophic questions raised. The intellectual was followed by a social feast, featuring wine and dancing girls. Isbahan turned out to be a haven of peace and an arena of scholarly productivity for the tired, unhappy shaykh.

Indeed he had not been intellectually inactive. In Jurjan he completed several treatises and began writing his great *al-Qanun* (the canon). While at al-Rayy he composed *al-Mabda' w-al-Ma'ad* (the beginning and return). At Hamadhan he completed *al-Qanun*, began work on his *Kitab al-Shifa'* (book of healing), and while in prison he wrote a book on colic and another titled *Hayy ibn-Yaqzan* (the living, son of the vigilant). And now in Isbahan he finished *al-Shifa'*, abridged it in *al-Najah* (deliverance), revised *al-Qanun*, and wrote a commentary on *Almagest*. Some of his writing is said to have been done when on horseback accompanying his campaigning patron. That he was able to produce what he did under such hardships of travel, including illness, flight and imprisonment, seems incredible.

Why that turbulent activity in the pre-Isbahan period, neither the master nor his confidant al-Jujzani, who continued the life story as a biographer, discloses. At times we notice al-Jujzani urging the master to write. Presumably the philosopher was trying to play a role for which he was not cast. It can also be assumed he did not get along with people. Behind that must have been some personality difficulties. Noticeably, ibn-Sina was an intellectually arrogant man, disdainful of mediocrity and jealous of superiority. He must in turn have been the subject of jealousy on the part of inferior confreres. In his disputes he was merciless in vilification. Al-Razi—who was his superior in originality—should in his opinion have stuck to "testing stools and urines."

Other professional detractors of ibn-Sina were fundamentalists charging him with heretical teachings. He gave them further ground for criticism by his unconventional conduct, which did not endear him to the ordinary Moslem. His image in folklore is—like al-Kindi's—that of a sorcerer. A lonesome bachelor, he sought solace in wine, women and food. Wine which once served him, then mastered him. His justification of its use involved a novel exegesis on the koranic text: "By religious opinion wine is illegal for the fool; by intellectual opinion it is legal for the intelligent." To women he was evidently as attractive as they were to him. How many concubines his harem comprised we cannot tell. Friends advising moderation received the same curt reply: "I prefer a short life with width to a narrow one with length."

A Persian anecdote confirms a character trait cited above, adding an assurance that the man was not entirely devoid of good sense. At the dawn of a cold day in Hamadhan he asked a pupil to fetch him a drink of water. The student demurred. Cold water at such an hour is bad for veins and nerves. The master rebuked him, reminding him that he was the greatest physician of the age. Then he went on to tell him why he did not claim prophethood as urged on him by this young man among others. "Four hundred years after the Prophet's death we obey his commands; while you, the closest to me, disobey my order for a drink. How then can I pose for a prophet?"

The student circle of the teacher-philosopher extended so widely as to include some in absentia. All queries were answered by him promptly and in person. A group of scholars from Shiraz in southwestern Persia took exception to something in his *al-Mukhtasar al-Asghar* (the minor epitome [of logic]), which he had written at Jurjan and later incorporated in *al-Najah,* and sent him their comments. The messenger arrived about sunset on a summer day. Calling for writing—and with it drinking—material, the master started to answer. His brother and al-Juzjani joined the drinking bout. About midnight the two got tipsy and were ordered to bed. Morning came and he was ready to hand the messenger a fifty-sheet reply. He did not want to delay him unnecessarily.

The pleasant routine of intellectual pursuit was at times interrupted by military affairs. The autonomous Buwayhid princes were frequently at each other's necks, while all of them were under threat from the rising Ghaznawid dynasty. In or about 1030 Sultan Mahmud dispatched his son against Isbahan. Ibn-Sina accompanied 'Ala'-al-Dawlah in evacuating the city for a time, and returned to find his library plundered and some of his books carried off to Ghaznah. Among them was his manuscript *al-Insaf* (equitable judgment), in which he proposed to arbitrate conflicting philosophical views. To avert another Ghaznawid attack, his patron headed his troops to meet the enemy and ibn-Sina, fearing the prospects of falling into hostile hands in case of defeat, joined the amir. He was then suffering from a severe attack of colic (*qulanj*) and injected himself eight times in one day. His condition took a turn for the worse and symptoms of epilepsy manifested themselves. This he treated with *mithradatum* while continuing the injections with the addition of celery seed. The seed aggravated the abrasions. Taking advantage of his weakened condition, his slaves, having stolen some of his money and fearing exposure, threw in opium with the injection. He had a narrow escape.

On another occasion 'Ala'-al-Dawlah undertook a military campaign to Hamadhan—of unhappy memories to ibn-Sina, but he felt it his professional duty to accompany the amir. A relapse set in and he felt his strength ebbing fast. He gave up all treatment with the remark, "He who has been managing me can no more do so. Nothing will avail." But his intimate biographer had another explanation. "The master was powerful in all his faculties. Of his passions that of sexuality was the most powerful, the most prevalent. In it he indulged to such an extent that it undermined his constitution." [1]

The end came in June or July of 1037, at the age of fifty-seven, and the burial was outside of Hamadhan.

II

Three stages roughly mark the intellectual development of our scientist-physician-philosopher. The first, covering his teens, was the one in which he mastered the sciences current among his people, beginning with the Koran and ending with medicine. The second, during his twenties, was that in which he gained possession of Greek sciences, starting with the alleged Aristotelian metaphysics as illuminated by al-Farabi and continuing through Aristotle, Plato and Plotinus. In his thirties he started on his own, theorizing, experimenting, criticizing, researching and finally constructing a comprehensive integrated system which could be called Sinaic. Even the old passing through his genius looked new. His system involved God, man and the universe independently and in their interrelationship. Meanwhile he was doing the same with the medical sciences and with the same result. Both of his systems dominated the East and were studied and utilized for centuries in the West.

Three encyclopedic works were authored by him, two in philosophy strangely entitled *al-Shifa'* (healing) and *al-Isharat w-al-Tanbihat* (directives and remarks), and one in medicine, *al-Qanun* (canon). All three are masterpieces. A third major work in philosophy, *al-Najah* (deliverance), is an abridgment of the first. *Al-Shifa'*, written at the urging of his devoted disciple, is the longest he wrote (6 volumes, Cairo, 1952–1965). In fact it is perhaps the longest book of its kind ever written by one man. It consists of four major books in logic, physics, mathematics and metaphysics. Each book is divided into sections subdivided into essays and chapters.

[1] Al-Qifti, p. 425; ibn-abi-Usaybi'ah, vol. II, p. 8.

This philosopher was primarily of the speculative type. His special interest lay in Aristotle's metaphysics and Plato's ideas, as reformulated by Hellenic scholars, and in their application to the tenets and practices of the religion he professed. The study of being (ontology) is central in Aristotle's metaphysics and so it is in ibn-Sina's theology (*ilahiyat*). To him God is pure being. He is supreme being. In Him being and existence are identical. He is the only necessary being. Self-subsistent, He causes but is not caused. In all this He is unique. He is antecedent to the universe, its originator, its creator, and is transcendent to it. His attributes of power and knowledge stem from His unchanging being. Clearly this Sinaic God is different from the Aristotelian deity (known as First Cause or Prime Mover) who neither created the world nor cares for it. It is the Semitic God reformulated in Greek philosophical concepts and identical with the Christian and Judaic scholastic God.

Following is a sample of his style in reasoning:

> Every series arranged in the order of causes and effects—whether finite or infinite—if it includes only what is caused, clearly needs an external cause linked to it at one end of the series. It is equally clear that if the series does not include anything uncaused, this is the end of the series, its limit. Every series therefore ends at the Being, which is necessary by itself.[1]

Other than God all things are of a dual nature. They are all possible—not necessary—beings, contingent in themselves and dependent upon God. Man consists of two substances: body and soul. This Platonic doctrine, accepted by him as well as Christian scholastics, satisfied their ethical and religious needs. Man's soul is a substance in itself, independent of the body but in need of the body to act. It is a part of the universal soul in the second emanation from God, the first being intellect, and the third matter. The soul then existed before the body and is more real than it. It is immaterial, incorruptible and immortal. (Aristotle denied its immortality.) The passing of the soul at death into another body is ruled out. There is more than one kind of mind.

---

[1] *Al-Isharat w-al-Tanbihat*, ed. Sulayman Dunya, parts 3-4 (Cairo 1958), p. 455.

The active mind's influence over the body is manifest in the movements of man and in his emotional reactions.

This psychological soul-body relationship is dramatically brought out in the best known poem of those composed by ibn-Sina. This poem, with its thesis that the human soul is a ray of Divine light, imprisoned in the darkness of the body and yearning for release to return to the source whence it came, is still memorized by Arab school children.

> Out of her lofty home she hath come down
> Upon thee, this white dove in all the pride
> Of her reluctant beauty; veiled is she
> From every eye eager to know her, though
> In loveliness unshrouded radiant. . . .
> Why then was she cast down from her high peak
> To this degrading depth God brought her low,
> But for a purpose wise, that is concealed
> E'en from the keenest mind and liveliest wit.
> And if the tangled mesh impeded her,
> The narrow cage denied her wings to soar
> Freely in heaven's high ranges, after all
> She was a lightning-flash that brightly glowed
> Momently o'er the tents, and then was hid
> As though in gleam was never glimpsed below.[1]

Prophethood, a fundamental doctrine in Islam, exercised all Moslem philosophic minds. As an institution it developed dimensions in this religion unparalleled before or since. The Greek concept of it was nebulous and remained uninstitutionalized. The Hebrews had prophets and designated them by the same Semitic word, but none of the Old Testament prophets attained the stature of Muhammad in the Koran. His prophethood was a koranic dogma second only to that of the oneness of God.

No Moslem philosopher—al-Razi excepted—ever challenged a koranic dogma. Their quarrels were with theological beliefs. Ibn-Sina not only acknowledged the validity of prophethood but argued to establish its necessity. Following al-Kindi, he held that this state represents the highest, the perfection of man's faculties.

---

[1] Arthur J. Arberry, *Avicenna on Theology* (London, 1951), pp. 78–79. Reprinted courtesy of John Murray, Ltd., London.)

The genuine prophet is endowed with superior intelligence, extraordinary intuition, vivid imagination and, equally important, ability to command respect and obedience. He receives his knowledge suddenly and directly, without benefit of human instruction. His contact with the ultimate reality is through Gabriel. His office is a necessity so long as men differ in their intellectual faculties both qualitatively and quantitatively.

The prophet's function is to communicate revelation. But in order to make his message comprehensible and acceptable to the masses he uses symbols, parables and metaphors, which should be taken literally by them. But the elite are not bound thereby. The pleasures of the afterlife, for instance, are spiritual; they pertain to the soul. Punishment and reward are not for the body (thus denying himself in heaven the continuation of what he indulged in on earth). The body does not share in immortality. Bodily resurrection cannot be sustained by reason. Besides, the world is eternal, has no end, and the resurrection view implies the contrary. The eternity of the world is implicit in the Sinaic theory of creation as a process of emanation (*fayd*) from God. It differs from the Aristotelian and materialistic view of the world as existing eternally with no God. In composing his books ibn-Sina kept in mind the needs of the common people and the needs of the intellectual. *Al-Shifa'* and *al-Najah* were written for the public, but *al-Isharat* for his disciples. *Hikmat al-Mashriqiyin* and *Hayy ibn-Yaqzan* belong to the esoteric category. In esotericism, we have seen, Isma'ilis were past masters. In an exoteric book he maintains that the resurrection of the body could be accepted by faith; in an esoteric one he rejects it categorically. His justification of wine-drinking comes to mind. Al-Ghazzali entertained this double-standard truth but made no such extensive use of it.

Other than prophethood the doctrine of predestination assumed unusual proportions in Islam. It involves problems relating to God's almightiness, man's free will and reward and punishment for deeds committed by him. But the doctrine is clearly koranic and deeply rooted in Islamic theology and society. Committed to the logical laws of cause and effect, ibn-Sina was bound to concede man's free will, with consequent responsibility, leaving to God the overall control of major forces. But the orthodox view held that predestination was a double operation: God's universal, general, eternal decree (*qada'*) and the individual application of that decree in time and place (*qadar*). Here then he earned his third condemnation, after the denial of bodily resurrection and the acceptance of the doctrine of the world's eternity.

Sufism, as an aspect of Islamic piety, interested ibn-Sina for personal as well as philosophical reasons. In his periods of frustration and depression he must have resorted to it for relief. It will be recalled, he once fled disguised in Sufi garb. Aside from its treatment in the last three chapters of *al-Isharat,* he devotes thirty-two titles to Sufism. In the *Isharat* he emphasizes the point that the highest form of happiness is more intellectual and spiritual than physical and that it cannot be attained by material means. Abstinence and asceticism are not enough. Man should seek intellectual illumination, available with the aid of angels as intermediaries with the celestial sphere. Behind this is clearly the Neo-Platonic theory of light and emanation and the Near Eastern theory of gnosis. Prayer is essential. In prayer man's soul seeks its perfection. Central in prayer is or should be contemplation, the contemplation of God with a view to joining Him and seeing Him spiritually, the vision of God being the ultimate goal.

Thus did ibn-Sina open the way for the philosophy of illumination (*hikmat al-ishraq*) inaugurated by his follower al-Suhrawadi who, at the age of thirty-six (it may be recalled), was ordered killed (1192) by Salah-al-Din.

This philosopher owes his fame more to medicine than philosophy. The medical works bearing his name number forty-three, the weightiest, longest and most enduring being *al-Qanun fi al-Tibb* (the canon of medicine). The first Arabic edition, printed in Rome (1593), is 883 pages, quarto, numbering about a million words. The book may be considered a systematization of the medical lore of the age, corresponding to *al-Shifa'* in philosophy. In it the author endeavored to synthesize the Hippocratic and Galenic traditions with the Indo-Persian and Syro-Arabic, adding his own experience and experimentation. Judged by its vogue in the East and the West the measure of success it achieved was unparalleled. It supplanted its predecessors and remained the authoritative work in the East until the twentieth century. It survived as a text in European medical schools till the seventeenth, and in one Latin American country till well in the nineteenth century. "It has remained," in the words of a historian of medicine, "a medical bible for a longer period than any other work." No small part of the credit for its success was due to its detailed classification, clear presentation, lucid style and comprehensive coverage.

The Latin version done by Gerard of Cremona (d. 1187) in Toledo, though in places it does not do justice to the original, went through many editions. The last third of the fifteenth century witnessed fifteen of them and one in Hebrew. By then the name of Avicenna (through Heb., Aven Sina) had become familiar throughout Europe's learned circles. For centuries thereafter the name was echoed and re-echoed from the cloisters of France to the colleges of central Asia. *Al-Qanun* recognizes the close relation between emotions and physiological conditions, considers posture in treating insomnia, and malaria in treating insanity. It emphasizes the importance of dietetics and the influence of climate on health. In surgery it makes use of oral anesthetic (such as medicated wine). The book also recognizes the contagious nature of phythisis and the spreading of disease by soil and water, distinguishes between mediastinitis and pleurisy and attributes ankylostomiasis to an intestinal worm. Its materia medica considers some seven hundred and sixty drugs and recommends the testing of a new drug by animal experiment.

A minor medical work draws its interest from its composition in verse. Using poetry for instructional purposes was an early device for facilitating retention. Ibn-Sina was the first to use it for medicine and logic. The meter (*rajaz*) is simple with easy rhyme and was a favorite of grammarians. One such *urjuzah,* composed by a Christian Lebanese, was still in use a few years ago. Ibn-Sina's medical *urjuzah,* in more than a thousand verses, was done into Latin early in the fourteenth century and published in Venice a century later. Its popularity was enhanced by ibn-Rushd's commentary on it.

As a philosopher this author had to cover all known sciences. His *al-Shifa'* has sections on physics, meteorology, zoology, botany, geology, psychology and mathematics. Unlike al-Kindi he rejects astrology, but like him he does accept the possibility of chemical transmutation. Logic to him was an introductory science (*madkhal*) and he uses it as an introduction to *al-Shifa'*. Music he attached to mathematics and emphasized its effect on the soul. He treated it in both *al-Shifa'* and *al-Najah* and in other works, only one of which has survived. He rendered what he wrote in *al-Najah* into Persian, his mother tongue, together with other parts of his philosophic output. He thereby introduced Greek philosophy into Persian and with it relevant technical terms borrowed mostly from Arabic.

In the magnitude of authorship ibn-Sina competes with al-Kindi for highest honors. Ibn-Khallikan credits him with a hundred books, but a modern bibliographer (Cairo, 1950) catalogs two hundred and seventy-six titles ascribed to him; of these some two hundred have survived. Princeton University library has one hundred and eighty-seven entries under the name of Avicenna.

Ibn-Sina has been referred to as the Arab Galen. He could as well have been styled the Arab Aristotle. His people bestowed on him the unique honorific double title *al-shaykh al-ra'is,* dean (of the learned) and prince (of courtiers). But theologians had another title for him: *kafir* (atheist). At their incitement the 'Abbasid al-Mustanjid made a bonfire of his books. With the lapse of time the evil was forgotten, only the good remained. Three nations—Turks, Persians and Arabs—held three celebrations of his millenary, according to lunar reckoning of his birth (370 = A.D. 980). His father was born in Balkh, southeast of Bukhara and once a Buddhist center and a Persian-Turkish meeting place. The name Sina is of undetermined etymology. It is not Semitic. The attempt to connect it with China (Sin) is unsuccessful; the two s's are different letters. The Teheran and Baghdad celebrations assumed international aspects and prompted the publication of several volumes.[1]

Sinaic influence in the East was not limited to his coreligionists. Syrian Christians studied his philosophy and greatly benefited

[1] (1) Lajnat al-Athar al-Wataniyah, *Kitab al-Mahrajan l-ibn-Sina* (Teheran, 1335); Iran Society, *Avicenna Memorial Volume* (Calcutta, 1956); Zabihollah Safa, *Le livre du millénaire d'Avicenne* (Teheran, 1953); Jami'at al-Duwal al-'Arabiyah, *Al-Kitab al-Dhahabi* (Cairo, 1952). For more on the subject consult Ahmad F. al-Ahwani, *Ibn-Sina* (Cairo, 1958); Soheil N. Afnan, *Avicenna: His Life and Works* (London, 1958); Seyyid Hossein Nasr, *Three Muslim Sages* (Cambridge, Mass., 1964).

by his medicine. One of their most learned scholars, ibn-al-'Ibri (d. 1286), mentioned before as having used al-Kindi, made more extensive use of his successor. He translated parts of *al-Shifa'* into Syriac and followed Sinaic views, especially those on the soul. The Syrian scholar produced books on physics, astronomy and medicine, in which at times he gave his Moslem predecessor credit, and at others criticized him.

With ibn-Sina the series of Eastern Moslem philosophers comes to an abrupt end. The momentum generated two centuries earlier under al-Ma'mun had by this time spent itself. Arab intellectual activity was now channeled into theological fields culminating in al-Ghazzali, whose attacks on philosophers may have accelerated the decline. The ensuing period of Crusader wars and Mongol raids favored the downward curve. Eastern Islam was entering upon its dark ages. Happily, as philosophic interest waned in the Islam of the East, it waxed in that of the West, reaching its meridian in ibn-Rushd of Cordova, a follower of ibn-Sina in more than one sense. The philosopher of history ibn-Khaldun of Tunis is another one of those who fell under ibn-Sina's spell. Their stories occupy the next two chapters.

The relevancy of Arab philosophy to Scholasticism lay in the simple fact that it had dealt with the same general problem of adjusting Greek thought to monotheistic belief. Hence its feasibility as a model, and its usefulness in suggesting methods of approach and procedure and possible solutions. First among the Scholastic scholars to appreciate this fact was a German Dominican who studied at Bologna and held professorial chairs at Paris and Cologne. Albertus Magnus (Albert the Great, d. 1280) sought to unite Aristotelianism and Christian theology, utilizing Moslem commentaries and interpretations. Besides writings, he left a host of students, the most distinguished being an Italian, Thomas Aquinas, also a Dominican. The pupil outstripped the teacher (though he died six years before him). Affecting him in his formative stage, the influence was lasting.

His study at Cologne over, the young Italian held chairs at Paris and in his native land. Perhaps better than any other Scholastic he systematized Catholic theology and was styled *Princeps Scholasticorum* (prince of Scholastics). In his writings, the most

influential of which was *Summa Theologiae,* Thomas repeatedly
mentions Avicenna and often quotes to criticize him. The philosophic system he left is now known as Thomism, its adherents as
Thomists. Through St. Thomas (both he and Albertus were can-
onized) Arab philosophy established a firm foothold in Western
Christian soil.

The impact reached the British Isles. An English philosopher
and man of science, Roger Bacon (d. 1294), studied at Oxford
and Paris, where he developed interest in Arab philosophy and
science. He considered ibn-Sina the greatest authority on philosophy after Aristotle. Bacon experimented in alchemy and optics
and was accused of dealing in black magic. He was also suspected
of heretical writings by the Franciscan order, to which he belonged, and was confined in Paris for several years. The writings
of another Franciscan and Scholastic theologian, Duns Scotus (b.
in Duns, Scotland; d. 1308), who also studied and lectured at Oxford and in Paris and Cologne, bear testimony to ibn-Sina's influence.

Abu-'Ali al-Husayn ibn-Sina, physician, philosopher, scientist
and poet, shaykh of the learned and prince of courtiers; dominated Moslem philosophical thought and Arab medical lore for a
thousand years and blazed the trail for the dominant Christian
philosophy and theology of the Middle Ages and early Renaissance.

Ibn-Rushd:
The Great Commentator

The first question addressed to me by the commander of the believers, after inquiring about my name, my father's name and my pedigree, was: "What are the philosophers' views about heaven [the world], is it eternal or created?" So abashed and terrified did I feel that I began to offer excuses, even denying that I ever dealt with philosophy. I had no idea then what the sultan-caliph and ibn-Tufayl had in mind for me.

—Ibn-Rushd

FOR some two centuries after its establishment Spanish Islam depended upon its motherland for intellectual growth and spiritual inspiration. The umbilical cord was not easy to cut. Spanish Moslem rulers followed the Umayyad pattern worked out earlier in Syria, while their citizens followed the thought patterns developed in Hijaz and Iraq. Graduates of schools in Cordova, Seville, Granada, Toledo sought advanced study in Mecca and Medina, Baghdad and Cairo with the same eagerness with which present-day Asian and African students seek graduate study in Europe or the United States. The early Arabian, we learned, had his graduate schooling in the desert; the early Spanish Moslem had it in the urban centers of Eastern Islam.

The holy pilgrimage provided a ready implementation. For an

ambitious student to join a caravan from his home town, perform his religious duty, then linger a year or more in some mosques' learned circle before accompanying a caravan back home was an attractive opportunity. We heard of such cases when studying al-Ghazzali. Armed with a paper testifying to his having audited some shaykh's lectures and been licensed by him, the returning scholar would feel assured of a future in the world of learning. His license constituted a card of admission. It qualified him for the position of teacher, preacher or canon lawyer.

It was a double-way street. Scholars, poets, traditionists, theologians, singers were invited from the heartland to grace caliphal or amiral courts or to occupy university chairs. Others invited themselves. To them al-Andalus (Andalusia, from Vandals, Iberian Peninsula) must have seemed as attractive as the New World later looked to emigrants. The "brain drain" began early. A grandson of 'Abd-al-Rahman I invited (822) the famed Persian musician Ziryab of Baghdad, met him outside the capital (Cordova), assigned him an annual emolument of 3,000 dinars and established him on a 40,000-dinar estate. The young tenor, who was also a wit and a poet and "knew the words and tunes of 10,000 songs," soon became the idol of the smart set. The East-to-West movement assumed high proportions under 'Abd-al-Rahman III, who in 929 proclaimed himself caliph, and under his son al-Hakam. Among those invited to occupy a chair at the university of Cordova was the celebrated philologist of Iraq, abu-'Ali al-Qali. Designated by the new caliph to deliver the oration at a reception honoring Byzantine and other envoys, the professor was so struck with stage fright that he could not utter a word after reciting the usual formula of praise to God and blessing on His Messenger. Another orator jumped into the breach and "extemporaneously" delivered an eloquent oration in rhymed prose covering two and a half pages in al-Maqqari's history of Spain. Al-Hakam offered a thousand dinars for a first copy of *Kitab al-Aghani* (book of songs) by al-Isbahani, a descendant of the Umayyads.

Traffic in books, a one-way street, was brisk and lively. Pilgrims and merchant caravans included newly published books in their return baggage. We recall how Malik's *al-Muwtta'* became a manual of law throughout Spain and al-Maghrib shortly after the death of the author, who was regarded as a saint. The peculiarities

of the Moslem way of life, with no political assemblies and the-
aters characteristic of the Greek and Roman societies, put a pre-
mium on books as a source of knowledge. A Cordovan scholar,
according to al-Maqqari, eager to acquire a certain book, chanced
on one in the market and bid on it until another customer outbid
him. The scholar finally told his rival that the price offered had
far exceeded the worth of the book and asked what interest the
man had in it. "I am not even aware of the contents of the volume," came back the answer, "but having set aside a large room
in my house as a library, to gain prestige among my fellow citizens, and finding on the shelf a vacant space which this book with
its attractive cover and elegant hand could just fill, I thought I
would pay any price for it."

Transplanted ideas, no less than transplanted plants, tend to
develop new characteristics in their new environment. This is
particularly noticeable in the case of poetry, which in al-Andalus
freed itself from old fetters and struck a new alliance with music.
The two arts developed new meters, new tunes and new themes.
The popularity these folk songs achieved paralleled that of the
jazz in our own day. The main theme was, of course, love—but of
the platonic type. Professional minstrels made their appearance
in the eleventh century and moved from court to court singing
the praise of the great, and from town to town reciting their love
compositions. The enthusiasm was contagious, and soon native
Christians were using the same lyric type. By the twelfth century
it was emulated by Castilians and southern Frenchmen, giving
rise to the institution known as the troubadour. These lyric poets
and poet-musicians spread into Italy and flourished until the end
of the thirteenth century.

I

Philosophy did not figure among the early intellectual imports
of Moslem Spain. We know of more than one scholar who in the
900's acquired Eastern higher education, including geometry and
logic—least objectionable among the philosophic sciences. We also
know of philosophical treatises finding their way into the Andalusian market about 1000. But we know of no major Spanish

Moslem philosopher who delved into metaphysics until the twelfth century. This does not mean, however, that that country had not produced scientists.

Astronomical studies were cultivated assiduously after the mid-tenth century and were encouraged by the rulers of Cordova. Most of the astronomers were astrologers, believing in astral influence as the cause underlying the chief occurrences between a man's birth and his death. They followed abu-Ma'shar (L. Albumasar), who flourished in Baghdad and died in 886. The earliest distinguished Spanish Moslem scholar was a Cordovan astronomer-mathematician named Maslamah al-Majriti (d. *ca.* 1007). Al-Majriti edited and corrected al-Khwarizmi's planetary tables, converted their basis from the Persian into the Moslem era and to some extent replaced the old meridian with that of Cordova. The greatest surgeon the Arabs produced was a Spanish Moslem, abu-al-Qasim (Abulcasis) al-Zahrawi (d. *ca.* 1013), court physician of al-Hakam, son of the first caliph. His medical masterpiece, translated into Latin, held its place for centuries as the manual of surgery in Salerno, Montpellier and other schools of medicine.

The twelfth was indeed the greatest century in the intellectual history of Moslem Spain. It opens with abu-Bakr ibn-Bajjah (Avenpace, Avempace), philosopher, physician, scientist, musician and vizir—all in the tradition of his Eastern coreligionists. But he deviated in being more Aristotelian than Neo-Platonist. Ibn-Bajjah was born in Saragossa, served for about twenty years as vizir of the Murabit (Almoravid) governor of Granada and later of Saragossa, and died in 1138 in his early forties, poisoned by a fellow physician at Fas (Fez). He based his metaphysics, physics and psychology on Aristotle, and wrote commentaries on him. His best known work is *Tadbir al-Mutawahhid* (the regime of the solitary), which aims to teach that the penetrative philosopher is in the world but not of it, and can attain perfection by isolating himself and seeking union with the Divine, this being the ultimate object of philosophy. Like ibn-Sina he regarded philosophy as an esoteric science reserved for the enlightened, leaving the literal interpretation of such colorful koranic doctrines as eschatology to the masses. This Spanish philosopher was given by his people's theologians the same treatment given his colleagues in the East.

Ibn-Bajjah was followed by abu-Bakr (L. Abubacer) ibn-Tufayl, likewise physician, philosopher and courtier. Born in the province of Granada in the first decade of the twelfth century, he was not personally acquainted with his predecessor. After practicing medicine at Granada he served as secretary to the Muwahhid (Almohad) governor and thus started another career lasting about twenty years. His second appointment was as secretary to another Muwahhid governor, that of Ceuta and Tangier. Here he attracted the attention of the sultan abu-Ya'qub Yusuf, son of the founder of the dynasty. Abu-Yusuf dreamed of making of his capital—Marrakush (Marrakesh, Morocco)—a new Baghdad. He himself studied philosophy and patronized scholars. Ibn-Tufayl served as his personal physician, court judge and if not vizir a consultant. It was his influence that brought ibn-Rushd to the court.

The only important legacy that reached us from ibn-Tufayl was *Hayy ibn-Yaqzan* (the living, son of the vigilant). The title, of course, is taken from ibn-Sina's mystical allegory. But the borrowing ends there. Ibn-Tufayl's *Hayy* is a mystical philosophical story of his own creation. In its introduction he pays tribute to ibn-Sina but criticizes him for indiscriminately mixing Aristotle's with his own views. He also criticizes al-Farabi for his superficiality, al-Ghazzali for inconsistency and ibn-Bajjah for dependence on logic and intellect to the neglect of research and intuition.

The hero of the story was born spontaneously on an uninhabited island in the Indian Ocean, where he was nourished and brought up by a roe. His discovery of superiority over his fellow animals was made when he realized his nakedness and used leaves as a cover and armed himself with a club. When he passed on to the hunting stage he replaced leaves with skin. The roe's death grieved him and taught him the difference between body and what makes body alive. He chanced on fire as it was spontaneously generated by rubbing the twigs of a dead tree. From the tangible sensation Hayy moved to the intangible and from the specific to the general, arriving, at the age of twenty-eight, at the conception of the soul as incorruptible and immortal and of God as wise, knowing and merciful.

Moral: man, unexposed to traditional beliefs and unsubjected to social pressure, can through reason and common sense gradually acquire knowledge of the ultimate truth and realize his dependence upon a superior Being.

The public was quick to recognize the charm and value of the story. In it the marriage of philosophy with storytelling was consummated. Published in Arabic by Edward Pococke as the first of its kind by Oxford University Press (1671), together with a Latin translation, it has since been translated into English (by S. Ockley, 1708), Hebrew and several European languages. It caught the attention of the Quakers, who made special use of it. *Hayy* was a forerunner of Rousseau's *Emile*.

II

The date is about 1164 and the place is Marrakush. The second Muwahhid abu-Ya'qub Yusuf is receiving in audience ibn-Tufayl's recommended friend ibn-Rushd, who reports:

> The first question addressed to me by the commander of the believers, after inquiring about my name, my father's name and my pedigree, was: "What are the philosophers' views about heaven [the world], is it eternal or created?" So abashed and terrified did I feel that I began to offer excuses, even denying that I ever dealt with philosophy. I had no idea then what the sultan-caliph and ibn-Tufayl had in mind for me. . . . Sensing my embarrassment he proceeded to discuss the problem he had raised with such remembrance of facts the like of which I do not recall having found even among specialists in this field. He persisted in his effort to put me at ease until I was able to talk and he had a chance to size me up.[1]

What the two had in mind was commissioning the young philosopher to continue the work, started by ibn-Bajjah, of making Aristotle intelligible. The sultan-caliph could not tell whether the difficulty lay with the Greek philosopher or with his translators. With the commission went a robe of honor and an honorarium. An appointment to the judgeship of Seville followed.

This episode marked the turning point in the scholarly career of abu-al-Walid Muhammad ibn-Rushd. Born in Cordova in

---

[1] Al-Marrakushi, *Al-Mu'jib fi Talkhis Akhbar al-Maghrib,* ed. R. Dozy, 2nd ed. (Leyden, 1881), pp. 174–75.

1126 into a family of learned jurisconsults, he had his early education in that discipline. Both his father and grandfather had served with distinction as Maliki chief justices in the capital. The grandfather had served as imam in the grand mosque. So the three were differentiated as ibn-Rushd the grandfather, the father or the grandson. Family and environmental background assured the boy the highest possible education. After studying language, poetry, Koran and hadith, he "memorized" *al-Muwatta'*. Cordova had become since the days of 'Abd-al-Rahman and al-Hakam the intellectual center of al-Andalus and one of the most cultured cities in Europe. Its royal library is said to have housed 400,000 titles, filling a forty-four-volume catalog. Al-Hakam, a bibliophile and perhaps the greatest scholar among Moslem caliphs, left marginal notes on some of its manuscripts. The university, housed in the great mosque, embraced among its departments theology, jurisprudence, astronomy, mathematics and medicine. Its certificate opened the way to the most lucrative posts in the realm. This institution preceded al-Azhar of Cairo and the Nizamiyah of Baghdad, and attracted students from the Iberian Peninsula and al-Maghrib. Here abu-al-Walid specialized in jurisprudence and medicine, the two fields worthy of an intellectual. With medicine at that time went philosophy, both bearing the same title (*hikmah*). The only record we have of a philosophy teacher of ibn-Rushd is that of his medical professor. He could not have studied under ibn-Bajjah, as claimed, because abu-al-Walid was only twelve years old when that philosopher died, and there is no evidence that he studied under ibn-Tufayl. He was their pupil in the sense that he studied their works.

On graduation the young physician-jurist practiced his double profession first in his native town and then in Marrakush, meantime pursuing privately his philosophical studies. His biographers, beginning with ibn-al-Abbar of Valencia and ibn-abi-Usaybi'ah of Damascus, agree that in both medicine and law he became the authority of his age. In both Cordova and Marrakush he lived under politically disturbed conditions. Born under a Murabit (Almoravid) sultan, he found himself at the age of twenty-two under a Muwahhid ruler, who the year before had wrested Marrakush from Murabit hands. The city was a Murabit foundation and capital. Seville, instead of Cordova, functioned as a subsidiary capital. The Muwahhids (unitarians), like the Murabits, were of Berber origin but followed a prophet who entitled himself mahdi and emphasized the unity of God as a reaction against anthropomorphic tendencies in orthodox Islam. But he was not the founder of the dynasty. The dynasty remained puritanic in its theology but became liberal in its patronage of philosophy, despite its overriding concern to press the holy war against the Christians in northern Spain. The patronage reached its zenith under the second dynast, abu-Ya'qub Yusuf (1163–1184), on whose court first ibn-Tufayl and later ibn-Rushd shed imperishable luster.

Abu-Ya'qub's appointment of his new protégé to the Seville judgeship carried prestige. More importantly the appointment gave the learned scholar security and an opportunity to write. The city was noted for its artistic achievement, as indicated by a remark ibn-Rushd made to his highly esteemed medical colleague ibn-Zuhr (Avenzoar), "When a scholar dies in Seville his books are sent to Cordova for sale, and when a musician dies in Cordova his instruments are sent to Seville for sale." Ibn-Zuhr, the most illustrious member of a family that boasted six generations of medical men, was then the most distinguished son of the city and a close friend of the judge. The two scholars must have been debating the relative merits of their native towns.

After a short tenure (1169–71), the judge was moved to occupy a vacancy in the office once held by two of his ancestors. The move was especially agreeable for providing richer opportunities for research. His tenure in Cordova lasted about a decade. In 1182, again on the recommendation of the aged ibn-Tufayl, the sultan-caliph invited ibn-Rushd to be his personal physician. Two years later abu-Ya'qub died; he was followed by ibn-Tufayl the following year (1185).

After his own succession abu-Ya'qub's son al-Mansur (1184–1199) summoned ibn-Rushd to an audience for renewing his court appointment. The warm reception tendered and the seat offered—above all his courtiers, one of whom was his own son-in-law—left no doubt that respect for the learned was in the regal legacy. Several years of seemingly cordial relations between patron and protégé were unexpectedly and unexplainedly severed by a royal decree banishing the sixty-eight-year-old scholar to an isolated place not far from Cordova. His books, as well as those of other philosophers, were committed to the flames in Spain and Morocco; only those dealing with medicine, arithmetic and astronomy were spared. According to one source the sultan was personally offended by a passage in his physician's work on zoology declaring that he had seen a giraffe in the garden of the "king of the Berbers." The author's explanation that the last word was a typographical error for *barrayn* (the two lands, i.e. al-Maghrib and Spain) was not accepted. According to another source the disgrace was caused by a different passage, "Venus was a goddess," extracted from its context and misinterpreted. The real reason, however, is not difficult to guess. The same fate that had befallen ibn-Bajjah, ibn-Sina and al-Kindi now befell ibn-Rushd.

The reinstatement in royal favor some two years later was as abrupt as the fall. The dictator must by then have felt that the massive pressure to which he yielded, at a time when he needed the theologians' support in the war against the Castilians, had spent itself. Meantime the aged philosopher had likewise spent himself. He fell sick after his return and on December 10, 1198, passed away, leaving one son who specialized in medicine and others who followed the family's juridical tradition. His remains, in accordance with his family's wishes, were removed three months later to Cordova. His patron died the following year.

The image left us of ibn-Rushd is that of a dedicated student, abstemious if not ascetic, humble and not self-seeking, neither power hungry, nor wine thirsty. "In all his life he never missed an evening without reading or writing except the day he married and the day his father died." Love poems he composed in his youth he later destroyed. Clearly he did not share with his confreres the characteristic trait of intellectual arrogance. He was generous to a fault. His generosity and dedication to intellectual pursuits were apparent in his clothing and scanty possessions. When criticized by friends for being charitable to enemies, his reply was: "There is no virtue in being generous to a friend; but he is virtuous who gives to an enemy." He would give to one who insulted him and advise him not to do it to someone else unless he wanted a punch in the nose. Tolerant in case of insult to himself, he was not tolerant when an unfair criticism was made of a friend. He once himself administered a beating to a poet for satirizing a learned friend. Like other Arab philosophers his faith in God was never shaken; it was rather strengthened. "He who studies anatomy," he wrote, "increases his belief in God." More than that he and they generally observed the religious ceremonials. In his infamous banishment edict al-Mansur admitted that fact but explained it on the ground of hypocrisy.

III

What writings of ibn-Rushd were lost to the world consequent to the royal ban cannot be determined. Surprisingly, the Damascene biographer of physicians who flourished half a century later lists no fewer than fifty titles by ibn-Rushd, with a large number of commentaries on Aristotle and Galen. The list comprises original works on philosophy, medicine and jurisprudence. Law, the author's first love, gave way to medicine, which in turn was replaced by philosophy. Of his legal works *Bidayat al-Mujtahid* (starting the industrious, volume I published at Cairo, 1966) was the only notable one. Two hundred years after the author's death, a poet sang his praises because of it. Throughout Arabic literature ibn-Rushd's name is associated with the title al-qadi (the judge), corresponding to al-shaykh with ibn-Sina's, al-faylasuf with al-Kindi's, and al-imam with those of both al-Shafi'i and al-Ghazzali.

Of his medical works *al-Kulliyat fi al-Tibb*[1] (generalities in medicine) was the most valuable. An early encyclopedic composition, it has sections on anatomy, physiology, health, disease, diagnosis, materia medica, hygiene and therapeutics. The book recognizes that no one is taken twice with smallpox and describes the true function of the retina. Translated into Latin (*colliget*, corruption of the Arabic word), it was short-lived in competition with ibn-Sina's *Canon*. The author closes his book on generalities with the remark that at his suggestion ibn-Zuhr was compiling a supplementary work on specific matters relating to medicine. Ibn-Rushd considered this friend the greatest clinician after Galen.

[1] Photographic reproduction by the Instituto General Franco (Marrakush, 1939).

Ibn-Rushd the physician was dwarfed by ibn-Rushd the philosopher. Faithful to the mandate received from the father of the man who disgraced him, the learned man devoted most of his time and energy to making the philosophical products of a master mind—written in a foreign language and under the influence of an alien culture—meaningful, relevant and palatable to an Arab Moslem audience a millennium and a half later. He himself knew no Greek. His procedure consisted in studying critically and carefully Aristotle in Arabic translations, comparing them with the translated Greek commentaries as well as with those of Arab philosophers, digesting and reproducing the entire output. At times he would take his Arab forerunners to task for passing counterfeit Aristotelian views, at others dissent from ideas of the "great teacher."

His presentation aimed at three levels: beginners, intermediate and advanced. The books produced were in three corresponding sizes. Certain works of Aristotle were given the triple treatment, others the double one, still others the single one. For beginners the commentator summarized, paraphrased and explained in his own words, rearranging the material and introducing data from other sources. The result was not a commentary in the accepted sense; it was a semi-original work and was loosely entitled *talkhis* (epitome).[1] Most of the surviving works in Arabic are so entitled. Ibn-abi-Usaybi'ah lists eight *talkhis* books on Galen.

The long commentary for advanced study was the real one (*tafsir, sharh*). Ibn-Rushd would begin by reproducing one paragraph after the other from Aristotle, following each by his own explanation, usually longer than the quoted text, keeping the original and the additional clearly apart. In this he evidently followed the model in koranic exegesis. His *Tafsir Ma wara' al-Tabi'ah*[2] (Aristotle's *Metaphysics*) is perhaps the weightiest in this category. It reveals the depth to which the commentator penetrated into the thought of the philosopher and the way he disentangled Aristotelianism from Neo-Platonism. It will be recalled

[1] For an illustration in English translation see Averroes, *Epitoma of Parva Naturalia* [*Al-Hiss w-al-Mahsus*], tr. Harry Blumberg (Cambridge, Mass., 1961).
[2] Ed. Maurice Bouyges, in *Bibliotheca Arabicum Scholasticorum*, 3 vols. (Beirut, 1938–48).

how for centuries Arab philosophers had been using a Neo-Platonic work masquerading as Aristotle's *Theology*. Most of the commentaries in this category have survived only in their Hebrew or Latin translations.

The intermediate commentary, as the name indicates, falls in between the other two. Entitled *jawami'* (*summa*, compendiums), it uses direct quotations but sparingly and treats the text, when condensed, by elaboration; when ambiguous, by clarification and when necessary by using examples; material from post-Aristotelian sources is at times used. Of the *jawami'* only few have survived in Arabic.

Ibn-Rushd's contribution was not limited to the commentarial field. The problem of philosophy-religion relation which for centuries had been the preoccupation of his predecessors did not escape his concern. In his voluminous critique of al-Ghazzali's *Tahafut*, which he entitled *Tahafut al-Tahafut* (incoherence of incoherence), he followed the commentary method, taking one section of the original text at a time and then refuting rather than explaining it. As a philosopher, he felt duty bound to defend his confreres against the great theologian's charges of heresy, punishable by death. An enemy of the faith is an enemy of the society. Besides, such strictures as those relating to belief in the eternity of the world and the denial of bodily resurrection and of God's knowledge of the particulars, though written before ibn-Rushd's birth, applied to him. Abu-Hamid (as he called al-Ghazzali) misunderstood the philosophers. In the matter of God's knowledge, what they maintain is that God's knowledge differs from man's. It is cause, while man's knowledge is caused. If man's knowledge partakes of the nature of God's, man then becomes a partner of God, who has no partner (sur. 6:163).

On another occasion ibn-Rushd asserted that God has no more knowledge of details than a governor has direct knowledge of the detailed execution of an administrative act. On the related problem of predestination the Rushdite view was intermediate. Man's acts are neither fully free nor fully determined. His will is conditioned by external forces working uniformly. *Tahafut al-Tahafut* is the work for which this Cordovan philosopher was best known —and unfavorably so—in Eastern Islam. It came at a time when philosophy had become a monopoly of theologians, a servant of dogma.

In another original contribution, entitled *Fasl al-Maqal* (the decisive treatise), ibn-Rushd addressed himself to the subject of harmony between philosophy and religion. Both *Fasl* and *Tahafut* were written about 1180 and represent his mature thought on the subject. Both were early translated into Hebrew and Latin. The author insists that truth attained by philosophy does not differ from that attained by theology and any apparent contradictions are subject to reconciliation by interpretation of the scriptural text—a line of thought not peculiarly his. Allegorical interpretation assumes that certain verses in the Koran have an inner meaning. Several koranic passages, for instance, speak of God's throne; in one (11:9) the throne is set on the water, which cannot be accepted in its literal meaning. Such interpretation, however, should be considered esoteric knowledge, not to be divulged to the masses. For any divulgence resulting in massive confusions, theologians—rather than philosophers—should be blamed.

His concluding words summarize his thesis:

> Philosophy is the friend and milk-sister of religion; thus injuries from people related to philosophy are the severest injuries [to religion] apart from the enmity, hatred and quarrels which such [injuries] stir up between the two, which are companions by nature and lovers by essence and instinct.[1]

In another connection he classified knowledge under three headings: demonstrative and subject to syllogistic reasoning, lying in the philosophers' domain; oratorical, based on authority and rich in symbols designed to meet the commonalty's needs; and—in between the two—didactic, relating to opinions and pertaining to the mutakallim theologians.

In a companion volume to *Fasl*, entitled *al-Kashf 'an Manahij al-Adillah* (exposition of the methods of proofs), ibn-Rushd based his proof of God's existence on the principle of causality.

1 George F. Hourani, *Averroes: On the Harmony of Religion and Philosophy* (London, 1961), p. 70.

Nothing comes to be without a cause; causes fall into a definite
series leading to a Prime Cause. To this philosopher the world is
a continuum of animate and inanimate objects interrelated
through the law of causality; the implication is that the law of
causality is permanent and so are the objects of the world. This
makes the world eternal by virtue of a creative, moving cause. The
creative process is one of self-renewal consequent on changes from
moment to moment. The creative power operates in perpetuity.
The Rushdite explanation of the world's eternal character thus
differs from the Sinaic and anticipates the modern theory of evolution. As for immortality, the Rushdite view is that the immortality of the individual soul cannot be philosophically proved,
and if the resurrection of the body does take place, the form cannot be the same. The philosopher of Cordova further accepts
prophethood and reiterates the necessity of maintaining a double-
standard truth. Other Near Eastern religions had earlier resort to
this device, which exists in embryonic form in Christianity (Matt.
13:10–11).

Ibn-Rushd's stance as a Moslem philosopher was as difficult to
maintain as that of any of his predecessors. He held two simulta-
neous citizenships: one—intellectual—in the Hellenic world, and
the other—spiritual—in the Arab world. In his mind the two
were compatible. There is no reason to doubt his intellectual
honesty in accepting the explanations he made. But what satisfied
him did not satisfy his people. To them, holding such a double
citizenship was no less acceptable than holding a dual political
citizenship today. In all his polemics the philosopher avoided a
head-on-collision with dogma. His approach was of the oblique
variety. Nevertheless he was more assailed than his forerunners.
In literature his name tops the list of atheists and his books top
the "black list." That a judge, son of a judge and grandson of a
judge, should turn out to be a turncoat was the bitterest dose of
all.

Hard as he tried to convince his people that traditional Islam
and Hellenic heritage could be reconciled, he failed. The many
koranic quotations with which he endeavored to buttress his interpretations were of no effect. No matter what explanation he

put on the world's eternity it contravened the Divine fiat: "Be" and "it is." No matter how he interpreted predestination and God's knowledge, he infringed on God's almightiness and all-knowingness. No matter what possibility he held for a resurrected body, it cast doubt on the promises of a colorful next world. Ibn-Rushd came to his people and his people rejected him. By Western as well as Eastern Moslems he was consigned to oblivion. Others—Jews and Christians—were more considerate.

IV

Rushdite original contributions to juridical, medical and philosophical thought were not of major significance. Wherein, then, does his distinct contribution lie?

The field in which it lies, commentary, does not rank high on our scale of modern research. But that does not mean it never did. For Aristotle unexplained was Aristotle unused, and if used ineffective. Ibn-Rushd was not the first commentator on the "first teacher." In fact he was the last of the many major Greek and Arabic commentators. But no sooner had his commentaries been translated into Hebrew and Latin than they rendered the earlier ones out of date. The Hebrew editions were started by Jacob Anatoli (Naples, 1232) and Judah Cohen (Toledo, 1247). Latin translations began with Michael Scot (1220) and Hermann the German (1240), both sponsored by Emperor Frederick II of Sicily. Thus within fifty years after his death Averroes' name became widely known in European learned circles. Improved Latin editions, especially those made from Hebrew, followed in rapid succession. In the fifteenth century, distinguished by the discovery of printing from movable type, more than fifty editions appeared in Venice. In the seventies of that century three editions of major works were published in Padua. The most accurate translation was done as late as 1553 in Venice. Averroism, studying Aristotle through Averroes' commentaries, became widespread. It established itself as a major discipline in university curricula, and for three centuries agitated European minds as perhaps nothing else did. Thus did a "Latin translation of a Hebrew translation of an Arabic commentary based upon an Arabic translation of a Syriac translation of a Greek original" spark a momentous intellectual movement in medieval Christendom.

Having laid so much stress on rational thinking, Averroism in due course aroused the same religious reaction that Rushdism had aroused. Thomas Aquinas used ibn-Rushd more for criticism than for approval. Paris spearheaded the attack. Its council in 1210 put the ban on the works of both Aristotle and Averroes. Twenty-one years later a papal injunction interdicted the use of their writings pending expurgation. In 1277 a Paris bishop pointed out more than two hundred errors in the teachings of these two men. Thus was the same battle fought in Christendom as in Islam, with the difference that, whereas in Islam tradition won the war, in the West rationalism won it. Modern liberalism can be traced from the eighteenth century back, through the thirteenth-century professors of philosophy at Paris and Padua, to the Averroist school of thought.

In modern times one of the early Europeans to revive interest in Averroes was the celebrated Frenchman Renan, whose study of Averroism (1852) earned him a Ph.D. and established his reputation. In this philosopher-Orientalist's opinion, Aristotle expounded the universe and Averroes expounded Aristotle. Centuries before Renan, Dante consigned the writer of the *gran comento,* together with Avicenna, to the illustrious company of Euclid, Ptolemy, Hippocrates and Galen. Michael Scot and Roger Bacon ranked him as second only to Aristotle.

In the modern East interest in ibn-Rushd was sparked at the dawn of the twentieth century by a Christian journalist born in Tripoli (now in Lebanon) who, drawing on Renan, published in his *Majallat al-Jami'ah* (Alexandria) several articles on the life of ibn-Rushd and his philosophy.[1] This aroused discussions and hot debate with the Egyptian modernist Muhammad 'Abduh, although he himself had made extensive use of the Rushdite theory of causality. The first Arabic edition of a work by ibn-Rushd was *Fasl al-Maqal,* supplemented by *al-Kashf 'an Manahij* (published by M. J. Müller, Munich, 1859; reprinted, Cairo, 1894–95). In recent decades several other works by and on ibn-Rushd have ap-

---

[1] Reprinted with rebuttals, Farah Antun, *Ibn-Rushd wa-Falsafatuh* (Alexandria, 1903).

peared.[1] Thus did this twelfth-century philosopher of rationalism, resurrected in the twentieth, contribute to modern Arab renaissance.

With ibn-Rushd the role played by Arab philosophic thought came to an abrupt end. The Andalusian philosopher left no progeny. The Greek thought which four centuries earlier was incorporated into Arab culture had since the fifth Christian century made no notable progress. It was al-Kindi and his successors who breathed new life into it and set it on a new career. Had they done nothing but transmit that thought to the Latin West and Moslem East, it would have been enough to make them benefactors of humankind. But they did more. They preserved, enriched and transmitted. Their major contribution lay where philosophy and religion meet, reason and faith conflict. The Greeks, with a multiplicity of deities—Zeus and Aphrodite, Sun and Moon, Victory and Fate—and a heterogeneity of myths—with stories about gods that are intentionally comic—never took their religion so seriously as the Semites. To them there was not much of a conflict. The Christians faced the same problem as the Moslems, though on a smaller scale in view of the uncreated-Koran dogma.

Greek and Latin church fathers were not unaware of the problem. They with relative ease appropriated philosophical concepts and bypassed or tangentially treated hot issues. Many of them were recent converts to Christianity and were already imbued with Neo-Platonic thought. Even the two great Latin ecclesiastical writers of North Africa, Tertullian (d. *ca.* 230) and St. Augustine (d. 430), did not go deep into the root of the matter. To St. Anselm, as to St. Augustine, religious faith is a reality defined in its context by revelation, in utter independence of personal preferences. It was not till late medieval times that Christian theologians—in the wake of the Islamic march—came to grips with the problem of reason against faith. Thomas Aquinas was an early champion in the struggle. He made extensive use of Averroes, as he did of Avicenna, and often criticized him. But in the opinion of a contemporary British philosopher (who is not sure what would

1 Majid Fakhri, *Ibn-Rushd: Faylasuf Qurtubah* (Beirut, 1960); 'Abbas M. al-'Aqqad, *Ibn-Rushd* (Cairo, 1953); Muhammad Y. Musa, *Bayn al-Din w-al-Falsafah* (Cairo, 1959).

have happened without St. Augustine) the work of St. Thomas Aquinas would not have been what it was without Averroes. Confirmed Averroists came to consider Averroes, Aristotle and reason as if synonymous. Through Thomas and other schoolmen the evolution of Chritian philosophy was profoundly modified by Moslem contributions.

As Arab philosophy passed into Europe over the two bridges of Moslem Spain and Sicily, science and other Arab elements of culture went along. The philosophers we have studied were also scientists. Mathematics, astronomy and medicine were the disciplines in which Arabs excelled. The large number of words which in their transliterated or translated forms found their way into European languages testifies to the richness of the legacy. Other than such well known words as algebra (*al-jabr*), zero, cipher (*sifr*), algorism (*al-Khwarizmi*), mention may be made by way of illustration of surd (L. *surdus,* tr. of Ar. *jadhr asamm,* deaf root) and sine (L. *sinus,* tr. of *jayb,* pocket). Arabic astronomical words can be recognized in such star names as Acrab (*'aqrab,* scorpion), Algedi (*al-jadi,* the calf), Altair (*al-ta'ir,* the flyer). Other technical terms like zenith (*simt*) and nadir (*nazir*) were borrowed. Especially numerous were the borrowed medical terms: soda (*suda',* splitting headache), syrup, sherbet (*sharab,* drink), julep (*julab,* rose water), alcohol (*al-kuhl*), alkali (*al-qali*). Dura mater and pia mater are Latin translations of *al-umm al-jafiyah,* (coarse mother, the tough membrane enveloping the brain) and *al-umm al-raqiqah,* (thin mother, the soft membrane).

The dawn of a new era in Europe characterized by rational speculation and scientific achievement—to which Arabs had so richly contributed—coincided with the beginning of the decay of Arab thought. From the early ninth to the late twelfth century the Arabs were probably the most learned people in the world. Their language could boast a greater output in literature, science and philosophy than any other, not excluding Latin. The creative spark after that was everywhere extinguished. To the all-encompassing blackout in the Moslem world, beginning with the thirteenth century, North Africa presented one notable exception. That will be the subject of our next study.

Ibn-al-Walid Muhammad ibn-Rushd—physician, philosopher, scientist, commentator—made Aristotle intelligible, fathered an enduring rationalist movement and substantially contributed to Europe's renaissance.

Ibn-Khaldun:
First Philosopher of History

*On the surface history is no more than
information about political events, dynasties, and occurrences of the remote past,
elegantly presented and spiced with proverbs. . . .*

*The inner meaning of history, on the
other hand, involves speculation and attempt to get at the truth, subtle explanation of the causes and origins of existing
things and deep knowledge of the how
and why of events. History, therefore, is
firmly rooted in philosophy. It deserves to
be accounted a branch of philosophy.*

—Ibn-Khaldun

NORTH Africa did not share in the golden age as it glittered to the
northeast and northwest, but it shared in the ensuing dark age.
The cultural pipe that ran from Baghdad to Cordova passed
through it but had no facets open to it. An outlying region, its
ethnic, religious and political structures were not conducive to
learned pursuits. Its soil from Libya to Morocco was more productive of the fruits of war than of peace. It rendered of the area
a nursery of rebels and schismatics. Learning in those days could
flourish only under caliphal or princely patronage conditioned by
stability and prosperity.

To the indigenous Berber population Phoenician and Roman

additions were made early and, more important, an Arabian addition consequent to the seventh century Moslem conquest. All three accretions, however, were along the coast. As the Arab blood flowed westward it got thinner. Language provides the safest criterion. In Libya and Tunisia the Berber-speaking groups form small pockets; in Algeria they become a minority and in Morocco more than a third of the population today uses the Berber tongue.

In our study of the establishment of the Fatimid empire we noted the way Berbers expressed their dissatisfaction with Islam by espousing dissident or heretical views. In the second half of the eleventh century, Fatimid caliphs set loose the banu-Hilal, a warlike and restless Arabian tribe long settled in Egypt, against the enemies of the state to the west. Vigorous and numerous, the Hilalis displaced or assimilated the Berbers and destroyed the relics of Roman and Byzantine civilization. They contributed appreciably to the process of Arabicization that is still in progress. Their heroic feats and love affairs have been immortalized in a romance-epic (*Sirat bani-Hilal*) still recited and sung in coffee houses throughout the Arab world. By the fourteenth century, the era we are studying, the population of North Africa had crystallized into four types: urbanized Arabs in country places and along the coast, nomadic Arabs to the south, Arabicized Berbers along the littoral and nomadic Berbers in the hinterland as far as the Sahara.

By the fourteenth century the mighty Muwahhid dynasty, the only one in the history of Moslem Africa which brought the area from Libya to Morocco under a single rule, had come to an end. Two powerful dynasties, both Berber, rose on its ruins: the Marinids in Morocco (al-Maghrib) and the Hafsids in Tunisia (Ifriqiyah), with present-day Algeria in between as a bone of contention. An Algerian city—Tilimsan for example—might defy both sides and establish a temporary amirate. Libya went with Tunisia.

The Marinids started with the advantage of holding Morocco, heartland of the defunct Muwahhid empire. The seizure of the capital city Marrakush (1269) was the culminating point in their conquest. But they built their own capital, a new Fas (Fez). The

Marinids fell heir to the Spanish territory, where they were con-
tinually threatened by the rising Christian powers. Their defeat
by the king of Castile in 1340 turned their eyes eastward. Shortly
after that the Marinid sultan abu-'Inan arrogantly assumed the
greatest title in Islam, commander of the believers. In this he followed the example of a Hafsid rival. The Marinid-Hafsid struggle for hegemony in the area became a central fact in the subsequent history of North Africa. Within both sultanates there were
times in which usurpers or provincial governors would seize the
throne or assert their independence.

The Hafsids, on their part, boasted that their founder abu-
Hafs was one of the first disciples of al-Muwahhid's prophet ibn-
Tumart and a lieutenant of the Muwahhid dynasty's founder
('Abd-al-Mu'min, 1130–63). A son of abu-Hafs was appointed
governor of Tunisia (1207). A grandson cast off al-Muwahhid suzerainty but contented himself with the title of amir (1228). But
a brother-successor (about 1250) added al-mu'minin to his title,
and was recognized as caliph by Mecca. The Hafsids therefore
claimed to be the real representatives of the Muwahhid tradition.
It was shortly before this time that a grandfather's grandfather of
ibn-Khaldun left Seville to join the Hafsid court. The Hafsids,
with whom the Khalduns had some early connections, were then
the most powerful rulers in North Africa.

Meanwhile a small state arose, between the two rival powers,
centered at Tilimsan (Tlemcen) on the northwestern frontier of
Algeria. Its rulers were of the mighty Zanatah tribe (treated before). The Tilimsan amirate was exposed to attacks from the east
and the west and shared in the vicissitudes of the area and era.
Tilimsan and Fas shared with Tunis the scenes of ibn-Khaldun's
activity. A few years after his birth a Marinid monarch penetrated Tunisia as far as al-Qayrawan, leaving the country in an
enfeebled state bordering on anarchy. The Hafsids outlived their
Marinid rivals, but their country succumbed to the Ottoman
Turks in 1574, after a rule of three and a half centuries, whereas
Morocco maintained its independence until 1912, when it became a French protectorate.

I

'Abd-al-Rahman abu-Zayd ibn-Khaldun was born in Tunis May 27, 1332, into a family justifiably proud of its Arabian descent and the achievement of its members, politically and intellectually, in both Seville and Tunis. The family traced its origin into Hadramawt (hence the designation Hadrami), whence an ancestor came to Spain in connection with the eighth-century conquest. In Seville his descendants, one after the other, served with distinction as judges and government officials, and when one of them shortly before Seville's fall into Christian hands (1248) moved to the Hafsid court in Tunis, his descendant there repeated the record of their predecessors in Seville.

'Abd-al-Rahman's early education, as reported by him, followed the pattern of most children on the same social level. It began at home with the father, continued through the mosque school and ended in circles under specialists—in this case mostly refugees from al-Andalus. Notable among them was Muhammad ibn-Ibrahim al-Abili (from Avila, Spain), who introduced him to mathematics and logic branching off into metaphysics and other philosophical sciences. When 'Abd-al-Rahman's formal education ended, at about the age of seventeen, his self-education began. By then the Hafsid power was hitting its nadir. In 1347 a Marinid, abu-al-Hasan, after reducing Tilimsan, marched victoriously through Ifriqiyah from west to east, landing at al-Qayrawan. In the following year he was forced to withdraw because of an uprising at home headed by his son abu-'Inan. In the wake of the victory several scholars, Moroccan and Spanish, came to Tunis and provided 'Abd-al-Rahman with the opportunity to concentrate on philosophy and logic, theology and jurisprudence. In the royal return retinue, not only these but Tunisian scholars were included. Prospects at Fas seemed brighter than in Tunis.

A more personal calamity befell the young man, the loss of his parents (1345) from the Black Death as it swept across the world. Some of his shaykhs, too, were among the victims. The father had shunned politics and devoted himself to religious pursuits. In his autobiography (*al-Ta'rif*) ibn-Khaldun mentions his mother only once, as a victim of the plague. The family must have had at least an elder son, Muhammad, and a younger, Yahya, who in the family tradition chose a political scholarly career. Supposedly the most elaborate autobiography penned by a Moslem intellectual, *al-Ta'rif,* fails to satisfy the curiosity of a modern reader. Throughout, it is lacking in human interest. No mention is made of the author's marriage—which must have taken place at about 1345—to the daughter of a Hafsid general and minister of war. She remained at least the principal wife until the day of her death.

Matrimony and the father's death prompted the twenty-one-year-old man to seek gainful employment. The first office he held was that of "master of signature" in the Hafsid court. While accompanying his patron on an unsuccessful military campaign, he deserted and went roaming from place to place, convinced that Tunis held no future for him. Thus ended unhappily his first experience as courtier. Nor was the second any happier. Accepting in 1354 an invitation of the Marinid abu-'Inan, then the most powerful sultan in North Africa, he joined his inner circle of philosophers, astrologers, theologians, poets and counselors, to some of whom he refers in his masterpiece *al-Muqaddimah* (introduction). Especially attractive to him was his favorite master (shaykh) al-Abili. Having a mind ever ready, sponge-like, to absorb knowledge, ibn-Khaldun rejoiced at the opportunity, but did not relish the position. It involved the recording of the sultan's decisions on petitions or documents. He, to borrow his own words, "had never known any ancestor to have done a thing like that."

Three years later, when abu-'Inan was planning a second invasion of Tunisia, he discovered that his Tunisian secretary was conspiring with a deposed Hafsid governor, so he considered it wise to keep ibn-Khaldun behind bars. There the trouble-beset politician remained for twenty-one months despite repeated petitions for pardon. His last petition took the form of a two-hundred-verse ode, of which a sample is given in his *al-Ta'rif* and which the sultan greatly admired. Abu-'Inan died, however, before the prisoner was finally restored to grace.

A new ibn-Khaldun emerges. Finding himself amidst cunning viziers, jockeying for power and using contestants for the throne as their ponies, he played the game. He would shift his loyalty from one contender to another and jump on the first victor's band-wagon. Abu-Salim, a banished brother of abu-'Inan, was such a victor. Ibn-Khaldun had worked for him and was now rewarded by appointment as the new sultan's chief secretary (amounting to secretary of state). For a time he was also made a special judge, for cases not covered by Islamic law. As a mere secretary ibn-Khaldun established a new style in royal correspondence, elegant, rhetorical and impressive, but as a politician his performance was—to say the least—dubious. At abu-Salim's death (1361) he again plunged into palace intrigues to the neck. From it he was lucky to escape with his head. This time the route northward was the only one open, no other was permitted him. His wife—whom he now mentions for the first time in his autobiography—he sent, with the children, to her brother at Qusantinah (Constantine).

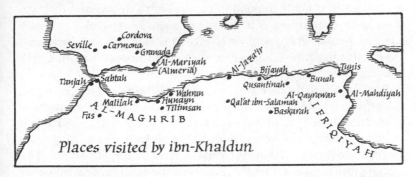

Places visited by ibn-Khaldun

On December 26, 1362 the expatriate landed in Granada, Islam's last foothold in the Iberian Peninsula. Its throne incumbent Muhammad V was once deposed and given asylum in abu-Salim's court. Earlier, when banished by his brother, abu-Salim himself had found refuge in this Muhammad's court. Muhammad was a descendant of Muhammad I al-Ghalib ibn-al-Ahmar (d. 1273), founder of the world-renowned Alhambra (*al-Hamra'*), construction of which this Muhammad completed. Strangely, ibn-Khaldun—who must have had his office therein—makes no mention of the palace by name. He devotes a couple of stanzas to the sultan's reception hall. While in exile in Fas, Muhammad was accompanied by his prime minister Lisan-al-Din ibn-al-Khatib. Ibn-al-Khatib was the most learned man in Granada, as ibn-

Khaldun was in Morocco. Besides, he was a great physician. He established a place for himself in the history of medicine for having recognized and proved by observation that the Black Death was a contagious disease rather than an "act of God." Ibn-al-Khatib and ibn-Khaldun at Fas soon became staunch friends and mutual admirers. No wonder the newcomer to Granada was showered with honors and gifts.

Shortly after arrival the new official was entrusted with a mission to negotiate a treaty with Pedro the Cruel, king of Castile, at Seville, his ancestral home and the one of all Andalusian cities he longed to see. The king knew all about this distinguished family from his Jewish physician. He received the ambassador with special honor, showed him the residential remains and offered to restore the estate in case he decided to stay and enter the royal service. Even if made in good faith, the offer's unacceptability was a foregone conclusion. But the gift of a she-mule with a gold saddle and bridle was gladly received. This was the only firsthand experience the future author of a universal history had in Christian Europe.

Back in Granada he felt so secure in the king's confidence and his prime minister's friendship that he asked the king to summon his family from Qusantinah. No sooner had he established a permanent residence, however, than he, in his own words, "began to smell the odor of alienation" on the part of ibn-al-Khatib. The prime minister was evidently jealous of the newly rising influence in the royal court. This coincided with an attractive offer from abu-'Abdullah, Hafsid sultan of Bijayah (Bougie). With a flattering "thank you" letter written by ibn-al-Khatib over the king's signature, ibn-Khaldun and family sailed from Granada's port al-Mariyah (Almeria) to arrive at Bijayah in March 1365.

> When I landed I found that the sultan of Bijayah had arranged for a ceremonial reception. His aides on their mounts were there, as instructed, to meet me. The populace rushed on me from all sides touching my garment and kissing my hands. It was indeed a spectacular day. As I presented myself before the sultan he greeted me and wished me long life. He then bestowed a robe of honor on me and ordered a mount for my use. Early the next morning I found his aides, by his orders, waiting at my

door. I thereupon shouldered the entire burden ot state affairs, all by myself.[1]

This abu-'Abdullah Muhammad was none other than the deposed Hafsid governor banished to Morocco on account of whom ibn-Khaldun had endured a long prison term. Undismayed, ibn-Khaldun later pressed the case of his friend before the new sultan in Fas, which resulted in his regaining his governorship and declaring his independence. Bijayah was a prosperous mercantile seaport (in eastern Algeria) with an exciting fourteenth-century history. Three times it achieved independence from Tunis, three times it repelled invasions from Tilimsan, but once (1347) it yielded to the Marinid abu-al-Hasan without striking a blow.

The Bijayan career of the new prime minister (*hajib*, literally chamberlain) began well but did not end well. This was the highest position he ever held, but between the zenith and the nadir the distance was short. In the following year a cousin of the sultan, abu-al-'Abbas, governor of Qusantinah, marched against Bijayah and killed abu-'Abdullah. True to his opportunistic character, ibn-Khaldun delivered the city to the victor and was retained in his service. But it was not long before he lost favor and narrowly escaped arrest. The episode ushered in a most precarious decade in a long precarious career.

Disillusioned in his quest for power and glory and yearning for the peace and tranquility of a scholarly career, the dejected politician turned his back on urban life. For residence with his family he chose the oasis of Baskarah (Biskra) in southern Algeria. But a man of his talents, experience and reputation would not be left alone. This time the sultan of Tilimsan, a son-in-law of abu-'Abdullah, requested his services. Ibn-Khaldun sent instead his brother Yahya, who had held a government post at Bijayah, been taken prisoner by abu-al-'Abbas and later been released. He was satisfied with the duty of instigating the tribesmen, mostly of the banu-Hilal, against his former master abu-al-'Abbas and on behalf of the new master in Tilimsan. While on a visit to Tilimsan, ibn-Khaldun learned that the Marinid 'Abd-al-'Aziz was advanc-

---

[1] Muhammad ibn-Tawit al-Tanji, ed., *Al-ta'rif b-ibn-Khaldun wa-Rihlatuhu Gharban wa-Sharqan* (Cairo, 1951), p. 98. The edition is based on two copies in Istanbul bearing the author's handwriting.

ing on the city. He lost no time fleeing to Hunayn in order to embark for Spain, but was pursued by Marinid troops and brought to the sultan's camp. Convinced that this *persona non grata* was not on his way to seek Granada's intervention in North African affairs, 'Abd-al-'Aziz set him free.

Returning to the desert ibn-Khaldun reversed his propaganda, serving this time as a Marinid agent against Tilimsan. He even decided to move his family to Fas (1372), and on the way they all had a narrow escape from death at the hands of Bedouins instigated by Tilimsan. The only loss sustained, fortunately, was in property. He arrived at Fas to find a new and unfriendly regime. After a short period of imprisonment he felt that all doors in al-Maghrib were closed in his face and to Granada he rushed, leaving his family behind. But no sooner had he arrived than he was extradited on representations from Fas.

This time there was no doubt about it. The man of politics in him receded to the background; the man of learning pushed to the front. Offered protection by an Arab tribe and residence in Qal'at ibn-Salamah, a castle and village of the Wahran (Oran) province, he moved there in the spring of 1375 with his family, his books and his papers, intent upon entering a new phase of his career. By forcing him to this situation his political enemies, indeed, did him and the world more good than all his friends. Then and there he began his monumental history of the world. The first book of the history he titled *Muqaddimah,* and that is the one to which he owes his fame. For about four years he labored, oblivious of the world, on the work by which the world was to remember him. Admittedly without those stormy, checkered political experiences, his history would not be what it is. In November 1377 he finished the first version of the *Muqaddimah,* an event to which he referred with these self-admiring words: "I completed this introduction, a unique composition with which I was inspired in my retreat. Ideas and expressions flowed through my head to be churned and yield their cream—a finished product synthesized and homogenized."

Five years of seclusion, of which the last was spent in bed because of illness, might not have sufficed to flush the author out of his desert hideout; but the necessity of consulting sources inaccessible there did. The natural place to look to was his birthplace, now under the control of his old friend-enemy abu-al-'Abbas. Magnanimously the sultan, currently the mightiest ruler in North Africa, offered him not only amnesty but patronage. Before long ibn-Khaldun was ready with a revised part of his history which he dedicated to his patron. But fate, or whatever brings bad luck, resumed his company. Intriguing courtiers convinced the sultan that his new protégé was a master intriguer and should not be trusted when left alone. The autobiographer specifies a jealous chief justice whose circle of auditors and admirers grew thinner and narrower as his own grew thicker and broader. Accordingly, when abu-al-'Abbas planned an expedition he summoned ibn-Khaldun to join him. The embarrassed man implored royal acceptance of his apology on the ground that he intended a holy pilgrimage—not even a tyrant could object to that. A ship chanced to be in the harbor and the habitual fugitive landed in Alexandria December 8, 1382, after about forty-five days, never to return to his homeland.

To Egyptians the Tunisian scholar and diplomat needed no introduction. Shortly after his arrival he was offered a teaching position at al-Azhar, the oldest and most distinguished university in the area. He later held professorships in two colleges and the presidency (shaykhdom) of a Sufi institute. Inaugural lectures in these positions, each introduced with a eulogy of the sultan, have been preserved in *al-Ta'rif*. His large learned audiences, he assures us, were greatly impressed. Additionally he accepted on six different occasions the Maliki judgeship, with the full realization that it was a political plum coveted by many local rivals. His attire remained Maghribi and so did his script. His college lectures centered on hadith and jurisprudence, with special reference to its Maliki form, and we can be sure he did not fail to make an occasional excursus of favorite political and social themes discussed in the *Muqaddimah*.

The second year after his arrival he was introduced to the new Mamluk sultan Barquq, originally a Circassian slave and now a usurper of the Syro-Egyptian throne. On ibn-Khaldun's request

Barquq asked abu-al-'Abbas to send the ibn-Khaldun family to Egypt. The expectant husband-father had no premonitory sign of what fate had in store for him. A brief report in *al-Ta'rif* tells the story:

> As my family coming from Tunis was near landing from the boat, a severe storm struck it and wrecked it. All my belongings, my wife and children were lost. The tragedy was great and the sorrow overwhelming. I felt like giving up the world and decided to resign my judicial post.[1]

What and how many were his children, he does not specify. Nor does he tell us whether he married again later.

In Egypt the education of the fifty-two-year-old scholar came near completion. Here he established for the first time direct contact with a higher form of culture as represented by Eastern Islam. Originally he had in mind limiting his history to Western Islam, Arab and Berber. To one coming from al-Maghrib and its Sahara, Cairo was indeed "capital of the world, the garden of the earth and the meeting place of nations." Its horizon is dotted with palaces and castles, mosques and schools; its sky is studded with the stars of its ulema; its soil is enriched by the never-failing bounty of the Nile, and its bazars are bursting with the products of the land. The new experience reaffirmed old theories arrived at under different conditions, and radically modified other theories. The author was more convinced than ever that economic prosperity and social development had embedded in them the germs of decay. But the theory that the reform of a society is contingent upon personal power exercised by a wise ruler gave way in favor of a duality of leadership: political and learned. The political assures stability and protection; the learned provides guidelines and regulations for individual and community conduct. Regulation, then, not rule, becomes the key to progress.

One more experience was essential to add a dimension of universality to the education of this world historian: a visit to Mecca and Medina. That came in 1387, five years after he had claimed he intended to undertake it. It lasted eight months and gave him a unique opportunity to meet scholars from Turkestan, India, East Asia and South Africa and add to his knowledge of differing

[1] Al-Tanji, *Al-Ta'rif*, p. 259.

societies. On his return he reported to his royal patron his rewarding experience.

In the following year (1389) Barquq was deposed by one of the military coups recurring in Mamluk history. When he regained his throne a year later he learned that, among other judges, his trusted protégé had signed a legal opinion justifying the deposition. Again resorting to verse, but this time in doleful meter, the disgraced scholar humbly apologized and asked forgiveness, assuring the sultan that the act was committed under duress and reminding him how in the past he had welcomed, protected and favored this poor stranger who had been deprived of his family and now of his position and possessions but still relied on the sultan's magnanimity. Barquq was touched and restored him to royal favor. For a few years in the stormy career of ibn-Khaldun there was no storm or, in his words, no clouded atmosphere. Besides teaching, judging and writing he played a part in establishing friendly relations between the rulers and peoples of his adopted home and those of his native land. He later undertook a journey to Jerusalem and Bethlehem but refused to enter the Church of the Holy Sepulcher, "claimed by the Christians to be built on the site of the Crucifixion." To the Moslems there was no Crucifixion.

The death of Barquq (1399) and the succession of his thirteen-year-old son al-Nasir Faraj signaled new disturbances in the kingdom coinciding with a serious threat from the north. Al-Nasir offered ibn-Khaldun a special honorarium to join his retinue as he headed his troops to repel the invader.

The site was a tent in a Tartar camp outside the walls of Damascus. The time was a cold January 10, 1401. The principals were the leading thinker of Islam and the Mongol Timur (Tamerlane), lord of Turkestan, conqueror of Persia, raider of Russia as far as Moscow and now invader of Syria. Timur had given Aleppo a treatment worthy of his nickname, "prince of destruction." Damascus was next on the agenda. Al-Nasir had got there before him, but hurried back to Cairo because of uprisings at home, leaving his aides inside the beleaguered Damascus. The military in the city resolved to resist, but not the civilians, Syrian and Egyptian, including ibn-Khaldun. Stealthily he had himself lowered from the same city wall whence Paul was let down in a basket, and made his way to the invader's tent. He was received with honor, and after greetings kissed the Mongol's hand.

The series of interviews between the two men through an interpreter lasted for some forty days and are counted among the most interesting of their kind in history. After asking his guest personal questions about his background and current post, Timur—with dreams of world conquest at the back of his mind—started quizzing him about the geography, rulers and general situation in Ifriqiyah and al-Maghrib. Ibn-Khaldun—with his and his colleagues' safety uppermost in mind—phrased his answers cautiously and—as far as he could—convincingly. Not satisfied, the insistent Mongol requested written answers. At one time the guest offered his host a copy of the Koran, a rug and four boxes of Egyptian sweets. Finally safe-conducts were issued. Timur asked for a she-mule for his way back and when he offered to pay, the donor remarked, "one like me does not sell to one like you."

The Egyptian party left Damascus to share the fate of its sister in the north. On the way past Safad they were attacked by Arab tribesmen and left "naked." On their arrival in Cairo ibn-Khaldun received the mule price forwarded in care of an Egyptian ambassador sent to negotiate with the Mongol conqueror.

The autobiographer dwells in elaborate details on this last episode in his life. One item follows in his *al-Ta'rif:* dismissal for the fifth time from the judgeship. That took place shortly before his sudden death, March 16, 1406, at the age of seventy-four. He was buried in the Sufi cemetery at Bab al-Nasr in the city where he labored for almost a quarter of a century.

II

The literary output of ibn-Khaldun, encyclopedic though it is, stands no comparison in volume with those of ibn-Sina, al-Kindi and other "lords of the pen." A descriptive catalog of his writings in 339 pages by an Egyptian scholar (1962) lists no more than seven minor works and one major. Of the minor, three deal with logic, arithmetic and Sufism respectively, two are commentaries on poems and two are abridgments of works by ibn-Rushd and a theologian.

His universal history *Kitab al-'Ibar wa-Diwan al-Mubtada' w-al-Khabar fi Ayyam al-'Arab wal-'Ajam w-al-Barbar* (book of instructive examples and a recording from beginning to end of the events of the Arabs, Persians and Berbers and those of their contemporaries who held supreme rule) is in seven volumes, the first of which is the *Muqaddimah*, the last volume is supplemented with the *Ta'rif*.

In its composition the author draws extensively on his predecessors, particularly al-Tabari and ibn-al-Athir, most of whom were annalistic chroniclers. But he follows the system of grouping historical events, with some interpretation, around peoples, dynasties and rulers, a system inaugurated by the third classical historian al-Mas'udi (d. 957) whom, surprisingly, ibn-Khaldun did not study. The emphasis throughout is political. Since the term 'Ajam (Persians) was used generally for non-Arabs, the author was committed to a world history. But his ceiling was rendered low by his sources' inadequate and inaccurate knowledge of ancient Semitic and Greco-Roman history, and his horizon was limited by the skimpy material on medieval Europe. He himself knew no foreign language. In fact he tells us that he considered the study of a foreign language by an Arab detrimental to his mastery over his mother-tongue. The only type of imperial rise and fall he studied in all its aspects was the Arab caliphate, built with the aid of religion by partly nomadic people, and succeeded by Turkish, Persian and Berber states on the nomadic level of culture.

His strength lies in his firsthand, intimate knowledge of North Africa—Arab and Berber—Egypt, and Granada, all of which he treats with an amazing degree of restraint and objectivity. Rarely does he flatter a personal friend or belittle an enemy. Ibn-Khaldun the historian stands in sharp contrast to ibn-Khaldun the politician. His history is considered an indispensable source for the study of such dynasties as the Marinids and Hafsids. Embedded in the text are occasional nuggets of information not to be found elsewhere. In Mali (Sudan), he reports a strange disease of lethargy which seems to be the earliest reference to sleeping sickness.

Valuable as it is, if all volumes of his book—minus the *Muqad-*

dimah—were lost together with all the author's minor works, his niche in the hall of fame would remain secure.

At the beginning of the *Muqaddimah* the author indicates his point of departure from the old as well as his starting point of the new:

> On the surface history is no more than information about po-
> litical events, dynasties and occurrences of the remote past, ele-
> gantly presented and spiced with proverbs. It serves to entertain
> large, crowded gatherings and brings to us an understanding of
> human affairs. . . .
>
> The inner meaning of history, on the other hand, involves
> speculation and an attempt to get at the truth, subtle explana-
> tion of the causes and origins of existing things, and deep knowl-
> edge of the how and why of events. History, therefore, is firmly
> rooted in philosophy. It deserves to be accounted a branch of
> philosophy.[1]

Having studied philosophy, theology and history and noted that philosophic concepts and rational reasoning had been applied to theology but never to history, ibn-Khaldun undertook the task himself. This seemed to him easier because history was still being made and he himself had taken a part in making it. The enter-ing wedge is logic. Historic events are related one to the other logically by a causal relationship (*'illah, sabab*). Social phenom-ena are then subject to laws that operate, though not with the same rigidity as in the natural sciences. This makes history a study of society in its social, economic and political aspects and renders it a branch of philosophy. As the historian seeks rational explanation of social development, he becomes a philosopher of history.

Society is not static. It is subject to change. Its evolution from the savage to the nomadic, and from the nomadic to the settled stage with its agriculture and industry, follows an observable pat-tern. Similar forces operating under the same conditions would produce the same results. The development is conditioned by var-ious elements involving climate, soil, food and mineral resources,

[1] Franz Rosenthal, *Ibn Khaldun, The Maqaddimah: An Introduction to His-tory* (New York, 1958), vol. I, p. 6; *Muqaddamat ibn-Khaldun*, ed. 'Ali 'A. Wafi, 2nd ed. (Cairo, 1965), p. 351.

These are more physical and geographical than biological or individual factors. Psychological considerations cannot be entirely ignored. The morale of an army on the battlefield may count more than numbers. Nor can the supernatural be dismissed. The phenomenal success of the Arab forces at the rise of Islam is a conspicuous illustration of Divine interference. Ibn-Khaldun's book on Sufism comes to mind in this connection.

As a community passes from the cattle-breeding to the agricultural stage, its economy is not only changed but enriched. Industry adds to the wealth. In an organized, highly developed state economy becomes more complex. The economy of a state remains healthy so long as the proper balance is maintained between individual enterprise and state control. Unreasonable restraints are detrimental to economic growth.

This science of society which ibn-Khaldun claimed to have discovered he called the science of civilization (*'ilm al-'umran*). At the core of social organization lies social adhesion or solidarity (*'asabiyah*). Solidarity is at its strongest in tribal organization, and if combined with religion the combination is irresistible. A society is born; it grows and flourishes under the influence of solidarity and of work for the common good. It reaches its heyday as a state. Its decline begins through inefficiency, pomp, luxury, corruption and extravagance on the part of the rulers, and indolence and addiction to pleasure on the part of the people. It becomes an easy prey for an enemy from outside.

The last book of the *Muqaddimah* is devoted to education. The author considered education a social phenomenon subject to change in response to social changes. The child should start with the simple and move gradually to the complex, with the general before the detailed. The Koran should not be used as a text in the elementary grades. Violence on the part of the teacher should not be exercised; it may react unfavorably on the child's character and social behavior. Teachers should be concerned with the development of skills (sing. *malakah*) and the right habits in their pupils, not only through direct instruction but through the indirect lesson they impart by their own example.

Neither ibn-Khaldun's philosophy of history nor his philosophy of education seems to have made any impression on his or later generations.

III

The fact is, this philosopher was born at the wrong time and in the wrong place. He came too late to arouse any response among his people, deep in their medieval slumber, or to find a would-be translator among Europeans. He had no immediate predecessors and no successors. No school of thought could be styled Khaldunic. His meteoric career flashed across the North African firmament leaving hardly a glare behind.

In fact ibn-Khaldun may be considered a luminary touched off by sparks from the fire ignited in Iraq six hundred years earlier and extinguished in al-Andalus four hundred years later. The spark carriers were refugees in the wake of the Christian reconquest; some of them were his teachers. He must have felt intellectually strange in the land of his nativity. Al-Andalus, whence his great-great-grandfather had come more than a century earlier, was his intellectual home. Viewed in this perspective, he towers like a Mont Blanc or an Everest rising with no Alps or Himalayas around.

Of all peoples the Ottoman Turks, builders of the mightiest and most enduring Moslem state in modern times, were the first to interest themselves in his theories. Those theories' relevance to their problems was apparent. Ottoman scholars beginning with the seventeenth century competed with one another in writing about or translating from this Arab author. In 1830 the first Turkish translation of the *Maqaddimah* was made.

The French came next. Selections in Arabic by the celebrated Orientalist Silvestre de Sacy appearing in 1806 were followed by an Arabic edition of the *Muqaddimah* by Étienne M. Quatremère (1852–56) and a French translation by William M. de Slane (1862–68). This latter *Prolégomènes* was the one responsible for making the Tunisian scholar known in the learned West. When then discovered, it was too late for ibn-Khaldun to exert any influence on European thought, the social sciences having been already formulated. But he aroused surprise and admiration —surprise at the realization that fathers of philosophers of history and the social sciences (such as the Italians Machiavelli and Vico, the French Montesquieu and Auguste Comte and the Englishman Adam Smith), had a precursor; and admiration for the relevance and modernity of certain political, social and economic principles brought out and laws deduced by him. In the last decades a large number of monographs and dissertations have been written on ibn-Khaldun's theories. The first complete English translation of the *Muqaddimah* was undertaken by the American scholar Franz Rosenthal.[1] Western appraisal of ibn-Khaldun's contribution found expression in Arnold Toynbee's *Study of History:* "He has conceived and formulated a philosophy of history which is undoubtedly the greatest work of its kind that has ever yet been created by any mind in any time or place."

Ibn-Khaldun's own people were late to rediscover him and slow to appreciate him. A few pupils, notably the Egyptian historian al-Maqrizi (d. 1442), expressed their indebtedness to the master but no impact of his teaching was generally felt. No complete Arabic edition of his history was published until 1867 (from a faulty manuscript), and no complete edition of his autobiography was published until 1951. The first modern Arab to make a serious study of him was the future dean of Egyptian men of letters, Taha Husayn. His study took the form of a dissertation in French (in 1917) and was published eight years later in Arabic, creating an image of ibn-Khaldun as an egoist, dishonest intellectually and Moslem only nominally. Even his "sorrow" over his lost family was a sham. Other writers in Egypt, Syria and Iraq echoed with additions the Husayn views. Hadn't he entitled one section in the *Muqaddimah,* "Arabs can gain control only over flat terrain", and another, "Places that succumb to the Arabs are immediately ruined"? And didn't he say somewhere that most of the great Arab scholars were Persians, that the Egyptians were characterized by gaiety, levity and disregard of consquences, and that the Fatimids were, in fact as in name, descended from Fatimah? He must then be anti-Arab, a Berber, a fabricator of his genealogy.

---

1 Three other American scholars wrote on ibn-Khaldun: Muhsin Mahdi, *Ibn-Khaldun's Philosophy of History* (London, 1957); Charles Issawi, *An Arab Philosophy of History* (London, 1950); Nathaniel Schmidt, *Ibn-Khaldun: Historian, Sociologist and Philosopher* (New York, 1930).

The anti-Khaldun feeling reached its climax in a recommendation (1939) by an Iraqi minister of education that his tomb be dug up and his books burned.

Gradually, however, the abused man was rehabilitated. Certain defenders argued—albeit not quite correctly—that the Arabs ibn-Khaldun meant were the nomads. So strong did the sentiment turn in his favor that in 1962 a memorial celebration was held in Cairo at which scholars from the Arab world vied one with the other in exalting his erudite contributions.[1] In the same year another celebration was held in his honor at Rabat, Morocco.[2] Meanwhile scholars in Persia, Pakistan and India were introducing him to their readers.

The question as to what place in history a man who bequeathed no timely heritage should be accorded has been well answered in these words:

> He who finds a new path is a pathfinder, even if the trail has to be found again by others; and he who walks far in advance of his contemporaries is a leader, even though centuries may pass before he is recognized as such and intelligently followed.[3]

'Abd-al-Rahman abu-Zayd ibn-Khaldun, historian, philosopher, social scientist, jurist, was the first philosopher of history and the last intellectual giant of Islam.

[1] Proceedings published as *A'mal Mahrajan ibn-Khaldun* (Cairo, 1962). For more on the life and work of ibn-Khaldun consult Muhammad 'A. 'Inan, *Ibn-Khaldun: Hayatuhu wa-Turathuhu al-Fikri,* 3rd ed. (Cairo, 1965); Sati' al-Husari, *Dirasat 'an ibn-Khaldun* (Baghdad, 1961).
[2] *Mahrajan ibn-Khaldun* (Rabat, 1962).
[3] Nathaniel Schmidt, p. 46.

Index